MODERN
SPEY FISHING

MODERN
SPEY FISHING

A COMPLETE GUIDE TO TACTICS AND TECHNIQUES
FOR SINGLE- AND TWO-HANDED APPROACHES

RICK KUSTICH
Fly photographs by Nick Pionessa

STACKPOLE
BOOKS

Essex, Connecticut
Blue Ridge Summit, Pennsylvania

STACKPOLE BOOKS

An imprint of Globe Pequot, the trade division of
The Rowman & Littlefield Publishing Group, Inc.
4501 Forbes Blvd., Ste. 200
Lanham, MD 20706
www.rowman.com

Distributed by NATIONAL BOOK NETWORK

British Library Cataloguing in Publication Information available

Library of Congress Cataloging-in-Publication Data
Names: Kustich, Rick, author.
Title: Modern spey fishing : a complete guide to tactics and techniques for
    single- and two-handed approaches / Rick Kustich.
Description: Essex, Connecticut : Stackpole Books, [2023] | Summary: "New
    approaches and uses for Spey techniques, including applications for fish
    species other than salmon and steelhead such as smallmouth bass, trout,
    and saltwater game fish. Also covers developments in rods and lines and
    is the only book on the market that thoroughly covers micro Spey or
    micro Skagit gear and techniques (light line, light rod). Includes
    technique photos as well as fly patterns"— Provided by publisher.
Identifiers: LCCN 2022039776 (print) | LCCN 2022039777 (ebook) | ISBN
    9780811739825 (hardback) | ISBN 9780811769754 (epub)
Subjects: LCSH: Spey casting. | Fly fishing. | Fly casting.
Classification: LCC SH454.25 .K87 2023 (print) | LCC SH454.25 (ebook) |
    DDC 799.12/4—dc23/eng/20220930
LC record available at https://lccn.loc.gov/2022039776
LC ebook record available at https://lccn.loc.gov/2022039777

♾™ The paper used in this publication meets the minimum requirements of American National Standard for Information Sciences—Permanence of Paper for Printed Library Materials, ANSI/NISO Z39.48-1992.

CONTENTS

ACKNOWLEDGMENTS

Producing a completed book seems to take a village. And I am entirely grateful to those that provided thoughtful and unwavering support throughout the process of creating *Modern Spey Fishing.* The story would be incomplete without the assistance and encouragement.

I first want to acknowledge and thank Nick Pionessa. His quality photography can be found throughout these pages and Nick's tireless effort to get the best images is greatly appreciated. But more importantly our hours of discussions on road trips or along the river that tapped into his expertise generated many of the thoughts included in the text.

I am truly honored that Simon Gawesworth agreed to write the foreword for the book as well as provide a few key details on Spey history. Simon's 2004 classic

There is an obvious human element to Spey fishing. Deep relationships are developed over a common passion. Here my late friend Keith Myott intently works the eye of a run.

book titled *Spey Casting* has been the main resource for so many casters and Simon's contribution to the world of Spey is without parallel in modern times. It is a humbling full-circle event to have one of my mentors contribute prominently to the final product.

A special thank you goes to accomplished distance caster and publisher of *Swing the Fly* Zack Williams who provided critical guidance on the cast, photography, and support in many other ways. I am very appreciative to Jeff Bright whose brilliant images add greatly to the visual aspect of the book and provide perspective on how Spey has spread to all corners of the world. Thank you to Joe Janiak for his beautiful salmon images. And special thanks to Jim Bartschi of Scott Fly Rods and Bob Meiser of R.B. Meiser Fly Rods who freely shared comments on modern rod design. Also, thanks to Jeff Bright and Bob Clay for thoughts on today's bamboo.

I also want to acknowledge two friends and experienced anglers Larry Halyk and Jerry Darkes who have provided support and assistance to much of my work over the years. These are friendships like many others that I have established based largely on our shared passion for fly fishing.

While the fly chapter provides only a basic cross-section of flies to be used in a wide range of Spey fishing situations, contributions were made by some of the very best tyers. A special thank you to Charlie Dickson, Steve Silverio, Nick Pionessa, Blane Chocklett, Greg Senyo, Jeff Hubbard, Justin Pribanic, Todd Hirano, Steve Yewchuck, Steve Bird, and Mike Schultz.

It's always a pleasure to work with editor Jay Nichols. His forward focused outlook encourages the fresh ideas that allow a book to be meaningful and impactful. Jay assisted in first framing the subject matter of the book and then providing guidance throughout while giving me plenty of space.

And at the foundation is family. A special thank you to my wife Karen who supports my crazy life in more ways than I'll ever know and has encouraged my growth as a person from the day we first met. To my daughter Sarah who has provided inspiration to keep moving forward in life. And to my brother Jerry who has always supported all that I do.

FOREWORD

Simon Gawesworth

Fly fishing has come a long way since the earliest recorded book on fishing. Written in 1496 by Dame Juliana Berners, *A Treatyse of Fysshynge wyth an Angle* is generally accepted as being the first book written about fishing. Among her discussion on the various fish you can catch, how to make your rod, how to make and color your line, and how to make your own hooks, she lists the many ways you could go fishing—to quote (and with cleaned up, modern-day English): *"Now that I have taught you how to make all your tackle, I shall tell you how to angle. There are six ways of angling.*

1. On the bottom for trout and other fish.

2. On the bottom by an arch, or near piles where the tide ebbs and flows for bleak, roach, and dace.

3. With a float for any kind of fish.

4. With a minnow as live bait, without weight or float for trout.

5. With a fly on a line of one or two hairs, for roach and dace.

6. With an artificial fly for trout and grayling."

And thus, in her sixth point, we get the first acknowledgment of fly fishing—more than 500 years ago and only four years after Columbus set sail from Spain to "stumble" on America. It seems like fly fishing has been around a while!

Since those early days, tackle has improved, a lot more people have taken up the sport, and fly-fishing techniques have evolved. Nowadays, fly fishers target any manner of species outside the trout and grayling of Dame Juliana's days, and I often wonder what she would have thought of people going fly fishing for carp, bonefish, tarpon, tiger fish, dorado, and peacock bass—to name a few.

Her directions for catching salmon were: *"The salmon is a gentle fish, but cumbersome to take.*

Usually, he is found only in the deep places of great rivers; and for the most part he keeps in midstream, so that a man cannot get at him. He is in season from March to Michaelmas (September), *at which time you should angle for him with these baits if you can get hold of them. At the beginning and end of the season with a red worm, and also with the grub that breeds on dunghills and especially with a sovereign bait you find breeding on the water dock. The salmon does not bite on the bottom, but at the float. You may sometimes take him, but it happens very seldom, with an artificial fly when he is leaping, in the same way as you take trout or grayling. The above are well-proved baits for salmon."*

So, even 500 years ago people fly fished for salmon (Atlantic salmon) in the United Kingdom and, by all appearances, found it as hard to get them to take a fly as modern anglers do. In 500 years, we have learned a lot about salmon, but to this day, it is still an elusive species to catch on the fly. Perhaps the greatest advancement in techniques was the creation of long, two-handed fly rods that could throw a hefty line out a long way and cover fish in the biggest rivers, and with those long rods, even more importantly, was the birth and advancement of Spey casting.

Credited with being a technique developed by anglers on the river Spey in Scotland in the mid-1800s, this style of casting has opened up so much water to the fly fisher. No longer does a fly caster have to have plenty of room behind them for a backcast in order to be able to cast the fly out, as the entire Spey cast family has virtually no backcast and, as a result, are perfect for fishing with any manner of obstructions behind.

Though Spey casting has been around for more than 150 years, it is only relatively recently that people have started to study it, to break it down and analyze it,

Modern Spey techniques have a wide application. Here, I load up the rod for the next cast against an early fall background. NICK PIONESSA PHOTO

to develop effective teaching techniques, and even to expand the number and type of Spey casts that can be made with a fly rod. Indeed, Spey casting is no longer the sole prerogative of the salmon angler, wielding a long two-handed rod on the great Scottish salmon rivers, but something every fly fisher can and should do—whether fishing for salmon, steelhead, trout, or even bonefish, and with a two-handed rod or single-handed rod.

Much has been written to feed the increased hunger of fly fishers for Spey casting—many books, magazine articles, and a rather prodigious number of videos, films, and social media posts. Interestingly, the majority of these resources concentrate on the act of casting itself and, with a few exceptions, not what to do once you have got the fly out there. For some time now, the fly-fishing world has needed a book that covers the whole enchilada—that discusses Spey fishing in its entirety, from gear to casting, from presentation, to fishing techniques, and even to the flies that work. Fortunately for the fly-fishing community, that wait is now over.

When Rick was kind enough to ask me to write a foreword for his new book on Spey casting, I had no hesitation in accepting. I have known Rick for many years and have had a long and deep respect for his angling skills and his ability to teach, explain, and educate people in a clear, concise language. I love Rick's style of writing as it is unpretentious, chock full of facts and important information, and he always makes it easy for anglers of all abilities to understand and enjoy—not an easy thing to do at all! I accepted his offer before I had read any of his manuscript because of his innate ability to entertain and educate and, for me, those are skills I deeply value.

When I finally got Rick's manuscript and read through it, I knew I had made the right decision. Rick does a marvelous job of weaving all the aspects of "Spey" into this one book. From learning the history of Spey casting, to an examination of the gear used—where Rick refreshingly talks about modern Spey tactics using switch rods, trout Spey rods, single-handed rods, as well as the traditional two-handed rods. His chapter on "Presenting the fly" is a wonderful read and clearly explains how to fish and present a fly in the best way for success. I also loved his "Tactical Spey Fishing" chapter, which gets more into the nitty gritty details that all Spey anglers should know. The opening paragraph, where Rick describes his "perfect pool," couldn't be a better start to a chapter and shows that Rick knows exactly what he is talking about. I quivered in anticipation of fishing the pool he describes and can imagine myself Spey casting and swinging a fly through such an incredible piece of water.

Perhaps it is wrong of me to pick out two special chapters that I thoroughly enjoyed, as I was enthralled by all of them. The entire book was an easy, enjoyable, and highly informative read, and I picked up some great tips myself that I can't wait to try out when I am next on the water.

I hope you enjoy this book as much as I did, and more, that it gives you a very solid base/platform to build on in this game of "Spey." By the time you have finished this book, you will certainly know more than just the casting aspect of Spey. Rick's easy writing style and his years of experience shine through in every word he writes, and as a reader, you can expect a glut of great information that will certainly help you out on the water.

INTRODUCTION

Getting connected—the ultimate objective of the Spey approach resulting from consistent casting and mindful presentation. Andy Dietrich battling a spirited fish in a peaceful setting.

Learning to properly Spey cast and fish a swung fly has been a long and captivating journey—one that is certain to continue through the end of my lifetime. The basics of the Spey cast can be gained in a relatively short period of time, given the equipment available today. But it is the application of the cast under various circumstances along with learning the intricacies of presenting the fly for a specific species, water condition, or holding structure that may take a lifetime to master. It is this draw that keeps the pursuit fresh and continually fascinating.

My interest in Spey fishing was inevitable. As fly-fishing techniques developed for the steelhead transplanted to the Great Lakes region, Spey casting enabled an effective approach to a growing interest in swinging flies. Defined as an efficient means for making a 90-degree change in direction cast while requiring little or no clearance behind the casting position, the Spey cast has a wide application to vast fishing opportunities.

At the outset, the technical advantage of keeping the fly in the water for a longer period of time coupled with the superior line control of a longer rod seemed to be the main advantage of this style of fishing. It allowed for significant water coverage while prospecting for active fish. However, in time, it became clear

The versatility of modern Spey techniques allows an angler to be effective on almost any type of water.
NICK PIONESSA PHOTO

Looking down on the Alaskan wilderness. Spey fishing can take us on great adventures to spectacular venues.

that the enjoyment of Spey was found in the casting and overall rhythm of the approach.

Cast, swing, step seems simple enough. But when employed on the currents of a river, the regular tempo becomes entrancing as hours simply melt away in the course of focused concentration of making good casts followed by controlling the fly in a way that best tempts the intended quarry into striking.

For me, Spey fishing has evolved into a craft or an art form. There are many aspects to mastering a craft. There are obvious physical skills required and being able to cast sufficiently is the starting point. Throwing consistent casts that stretch out over the surface provide the conduit for properly covering the water. My objective is to make the best cast I can with each forward stroke, admiring the balance of finesse and power as the line sails away in search of hidden treasures. Each cast reminds me of the stroke of a brush on the canvas of the day. Every movement is part of a succession that makes each outing unique.

But simply learning the basic casts is not enough. It is the utilization of this delivery method where the learning curve seems to extend into perpetuity. Wind, depth, flow, and riverside obstructions add to the complexity and difficulty factor of the cast—factors that make each delivery a unique entity within itself. It is a pursuit that can rarely be perfected, although hours are spent practicing toward that end. Identifying holding water and structure is an equally important piece of the puzzle. Trial and error, along with experience, will determine the proper rod, line, tip, and overall rigging for each situation and water type. But in the end, the objective is to make fishable casts that present a fly in that sweet spot that is irresistible to a holding fish and that turns dreams into reality.

In addition to the rhythm and constant connection to the water provided by Spey fishing, I enjoy the act of swinging a fly. It is a style that provides the sense of truly fishing the fly. At the onset, it may seem like simply casting and letting the fly swim. However, almost every factor of the presentation, including depth, speed, and action of the fly, can be controlled and varied. It may be this connection to the fly that I enjoy the most. When fishing subsurface, I try to envision how the fly is fishing—how it is showing itself to a holding or feeding fish. While we all strive for the take, the grab, the tug, I place more emphasis on fishing the fly well, allowing hookups to be the byproduct of proper presentation.

So what is modern Spey anyway? In this context, the term modern implies a current state that has departed or evolved from the past. It describes an advancement brought about by the intersection of technology with the inquisitive spirit of the fly angler to apply the concept of Spey fishing to a wider array of water and species than for what the technique was originally designed. While Spey fishing originated with long rods and long casts, the application of an efficient change of direction cast requiring little room for a backcast is now seen as a valuable approach not only on large rivers but on smaller water as well. Shorter, lighter, two-hand and switch rods are now manufactured that match well with just about any water and any species. Rods and lines built for one-hand Spey have continued pushing the boundaries of Spey fishing.

Modern Spey Fishing isn't designed to only explore the new developments in this style of fly fishing but rather the totality of what Spey casting, Spey fishing, and the use of two-handed rods have to offer in its current state. The objective is to dive into the areas where this approach has traditionally been utilized by analyzing casting and introducing new techniques while exploring the continued expansion of Spey fishing beyond its historical boundaries. Many anglers are discovering that the use of the Spey approach is allowing for a fresh way to approach their fisheries and that Spey casts are quite useful in certain situations when fishing with a single-hand rod.

The use of the Spey and two-handed setup also now extends into fly-fishing tactics that have not traditionally been associated with this style of fishing. There

are casts and setups to be utilized in a wide array of fishing situations that do not involve swinging the fly. Spey and Spey-like approaches are finding a way into the mainstream of fly fishing—techniques that almost any angler would find useful.

While designing the outline and writing its chapters, I often wondered who would be interested in this book. There has already been so much written on fishing for salmon and steelhead that includes Spey casting and presentation instruction specifically for these species. But Spey has evolved into so much more and should appeal to any angler interested in expanding their skills and enjoyment of the sport of fly fishing. The objective of the book is to provide a detailed basis of rigging, casting, and techniques that can be applied to a wide range of species and fishing situations while opening doors of opportunity to bring Spey fishing and two-hand casting techniques into your regular fishing outings. The hope is to demystify Spey casting and fishing. There is no secret society but rather an approach that can be incorporated into an expanse of fishing situations.

The possibilities seem endless, limited only by imagining how this style of fishing can be used for enjoyment and to provide solutions for certain fishing challenges. Providing a solution has always been at the heart of the development of Spey and two-handed techniques, and that spirit is embodied in the current modern developments.

Modern Spey Fishing certainly won't be the last word on this complex subject but rather a piece of the story in this ever-developing approach to fishing with a fly. While Spey fishing has historically represented a relatively small percentage of fly anglers, the recent expansion into a wide range of water, species, and applications is certain to continue as more anglers realize the joy in effortlessly stretching a beautiful cast across the pool and making use of its many tactical advantages. The timing seems right for a book that explores all that Spey casting and fishing with a two-hand or one-hand Spey rod has to offer and its applicability to a wide range of fly-fishing situations.

HISTORICAL PERSPECTIVE

Often, the present can be best appreciated by looking through a historical lens. The world is changing rapidly through constant technological expansion in nearly every aspect of life. But the path of history can teach us much about the current state. Understanding the steps of past development provides important context for appreciating current methods and the continued expansion into the future.

It has been fairly well documented that the art of Spey casting originated around 1850 on one of Scotland's top Atlantic salmon waters—the River Spey. This style of casting was developed to solve a fishing problem. The river is wide with swift flows making it difficult to wade far enough from the tree-lined banks to make a full backcast. The concept of making a cast where only a limited amount of line passes behind the casting position was born from necessity. With this approach, water could be covered with a fly where it wasn't possible with an overhead cast.

The rods used to make these early innovative casts were immense, with a length of 20 to 22 feet. Most were constructed from a heavy wood called greenheart. While these rods would be considered quite cumbersome and hefty by today's standards, the length provided significant leverage to facilitate a forward cast without a standard backcast. And the sheer weight of the rod required two hands to control its movement. Various types of split cane rods were also developed as the use of two-handed rods became increasingly

Spey started in Scotland but has found its way around the world. Here anglers ply the fabled waters of Argentina with two-hand rods in search of sea-run brown trout. JEFF BRIGHT PHOTO

1

Spey fishing and beautiful places go hand in hand. An angler covers an Atlantic salmon river in the early morning light. Atlantic salmon have played prominently into the discovery and development of the Spey approach. JOE JANIAK PHOTO

popular for salmon fishing in Europe throughout the remainder of the nineteenth century.

By most accounts, the early casts aimed at casting the fly with little line passing behind the angler's position seemed fairly crude and difficult to accomplish. The early versions of the cast were known as the switch, Welsh, or Spey cast or "throw" and were used to describe this developing style of waterborne casting. At some point, Spey emerged as the consistent description for the cast.

Early written accounts of the original switch, Welsh, or Spey cast were generally incomplete and difficult to follow. A handful of authors in the mid- to late 1800s attempted to provide the mechanics of the cast in a written form, including George Kelson, who included some basic description of the cast in his book *The Salmon Fly*, published in 1895. But it wasn't until a book published in 1931 written by Eric Taverner called *Salmon Fishing* that there was some clarity to the working components of this casting style. While the author credits some of his predecessors for laying the groundwork, Taverner provides detailed descriptions of the Spey cast (by this time it appears that Spey had emerged as the accepted moniker for this style of casting) along with illustrated images showing the casting steps. It was also the first account of two variations of the cast—the single Spey and the double Spey. With the two variations, an angler could accommodate both an upriver and downriver wind.

A discussion of the history of Spey casting must include a look at one of the all-time masters, Alexander Grant. He was known throughout Scotland and beyond for both his casting and fishing prowess during the late 1800s and early 1900s. Grant's contribution to the sport was not just while on the water. As a craftsman and musician that produced beautiful violins, he applied his understanding of the working elements of a finely constructed tool to the art of rod making. In the late 1880s, the Grant Vibration rods were designed with a precision taper to distribute the load of the line evenly and best accommodate this new style of casting. The rods were constructed from greenheart featuring a unique joint that allowed the Vibration rods to flex smoothly, eliminating the dead spots that had plagued earlier rods of that era. Eventually, the patent to the Vibration rod was sold but continued as a top-of-the-line rod for two-handed casting into the middle part of the twentieth century.

Grant's casting and fishing abilities were apparently even more impressive than his rods. His casting approach was well documented in a book authored by Jock Scott titled *Fine and Far Off* published in 1952. The book is complete with diagrams, photographs, and descriptions of the cast that Grant referred to as the "switch cast." There is some debate as to the origination of the name of the cast, but it seems to be generally accepted that it refers to the change or switch in direction from the beginning to the end of the cast without utilizing a traditional backcast.

The switch cast depicted in *Fine and Far Off* is essentially a single Spey. It has been refined over time, but the general elements and objective of the cast are the same by placing the fly off the upriver shoulder to set up the forward stroke. Grant could utilize his switch cast to cover incredible distances and reach salmon holds where other casters fell well short. This was accomplished with all the line beyond the tip of the rod prior to beginning the cast while shooting no additional line. In a competition, Grant made a cast of 65 yards, a record that existed for many years.

Split cane was also used for two-handed casting rods during the 1900s. Like greenheart, split cane rods were quite heavy. In the 1950s, fiberglass gained quickly in popularity throughout the fishing industry. The lighter, less-expensive material allowed for greater production at affordable prices. And while split cane maintained a share of fly rod sales, the lighter fiberglass material became well accepted by anglers although somewhat limited in the production of two-handed rods.

In my formative years of fly fishing, I was fortunately introduced to the work of Roderick Haig-Brown, who spent a great amount of time on his beloved salmon and steelhead rivers on Vancouver Island in British Columbia. His words can all at once paint a brilliant picture, tell a fantastic story, and provide valuable fishing information. I attempted to collect most of his writings. In one of his books titled *A Primer in Fly Fishing* first published in 1964, Haig-Brown discusses the single and double Spey casts as a variation of the roll cast that allows for control over changing direction. While he recognizes that Spey casts were commonly utilized on European salmon rivers using long two-handed rods, *A Primer in Fly Fishing* discusses adopting the casts to a single-handed rod.

Haig-Brown provides detailed instruction of the two casts. And while the instruction is fairly easy to follow, it is just text and no diagrams. He recognized the Spey cast as an important tool when fishing with vegetation-lined banks. Haig-Brown also discussed developing enough power to shoot additional line to add distance. This seems to be one of the first references in Spey casting to add distance through shooting-line. As a skilled angler, he was able to realize the versatility of the Spey cast for fishing a range of waters and also felt that the art of Spey casting is a "smooth performance, not without considerable grace." This was a significant recognition of Spey fishing as not only utilitarian but to bring a certain element of elegance and style to working the water with a swung fly.

In 1984, a book titled *Salmon Fishing* written by expert angler Hugh Falkus was released and provided substantial information on Spey casting. Complete with detailed descriptions and photographs, the book quickly became an important reference for salmon fishing but even more importantly for Spey casting. While Falkus may have been best known for his angling books, he was also a well-known filmmaker and broadcaster for the BBC.

Salmon Fishing provided an inspiration for me to learn about two-handed rods and Spey casting. Its pages are where I learned enough to begin thrashing the surface of some local waters. *Salmon Fishing* proved to be a very useful reference volume in making incremental casting improvements. Falkus followed this book with another very important work published in 1994 dedicated to the Spey cast simply titled *Speycasting*. It quickly became the definitive word on the subject in Europe and made its way to North America, where the book also had a significant impact on introducing Spey and teaching many how to cast properly.

The mid-1970s through the 1980s represented an important era in the development of the popularity of two-handed rods and Spey casting. New technology in the name of graphite fiber began to change the game in terms of rod design. The lighter, stronger material took over the fly rod industry as manufacturers moved from cane and fiberglass to various formulas of graphite.

Two-handed rods made their way to North American steelhead rivers by the mid-1900s, beginning a movement and popularity that continues today, particularly on rivers along the Pacific Coast. Jeff Fisher swings a fly on a British Columbia river.

From a two-handed rod perspective, rod builders could now build 15- to 16-foot two-handed rods that were significantly lighter than the previous materials. This opened up the opportunity for innovation and growth in the two-handed rod segment of the industry.

There are anecdotal tales of two-handed rods being used in North America in the mid-1900s on Atlantic Coast rivers in the Canadian maritime provinces. But prior to graphite the popularity of longer rods and Spey casting on the continent seems limited and books written by North American salmon anglers include little discussion of this style of fishing. That would change quickly as graphite two-hand rods became more available.

There is evidence that two-handed rods and Spey casting made their way to the steelhead rivers of the West Coast in the late 1950s. Mike Maxwell learned

the craft of Spey fishing in England and brought this approach to some of the famed rivers in British Columbia. Maxwell inspired many anglers over the years to pursue the two-handed rod for its control of presentation, ease in casting, and overall effectiveness. He was an advocate of fishing a fly on the surface or up in the water column on his home waters of the Bulkley River.

Maxwell's enthusiasm for Spey casting and the related fishing techniques spilled into the creation of his book, titled *The Art & Science of Speyfishing*, which was released in 1995. It became a very important work related to both casting and fishing with a two-handed rod. The book not only includes details on casting but also makes the case for the many fishing advantages of the longer rod. For many years, Maxwell operated a guide service in British Columbia along with his wife Denise. After his passing in 2004, Denise has continued to operate their guide business.

Maxwell was not the only angler to bring two-handed rods to western North America well before the style of fishing gained popularity. Graphite rods produced in the late 1970s and early 1980s were generally in the 15- to 17-foot range. The tapers varied widely as manufacturers slowly worked through the growing pains of designing a tool that only a few were using in North America. In an article published in *Swing the Fly* magazine in 2017, Art Lingren discusses his part in pushing the use of two-handers and Spey casting on British Columbia rivers in the mid-1980s. In his assessment, rods that were built for the European market by Orvis or the British company Bruce and Walker best met the fishing demands of larger steelhead rivers. One interesting aspect of the early part of Lingren's journey is that he discusses looping a sinking-tip line to the front of a floating Spey line. This would begin a very common practice in modern Spey of the exchange of tips for various conditions and pools.

In the late 1970s throughout the 1980s, a handful of United States rod manufactures began to produce quality two-handed graphite rods. While rod lengths generally remained around 15 to 16 feet, experimentation began with shorter lengths. At the time, some shorter two-handed rods were also being produced in Europe. Rod designs may have been a step ahead of line development. The common Spey tapers at the time were long bellied and similar to a double-taper. This style of line matched well with longer rod lengths and was mainly designed to cast whatever length was beyond the tip without shooting additional line. Also, the lines at this time were mostly floaters that fished a fly well up in the water column but were at a disadvantage for reaching fish that weren't surface oriented. While fishing on or near the surface was highly effective for Atlantic salmon, it was not necessarily a high-percentage approach for winter steelhead and Pacific salmon.

Jim Vincent was introduced to Spey casting in British Columbia in the 1980s. After teaming up with Spey master Simon Gawesworth for some lessons, Vincent moved into the Spey game full speed ahead. When he founded RIO Products in 1990, his objective was to create a line that would allow anglers

The WindCutter Spey line designed by Jim Vincent became the first tactical line for two handers and considered the first step in the modern Spey revolution.

to become more efficient Spey casters and tactical anglers. The RIO WindCutter is considered the first "modern" Spey line with the concept of a forward taper that could shoot additional running line for added distance. The WindCutter was designed with a mid-length belly and integrated running line and quickly became the line of choice for North American Spey anglers. This line design assisted in populariz-ing two-hand casting and Spey fishing on many rivers in the late 1990s.

One of Vincent's most significant innovations that changed the game for steelhead anglers was the WindCutter VersiTip or exchangeable tip line. With a loop-to-loop system, this allowed one line to act as a floating line or easily convert to a sinking tip line with a selection of balanced tips of various sink rates. The versatility of this line continued the development of matching Spey fishing to a much wider application and to increase its popularity. During this time, the Accelerator line was also developed as the first long belly Spey line for bigger rivers and longer rods.

There were also some advancements in long bel-lied fly line design in the mid-1990s that originated in Europe. A group of anglers attempted to design a continuous taper and long-bellied line similar to the taper used by Alexander Grant to attain long dis-tance. Expert caster Derek Brown was one of the first to attempt developing the proper taper. Way Yin and Steve Choate took the concept of a continuous taper to a commercial level by working with the company Scientific Anglers to design the XLT Spey line. The XLT was designed as a fishing line but was capable of casting great distances with shooting an additional length. In fact, the line was used by international cast-ing champion Scott MacKenzie in 2005 to break Alex-ander Grant's distance record that had been in place for more than one hundred years.

My own journey into Spey fishing began in the early 1990s. Through discussions with some of my fishing acquaintances and by referencing the works of Hugh Falkus and then Mike Maxwell it was clear that the general concept of this style of fishing matched with what we were trying to accomplish in the Great Lakes. The approach of making a change in direction with no backcast was a perfect solution for many of the waters where we fished a swing the fly approach. But it would be a few years before we could refine this system to work properly.

The main hurdle to clear was matching the equip-ment to the local Great Lakes rivers. My first two-hander was a 15-foot for a 9-/10-weight, and if casted just right, it could get a double-taper floating line out there a good distance. But just about everything seemed wrong with this rig for the water we were fishing. The rod was overmatched for the average 6- to 12-pound fish that made up a large percentage of our catch. And instead of pounding out long casts, we needed to be effective at shorter distances since many of the rivers are of a moderate size. And even the largest rivers required more control along the edges instead of distance. We also needed to get the fly down when the water turned cold.

My enthusiasm changed after I first put my hands on the Sage GFL 7136-4. The 7136-4 is a 13½-foot for a 7-weight two-hander with a much lighter, softer feel. It was immediately clear that this rod was a significant step toward greater versatility. Not being able to find a Spey line at the time that could turnover tungsten leaders or weighted flies I had to improvise. We needed a heavy, exaggerated forward taper and found the best match to be a Cortland pike taper. This allowed for a good load in the rod and made effective casts of 50 to 60 feet. I used this rig for a number of years until the line nearly disintegrated. A couple years later, I worked with Sage rod designer Jerry Seim to provide ideas on shorter rods that better matched smaller waters using an exaggerated front taper. Sage then produced some shorter two-handers, including the GFL 8113-3—an 11-foot-3-inch 8-weight that effectively became one of the first production switch rods and was my go-to choice for smaller water for many years.

During the first decade of the twenty-first century, several developments occurred that would greatly move forward the popularity of Spey casting and fish-ing. Spey fishing had become quite popular for the pursuit of steelhead during this time. West Coast steel-head guides Scott O'Donnell, Mike McCune, and Ed Ward utilized homemade lines to cast heavy tips and flies to effectively cover winter steelhead holds. Jim Vincent worked with O'Donnell, McCune, and Ward to develop the first Skagit line—a short shooting taper with significant mass to easily carry heavy tips and weighted flies.

The story behind the Skagit concept is quite inter-esting. In the late 1990s and early 2000s, Jim Vincent was getting requests from anglers all around the world

The desire for a more versatile approach to presenting a steelhead fly resulted in the development of the Skagit head—an important advancement in the modern Spey movement.

for heavy double-taper lines for two-hand casting. Many anglers weren't convinced about the new Spey designs and wanted to use traditional double-taper lines. Many line manufacturers stopped producing heavier double-taper lines from a lack of demand. RIO produced a double-taper 10- and 12-weight to satisfy these very small markets. O'Donnell, McCune, Ward, and a few other of Vincent's friends persuaded him to produce a double-taper 14 and 16–all level (so technically not a double-taper at all) and then would chop off varying lengths to create a custom taper. It was these homemade lines that would have sections of various double-tapers spliced together that solved many of the casting problems encountered by Pacific Coast winter steelheaders. After consulting with O'Donnell, McCune, and Ward, Vincent began building lines to match the homemade tapers, and the first Skagit heads were born. This new concept brought a great deal of versatility to the Spey game and cut the learning curve for casting a two-handed rod—a revolutionary step in popularizing Spey fishing.

In 2004, Simon Gawesworth released his game-changing book, entitled *Spey Casting.* It is a significant

work that focuses not only on how to make proper Spey casts but also on troubleshooting what can go wrong during the setup and forward stroke. A caster at any level can benefit from the insight provided in Gawesworth's book. A number of instructional videos followed, such as *RIO's Modern Spey Casting, Skagit Master* featuring Ed Ward, and *Skagit Revolution* featuring Tom Larimer.

Around the same time that line designs were advancing in North America, Spey anglers on the other side of the Atlantic Ocean discovered that the concept of the shooting taper worked well on their salmon rivers as well. The shorter heads were especially effective on Scandinavian rivers with limited room for a backcast since the shorter head resulted in a smaller D loop. Scandi heads were designed to be longer than a Skagit head with a finer front taper and to generate significant line speed and distance. Floating Scandi heads combined well with lighter flies and tapered monofilament or poly leaders.

The advancements of the last 10 years have been significant but not always smooth. Lighter, shorter two-handed rods have changed the complexion of

Shorter head lines and lighter, shorter rods have been the major development in Spey in recent years. Shorter heads and rods provide the perfect match for intimate river settings. NICK PIONESSA PHOTO

the sport. And there has been a movement toward shorter shooting tapers to combine with the shorter rod lengths. But there has also been confusing aspects of line and head development that has baffled many a beginning Spey angler. To make Spey casting easier for more anglers, a certain level of complexity has resulted in available line and head options. However, more guidance is becoming available to assist in alleviating the confusion.

But as we roll into the third decade of the twenty-first century, the most significant recent developments in the long history of Spey fishing involve the expansion of the sport past traditional salmon and steelhead fishing. Rods and lines are now available to match, with a wide variety of applications from trout to warm water to salt water. These new applications are leading the sport into the new period of modern Spey.

2

RODS, REELS, AND LINES

All aspects of fly fishing have benefitted from the tremendous advancements over the last 20 to 30 years. Technological changes have allowed equipment to be lighter and perform at a high level as compared to equipment of the past. For some anglers that value the traditional aspect of fly fishing, the advancements are not always welcomed, as the technology can be viewed as chipping away at the soul of fly fishing. But for many, the advancements represent a natural evolution as men and women have an innate propensity to continually push boundaries. While this propulsion forward now occurs in nearly every aspect of life, it is little surprise that fly fishing is no different, given the industrious and passionate individuals that are attracted to the sport.

Rods rigged and ready to go along a Quebec Atlantic salmon river. Being properly prepared is the first step to enjoyment and success in Spey fishing. JEFF BRIGHT PHOTO

Two-handed rods today are available in a wide range of lengths and configurations. This lineup of varied rod, reel, and lines is ready for the challenges of the Skeena River system in British Columbia.

The combination of rod, reel, and line creates the basis for the Spey experience. An individual angler's choice of equipment and rigging can be based on as much personal preference as it is matching up with a specific water type, fish species, or fishing condition. Spey provides an angler the opportunity and versatility to create their own approach to address a combination of fishing success and overall enjoyment.

I have long viewed Spey fishing and casting through both a pragmatic and esthetic lens. Spey fishing represents an efficient tool to accomplish fly presentations that would be difficult or impossible with single-hand overhead casting. But Spey casting and the resulting presentation of the fly is also an activity on its own that I greatly enjoy. In this combination, I continually look for balance between the right rig for the situation along with equipment that casts well and feels right on the water being fished. It should also match well with the quarry to not overpower a fish during the fight but rather enhance the experience in bringing a fish to hand.

This chapter explores the myriad choices available to Spey anglers today that create a nearly infinite combination of elements. Two-handed rods as well as some designed for one-hand Spey form the basis for this style of fly fishing. Many rods are designed for a specific purpose, but most can have a wide application. This chapter looks at how recent developments have helped shape modern rod offerings and impacted rod designs from traditional rod makers.

No element of the sport of Spey fishing is as complicated as the choice of lines. This complexity has created a barrier for new anglers and, in some cases, has scared off would-be Spey fishers. This chapter also breaks down line choices to create a better understanding of the line type to match with a rod, particular species, water type, or condition. It also discusses the recent movement of Spey line recognition to focus on the grain weight of the head of a line as opposed to the line weight designation that has been used for years for two-hand rods and is still the standard for single-hand rods.

Rods

Technological advancements can be observed across the spectrum of fly rod design. From the perspective of an observant angler, rods have become lighter, thinner, and stronger, resulting in a more-versatile fishing

tool. But from a rod-building perspective, "a reduction in swing weight, greater directional stability, and increased versatility in handling various lines" have been the most significant changes in recent times according to Jim Bartschi, President of Scott Fly Rods, who has designed two-handers for more than 20 years. He believes that the key to a quality Spey rod of any size is "the combination of bending deeply and then unbending quickly to form quality and pleasurable casts. The rod should be finished with superior components like quality cork, light and corrosion proof guides, and a reel seat that can be operated in the cold."

Bob Meiser, founder of R. B. Meiser Fly Rods, has been designing rods for the better part of a half century. Unlike the dramatic step up in materials from greenheart to bamboo and then bamboo to graphite, the advancements of graphite in the last 30 years have been gradual. "Incremental changes have led to a more finely tuned instrument that has greater feel. Unlike the original low modulus graphite, today's materials allow for broader diversity of actions and finely tuned tapers. Lighter weight, ability to handle a wider range of line weights and configurations, and greater speed recovery allowing for more sensitivity are all characteristics of modern two-handed rod design."

When it comes to rods for Spey fishing, there are a wide range of sizes and styles designed to cover various rivers, fish species, and fishing opportunities. Rods for Spey fishing can be roughly broken into a handful of categories.

LONG SPEY RODS

The first rods built for Spey casting were quite long, some exceeding 20 feet. Even with light graphite material available today, few rods are commercially produced that exceed 16 feet. Rods that fit into the long category are of 14 feet or greater. These longer rods are generally used on big water in situations where covering more of a river's width can pay dividends. Due to the leverage created by their length, this size rod creates the mechanism for bombing out long casts.

According to Jim Bartschi, where advancements in materials have really impacted two-handers is on the longer rods as weight and instability create a design challenge. "Super lightweight unidirectional prepregs, new toughened epoxy resin systems, and blank construction techniques have really improved performance."

Longer two-handed rods are useful tools on larger salmon and steelhead rivers to handle longer head lines and cover more water with efficient distance casting.

The longer rods also match well with longer lines or heads for casting. A longer line or head requires less stripping of line in between casts than a shorter head and creates a very efficient system for placing the fly back in the water. Analysis has shown that the fly is in the water and fishing a substantially greater amount of time when using a longer head.

Longer rods are generally heavier and stout in the butt, matching well with big anadromous fish by providing the leverage necessary to win a battle even in heavy water. I tend to rely on larger rods when fishing big water and long heads in the upper portion of the water column or on the surface. I also choose greater length when the water being fished calls for continuous deep wading. From an esthetic standpoint, longer

rods afford the mechanical advantage to command the water while providing a certain challenge in casting that requires a more refined technique and timing than with shorter rods and lines. I enjoy the experience of casting and fishing a longer rod when the situation is right, along with enjoying the connection to the traditions of Spey.

Longer rod lengths are commonly used in Spey casting distance competitions. The rules for the annual world championships allow rods up to a length of 15-feet-1-inch.

SHORT / MID-LENGTH SPEY RODS

Rods of 11-feet-6-inches to under 14-feet would generally fall into this category of rods. Shorter rods have been a relatively recent development in Spey fishing. Advanced technology created the ability to commercially produce light rods that can generate significant power and line speed.

Bob Meiser was one of the first rod makers to introduce shorter rods to the market years ago. According to Meiser, today's shorter rods are designed to accommodate the popularity of shorter heads and to meet the requirements of tighter casting on a wider range of waters. It's a matter of lining up the proper tool for the task. Meiser designs shorter rods with a similar approach to longer models by placing the power in the top two-thirds of the rod with a progression for feel deep into the butt and cork.

Rods in this size range are still capable of casting a long line. Rods at the longer end of this range can handle mid-length lines, but generally, the short rods match best with shorter lines and heads. The generation of line speed can carry a shorter head a significant distance by shooting running that has been stripped from the reel.

Rods built for heavier line weights in this range are capable of handling everything from floating lines to heavy tips and flies as well as being able to tame large anadromous or saltwater fish. Also, rods in this size range have the general advantage of being able to operate in tighter areas where there may be overhanging brush, rock walls, or other items that can obstruct the cast.

Lighter rods on the shorter end of this range match well with smaller fish and more intimate waters. For migratory fish in the 4- to 8-pound range, it is most enjoyable to feel the fight and power of the fish by

Shorter length two-handers and switch rods have grown in popularity in recent years, providing versatility in fly presentation, casting advantages in tight areas, and matching well with smaller waters.

utilizing a lighter rod. The lighter, shorter rods have long been my choice in the Great Lakes and match well with fish such as smallmouth bass.

TROUT SPEY

The concept of two-handed swing rods for trout has earned its own classification. These rods are generally 10-feet to 11-feet-6-inches in length. Being built for lower line weights, trout Spey rods have a light feel and are designed to match with the average size of a resident river trout. Most trout Spey rods are built with a line designation from 2- to 5-weight, but as discussed later in this chapter, understanding how the rod matches with the grain rate of the head of the line is often of more importance.

The lighter trout Spey rods work best with floating lines, long leaders, and wet flies or emergers prior to or during a hatch. These rods are designed for pleasurable casting on trout water of all sizes. Heavier trout Spey rods match better with the ability to add a tip and large flies such as streamers and mouse patterns. Some of the more powerful options in this classification of rods can cast long distances. The heavier trout Spey rods can also match with other species such as smallmouth bass.

SWITCH RODS

The term switch rod is used somewhat loosely but can be defined as having a similar length as trout Spey—10-feet to 11-feet-6-inches—but are generally built to handle heavier lines and larger fish. A switch rod has a long enough extended butt that it can be cast with two hands but light enough to also be cast with one hand. This allows the rod to be used interchangeably for Spey casting and swinging a fly or single hand over head cast and a high-sticking approach. It can be a good choice when using both approaches during an outing or for an angler that is just learning the Spey game. While this style of rod can be handled with one hand, some of the heavier weights are fatiguing to handle all day with one hand.

The shorter length of a switch rod generally matches well with shorter head lines that only require a small D loop to cast effectively. The small D loop allows for casting in the tightest of areas and is perfect for when backed right up to casting obstructions. From my own perspective, I enjoy how a lighter, shorter switch rod enhances the experience when fighting fish in the 4- to 10-pound range. Switch rods match up so well with smaller, intimate rivers and creeks. Matching the size

One-hand Spey techniques are very effective and a joy to fish on smaller trout streams and rivers, providing a definite advantage where backcasting room is limited. NICK PIONESSA PHOTO

of the rod to the water is important in terms of presentation control and overall experience. Switch rods allow me to enjoy smaller waters that I previously avoided with longer two-handed rods.

ONE-HAND SPEY

Spey casting isn't just for two hands. There are some rods manufactured light enough and with the proper balance to comfortably perform all the basic Spey casts with a single hand instead of two. This style of rod is generally 10-feet to 10-feet-6-inches. One-hand Spey rods typically combine well with a short head but are capable of shooting a significant amount of line. While some power is lost in one-hand Spey without the advantage of the lower hand, the second hand can still be involved in the cast. Performing a haul on the forward stroke can increase line speed and deliver a tight casting loop.

One-hand Spey matches up well for migratory fish on smaller waters and tight areas with casting restrictions. I have found one-hand Spey to match perfectly with smaller trout rivers while presenting streamers with precise casts close to structure. The lighter design of a one-hand Spey rod also works well on larger trout water with wet flies or streamers. One-hand techniques are equally at home on larger water for covering specific structure and pockets.

Almost any fly rod of nine feet or longer can be used to Spey cast with one hand when matched with the proper line or head. And single-hand Spey casting techniques can be utilized in many fly-fishing situations to begin a standard cast or to avoid obstructions to a basic backcast. The use of one-hand Spey in ever-expanding circumstances blurs the definition of Spey fishing.

OVERHEAD RODS

Although technically not Spey casting, overhead casting with a two-hand rod still fits into this discussion of leverage resulting from the use of two hands. The rod loads with a standard backcast, but the forward stroke and delivery are nearly identical to a forward stroke of a Spey cast.

Overhead two-hand rods are typically shorter than two-handers created for Spey casting and are usually found in the 9- to 10-foot range while some are a foot or two longer. This style of rod has a pronounced lower grip although not as long as found on long, full-sized two-handers. Overhead casting with two hands is efficient and may require only one false cast to shoot a significant distance of line. According to Bob Meiser, "two-hand overhead rods have a similar design to those used for Spey casting—a powerful tip with progression into the butt for efficient energy transfer."

The most common applications for two-hand overhead casting are fishing beaches for striped bass and other near-shore saltwater species and for musky and pike in lakes and rivers. Both beach fishing and musky/pike fishing entail stripping the fly back near the tip of the rod. The power of the two-hander allows for placing the head of the line beyond the tip with a roll cast and then a quick delivery of the fly back into water after the single backcast. This style of rod can also be used for limited Spey casting that may be a good approach when fishing beaches that have backcasting obstructions or where very quick presentations are required.

BAMBOO

It may seem like bamboo is out of place in a discussion about rods for Spey fishing in modern times. While bamboo rods have figured prominently in the development of fly fishing, the spirit of bamboo has allowed it to not simply be stuck in its historical contributions to the sport. Those who value bamboo point to its feel and using equipment with soul as opposed to today's carbon-fiber rods built more for performance. It's an appreciation for a finely hand-crafted tool that is a joy to cast balanced with a profound connection to our fly-fishing roots. It is a connection that many anglers find valuable as part of their fly-fishing journey.

Bamboo rods built for Spey casting are not to be confused with soft, wispy models designed for trout fishing. These are powerful tools capable of handling a range of modern lines. Due to weight considerations, lengths in the range from 11 to 12 feet are the most popular. But bamboo rods up to 14 feet built to handle long belly lines, long casts, or heavier tips are quite manageable when properly balanced with the correct reel.

Nearly every aspect of fly-fishing equipment has experienced a continuous progression in design, and bamboo construction is no different. Improvements in design and advancement in components allow for lighter rods that cast efficiently and fish effectively. Master bamboo rod builder Bob Clay lives on the banks of the famed Kispiox River in British Columbia. For the last two decades, he has been leading the way

Advancements in design have allowed today's bamboo rods to be constructed in a manner that balances tradition with function to handle modern line designs. Here, expert rod builder Jerry Kustich swings a steelhead fly on bamboo.

in two-handed bamboo rod designs where the past meets the present of modern Spey. Clay's beautifully crafted Riverwatch rods define a new age of bamboo construction. This is a tradition that will be hopefully upheld well into the future.

In an interview by author Jeff Bright that appeared in *Swing the Fly 2021 Anthology*, Clay was asked how modern bamboo two-handed rods have evolved or changed from those built prior to fiberglass and graphite. "Modern bamboo rods are lighter, therefore faster, and generally shorter than rods of yesteryear . . . Where bamboo really shines is in the shorter lengths, where it becomes light in the hand and quicker than longer rods. This has been achieved by refining tapers, hollow-building, and the use of modern glues. Although one must be an experienced Spey caster to get the most out of a shorter rod.

"The biggest challenge is dealing with the stresses put upon a rod in the course of two-hand casting. Making rods both strong and light will continue to be the goal. In days past, adhesives were not as strong as

today. Much stress is put upon the rod while Spey casting. The sudden load, the change of direction, and twisting stresses every rod. Modern graphite rods have been refined to handle such stress. With bamboo rods, the advent of new adhesives allowed rod builders to lighten their rods by hollowing. Lighter rods are quicker and consequently can cast further and with more ease. It's the combination of several factors that allows us to advance the art of making the bamboo Spey rod."

Clay goes on to explain the importance of ferule design for two-handed bamboo rods. "The trouble with conventional metal ferrules is they do not bend at the same rate that bamboo does. This causes a stress point and often failure at the joint. Spliced joints allow the rod to behave like a one-piece rod, transferring the stresses smoothly along the entire length of the rod. Alexander Grant and Sharpe's of Aberdeen both used this method on their rods with great success."

Clay has developed a composite ferrule design that relieves the stress point enough to be effective.

Though not as efficient at energy transfer as the splice design, the composite ferrule is a much better choice for rods where setup and breakdown occurs regularly.

Bamboo remains a viable option for anglers looking for a balance between feel and performance, current times connecting with the past. Recent bamboo advancements allow these rods to handle today's modern line designs effectively. Some distance is possibly sacrificed when compared to graphite, but to those that enjoy the experience of bamboo, it is a non-factor. Older bamboo and fiberglass rods can be quite soft and may require slower, more deliberate movements during the setup and forward stroke to allow the rod to work with as opposed to against the caster. However, modern-designed bamboo rods have a faster, stronger feel and match well with today's heads and lines.

Reels

The proper reel plays an important role in a Spey fishing setup. While not as prominent as the rod and line selection, matching the reel for a particular purpose can be both a personal and tactical decision.

A key consideration of the reel is its weight and the ability to balance the rod. The concept of weight balance is important when casting but critical during the act of fishing for long hours. When the rod is set on one or two fingers where it is normally held when fishing, it should lay mainly parallel to the ground or water's surface. I prefer to test this with the reel spooled up the way it will be fished and the line through the guides in the same way as when fishing. If the rod tips down, then there isn't enough weight in the reel, and if it tips up, the reel is too heavy.

When fishing, I attempt to maintain a mostly parallel rod position. While a slight imbalance may seem insignificant, the extra strain on the wrist, arm, and shoulder to raise or push down the tip throughout a day of fishing takes its toll on muscles and tendons, and I have experienced the pain of imbalance firsthand. Slight adjustments can be made by changing

With so many choices, selecting the right rod based on size of river, casting requirements, size of fish, and simple personal preference is extremely important. Jeff Bright found the right tool to land this beautiful sea-run brown from a river in Argentina. JEFF BRIGHT PHOTO

the balance point by sliding the hand up or down on the rod grip. And provided it is comfortable to hold the rod in that position, this is the easiest solution to correcting an imbalance. But in situations where the rig is significantly out of balance, a different reel may be required.

When I first started Spey fishing, most of the available rods were long and quite heavy. It was a common challenge to find a reel heavy enough to balance some of these rods. Various strategies were devised for adding weight to the butt of the rod for balance. With the shorter, lighter rods available today, it is much easier to balance a rig. Reels have become lighter as well, and some are even too light to act as effective Spey fishing tools.

Longer rods manufactured today still require enough heft to properly balance the rig. This also goes for bamboo rods that are heavier than graphite by the nature of the material. Often, you find classic reel designs on both longer rods and bamboo. And while

The reel on a two-handed rod provides balance and the desired drag mechanism. The classic click and pawl design provides some tactical advantage for successfully hooking fish and emits a lovely melody as a line leaves the reel.

a classic or antique reel provides a great look and feel on a rod, especially bamboo, the weight of older reels assists in overall weight balance.

Reels for two-handed rods are generally much larger than those used to outfit a single-hand rod. And it's not all about weight of the reel but also the capacity for holding line. The double-taper lines traditionally used for Spey casting were long and thick with mass to place a powerful load in the rod. A reel with significant capacity was required to accommodate the general size of the line. And for the long belly lines still used today, reel capacity is an important consideration.

Even though mid- to shorter-head lines have become quite popular, the thickness of these lines still requires a fair amount of capacity. When fishing for large migratory salmon, 200 yards or more of 30-pound backing may be required along with running line, the fly line head, and possibly a tip. This can take up a significant amount of space. Today's larger arbor reels help to control weight while offering capacity to easily hold backing, running line, and head. The larger arbor also assists with line pickup for situations when a hooked fish runs in your direction.

The choice of drag systems on reels for Spey fishing is impacted by both function and preference. There are two drag choices—a click and pawl system and mechanical drag. The click and pawl represents tradition and is a relatively simple design of a spring mechanism providing enough tension for the spool to not backlash when line is taken out. This style of reel dates to the 1800s. The gold standard of these historic reels is the Hardy Perfect and are well sought after by collectors and anglers alike. These reels still adorn two-handed rods today on salmon and steelhead rivers. Many Spey fishers prefer the sound and feel of tradition, and there are several makers designing and creating beautiful click and pawl reels attempting to match the magic of the Perfect. Most click and pawls are loud when line is pulled from the reel. This sound is like music to the ears of an angler when a hooked fish tears line from the spool as it runs across the river.

Mechanical drags create tension by two surfaces in contact with one another like a car break. Unlike the click and pawl that can offer slight tension adjustments, mechanical or disk drag systems can be highly adjustable, and the best reels allow for light tenson or heavy enough that it becomes difficult to pull any line from the reel. Drag systems that are sealed prevent water and dirt from compromising the performance of the drag. I prefer an adjustment mechanism that has a click between settings and is numbered or denoted is some way to provide a reference when setting the drag for a specific situation. I also prefer that the reel makes a discernable noise when line is taken from the reel. This isn't only for the esthetic value of hearing line leave the reel from a big fish but also allows you to maintain a gauge of how much line or backing the fish is taking from the reel.

While click and pawl reels typically emit a pleasing melodious sound when an energetic fish peels off line, there are some challenges handling big fish with minimal drag tension. The tension on a click and pawl is generally set light so that line is pulled off easily. Extra tension or drag can be added manually by allowing the line to run through the index and middle finger and squeezing the fingers together. Also, an exposed outer rim allows for extra tension to be applied by the palm of the hand as well as allowing the thumb or other fingers to rub against the outside of the spool. These techniques for adding tension take some experience to gain proficiency but add a fun challenge to playing a fish. I tend to use click and pawl drags when fishing areas where a fish has room to run.

From a tactical fishing perspective, I use a click and pawl drag as a high percentage approach to hooking a fish. When a fish grabs, I typically allow it to take a few clicks of drag before sweeping or raising the rod. The tension of the drag is normally enough to bury the hook point, and by waiting for a few clicks, there is less chance of setting too early. There is more discussion on proper hook setting in a later chapter.

The disk drag allows for more control and tension to be added or reduced, even during a battle with a fish by making an adjustment. A disk drag is my choice when fishing areas that have confined room for fighting a fish. It is important to keep a fish away from elements such as boulder fields, logjams, or rapids where a fish can't be followed when hooked. A disk drag provides that option. I also like disk drags on extremely large fish. While I enjoy the click and pawl, allowing a fish to get too far away can spell disaster. I vividly recall losing a large British Columbia steelhead that too easily took drag and used a mid-river boulder to leverage the hook from its mouth. If I would have kept the fish closer to my position, the encounter may have ended favorably.

A disk drag provides an advantage when fighting powerful fish in restricted areas. Making this bright king fight for each foot of line against a tight drag allowed me to keep its power in check in an area that allowed for no opportunity to follow a long run downriver.

Any reel used when Spey fishing should have no startup inertia. In other words, there should be no hesitation or extra force required when line is first pulled off the reel. The drag should be smooth right from the beginning and all the way through a fight with a fish.

Lines

Knowing that the selection of a line for Spey fishing is a complex topic, it requires careful consideration in *Modern Spey Fishing*. Understanding the advantages and disadvantages of the various line types provides a basis for the proper choice given the situation. One constant that tends to be found throughout Spey fishing is that the choice of a line can be tactical or personal preference or some of each. But since the objective of Spey fishing is to enjoy the act, personal preference usually plays a role.

One concept in lines born from the modern era of Spey is the idea of a head as opposed to an entirely integrated line. A Spey head has loops on both ends and is added to a running line at the rear using a loop-to-loop connection. On the front end, a leader or tip is added also with a loop-to-loop. A head typically

It's easy to be overwhelmed by Spey line options. Understanding the advantages of various designs along with the needs for water being fished can lead to the proper choice. Nick Pionessa covers a pool on a Great Lakes river with a Scandi head.

includes a front and rear taper. The clear advantage of a head is the ability to make a quick, efficient change in lines when on the water without carrying an extra reel or spool. In fact, by carrying a wallet of Spey heads, it's possible to have a variety to meet any challenge. There is also some cost savings in purchasing a Spey head as opposed to a full line. Having a loop connection in the line may take some time to get used to, but the loops will almost always be past the tip of the rod when casting. With a head that is properly balanced for the rod, the head and a small amount of running line extends past the rod tip when loading up and making the cast.

Fully integrated lines can also be readily found as a Spey choice. Most modern full lines are designed with a head integrated into a running line. The head of the integrated line normally has a rear and front taper and is quite similar in design to a separate head system. There is normally a change in color between the head and running line for an easy visual in making sure the full head is beyond the tip of the rod when casting. I

prefer full lines when using techniques that require the fly to be retrieved all the way to the rod tip or in cold weather when ice may develop in the guides. With a full line, there is no concern with loops hanging in the guides on the retrieve or when setting up the next cast.

Identifying a separate head or the head section of an integrated line by its grain weight is another concept that has evolved in the modern Spey era. The grain weight identification is often used instead of the standard line weight designation. The packaging of most Spey lines and heads includes only the grain weight or both a standard line weight designation and the grain weight.

The standard line weight designation on a two-handed rod is not the same for single-hand rods. There is a difference of approximately two to three line weights. In other words, a 6-weight two-handed rod may load with approximately the same line weight of an 8- or 9-weight single-hand rod.

Using grain weights assists in providing a constant when selecting a line for a particular rod. The grain weight designation measures the weight of the entire head. In comparing this to the standard line weight designation for single-hand rods, the weight of the first 30 feet of line minus level tip is considered. For example, a line for a single-hand rod that weighs 210 grains over its first 30 feet would fall in the range of an 8-weight according to the standard table established by the American Fly Fishing Trade Association (AFFTA). A similar standard also existed for lines for two-handed rods and was established at a time when double-taper lines were the norm for Spey casting. And like the single-hand standard, the two-handed system assigned a line designation for the first 30 feet of line minus level tip.

As Spey casting and fishing moved into the twenty-first century, it became apparent that the system for establishing line weight designations for two-handed rods had become antiquated. The movement toward casting with the entire head past the tip given that different style heads have various lengths created the need to reimagine the two-handed fly line standard. Due to the way the rod loads during Spey casting, the grain weight that a rod can adequately handle varies by the length of the head. With this as a driving factor, a committee of two-handed casting experts devised a sliding scale for the two-handed line designation standard. This standard focuses on the grain weight of the total head length including the back taper.

The Spey line standard represents a basic guide to the proper grain weight for a particular rod and line style. But it is far from a complete tool to match a head to a particular rod. As line/head styles have continued to advance, this standard needs an update for more specific line styles and for line definitions to be in concert with those currently on the market. Many rod manufacturers produce their own tables that show a recommended grain length for each style of head for a given rod. This is typically posted on their website and provides very useful information for dialing in the proper setup for a line style. However, we all have our own casting preferences, and the right head for a particular rod can vary somewhat from one individual caster to another. Balancing a rod with the proper grain weight for a casting style is a key step toward getting the best performance and feel from a rod. It often takes some trial and error. And you may

Carrying a few head options on the water allows for quick and easy adjustments as dictated by the fishing conditions or based on personal preference. Today's lines are all marked to keep things organized. NICK PIONESSA PHOTO

AFFTA APPROVED SPEY LINE WEIGHT STANDARDS

Line wt.	Line style Head length Weight point Increment	Shooting Tapers H 30'–50' 40' Grains/grams	Short Bellys S 50'–60' 55' Grains/grams	Medium Bellys M 60'–70' 65' Grans/grams	Long Bellys L 70' plus 80' Grains/grams
6		250 / 16.2	420 / 27.3	460 / 29.9	600 / 39
	50				
7		300 / 19.5	470 / 30.5	510 / 33.1	650 / 42.2
	60				
8		360 / 23.4	530 / 34.4	570 / 37	710 / 46.1
	70				
9		430 / 27.9	600 / 39	640 / 41.6	780 / 50.6
	80				
10		510 / 33.1	680 / 44.2	720 / 46.8	860 / 55.8
	90				
11		600 / 39	770 / 50	810 / 52.6	950 / 61.7
	100				
12		700 / 45.5	870 / 56.5	910 / 59.1	1050 / 68.2

find that your preference for selecting a grain weight is slightly higher or lower than recommended by the rod manufacturer, a factor that you may be able to use when selecting a head weight.

Some rod manufacturers are listing the grain weight range for a rod on the butt section along with or in lieu of the line weight designation. In time, I believe this will become common practice for two-handed and one-hand Spey rods.

DOUBLE-TAPER LINES

Prior to the relatively recent developments of current style lines, the double-taper was the common design for Spey casting and fishing. As the name implies this style of line is thickest in the middle, tapering down to each end so that there isn't a designated front or back. While the double-taper has largely been abandoned for modern styles, it still has its place. A major advantage of the double-taper is that after the swing is complete the next cast can be made without stripping in any running line. This keeps the fly in the water significantly more than when using a line style that requires stripping back to the head. Another advantage of the double-taper is the line can be reversed when the front end shows wear from use.

A double-taper generally requires a longer rod to pick up and cast the line. This style of line generally does not provide the versatility of fishing sinking-tip lines or weighted flies. Double-taper lines for Spey casting are not readily available from most line producers, but there are some still manufactured for this purpose.

LONG-HEAD LINES

A long-head line generally has a head length of 60 to 65 feet and above with a relatively long front taper and short rear taper. The term long-head or belly relates to different lengths among manufactures, and most are shorter than the definition as stated in the AAFTA Spey line weight standards chart. A typical long head

Long- and mid-range head lines work best on big water with sufficient room for a big D loop. The longer head requires stripping in less line to begin the next cast and provides for more efficient water coverage.

is around 600 grains for a 7-/8-weight up to over 800 grains for a 10-/11-weight two-handed rod.

Most long-head style lines integrate into a running to shoot for extra distance. Modern integrated lines typically have a clearly marked loading or handling section that should be positioned at or very near the rod tip for maximum casting efficiency on the setup and forward stroke.

The advantage of the long belly is that it requires less or very little line to be stripped in after the swing to begin the next cast. The long head also allows for effective mending and line control on long casts. This style of line performs best with a long rod of 14 feet or longer. A good rule of thumb for rod length for a long belly line is that the head length be in the range of four to four and a half times the length of the rod.

Long-head lines perform best when fishing on or near the surface. Using a poly leader or a lightly weighted fly allows for presentation down a few feet in the water column. And interchangeable tip lines could allow for even greater depth. Long belly lines have

lost popularity due to a somewhat limited application and the more refined casting abilities required. This style of line is not offered by all manufactures of Spey lines. Even though the trend is for shorter rods and heads, longer belly lines should continue to occupy a place in the future of Spey fishing.

MID HEAD LINES

The head length for lines marketed as a mid-belly are generally in the range of 50 feet to 60 feet in length and match well with mid-range rods of 12-foot-6-inches to 14 feet. The four to four and a half times rod length rule also applies to mid-range heads as well. Like a long belly, this style line has a long front taper and a relatively short rear taper. Most mid head lines are fully integrated with the running line but can also be found as a head to be looped onto running line. A typical mid-head is around 550 grains for a 6-/7-weight up to near 800 grains for a 10-/11-weight two-hand rod.

Mid belly lines match well with medium to larger rivers and enjoy some of the advantages of the long belly in that not as much line is required to be stripped in between casts as when utilizing a shorter head. This length also mends well and is easier to handle from a casting standpoint than a long belly line. From my perspective, this length line offers the ability to use a longer head that can be comfortably casted with a light mid-length rod and is often my choice when fishing a fly on the surface or up in the water column on larger waters. Some interchangeable tip lines in this head length are also available that allow the fly to be fished down in the water column.

SHORT-HEAD LINES

The classification of Spey lines becomes more complex when moving into shorter head lines. There are several specialty heads and lines that fit into the short category and are covered in more detail under shooting tapers. Most lines marketed as short-head or belly have a head length of 40 to 50 feet. Like the long- and midhead, a typical short-head line would have a graduated front taper and a short rear taper. This head length comes in at about 10 feet less the short belly defined in the AAFTA chart.

A short-head line is easier to handle than a long- or mid-length head and can be used on rods under 13 feet in length. This style of line excels in tighter casting areas since it forms a smaller D loop during the setup. Short-head lines are typically integrated with the running line but are also found as a separate head with loops. A full short-head line may have an exchangeable tip to convert from a floating line to a sinking-tip line.

SHOOTING TAPERS

In a sense, the modern Spey movement has largely been defined by the popularity of short shooting tapers. Short heads are easy to cast and with proper running line management capable of reaching out significant distances.

There are two popular style of heads that are used by a high percentage of Spey anglers—the Scandi head and the Skagit. These two head designs were developed in specific geographic areas to address certain casting and presentation challenges. These styles of lines are typically found as a separate head, although some manufacturers have integrated the head and running. The separate head concept allows easy exchange and versatility on the water.

Scandi heads were developed on the rivers of Scandinavia. The steep banks typically found in this region make it difficult to cast long-head lines due to the limited room for the setup. A short head that develops significant line speed in tight spaces helps solve the problem. In the history of Spey fishing, developments have almost always resulted from meeting a specific challenge. Scandi lines also have a long front taper that provides for a smooth casting feel and delicate presentation. Standard Scandi heads are typically 30 to 40 feet in length, however, heads are available up to 50 feet from a few manufacturers.

Scandi heads are generally full floating lines, but some manufacturers have developed versions with a sinking portion or exchangeable tip. To the front end of the Scandi head is added a monofilament leader or poly leader with tippet. The long front taper that provides its smooth feel can't turn over too much weight so the standard Scandi performs best with unweighted or lightly weighted flies and lighter to moderate sink rate poly leaders.

The Scandi head is a good choice when fishing the fly up in the water column or during low-water conditions. The shorter head length allows for the use of a mid-length rod. A good rule of thumb for Scandi heads is that the head length be approximately two and a half to three times the length of the rod. When the proper conditions exist, a Scandi head provides for an enjoyable casting experience and delicate presentations. And as discussed in a later chapter, the longer taper and lighter feel of the Scandi head lends itself well to the touch-and-go type of Spey casts.

The Skagit head (named after the well-known steelhead river in Washington State) was developed on the West Coast by steelhead guides Scott O'Donnell, Mike McCune, and Ed Ward. This style of line was designed to meet the challenges of winter steelhead fishing in the Pacific Northwest. It is a short head with significant mass that can easily handle heavy sinking-tip lines and weighted flies. And due to its mass, it is capable of casting great distances. A standard Skagit head is generally in the 22- to 26-foot range with a short front taper. Most Skagit lines on the market are in the form of a separate head, but it is possible to find this design in an integrated head as well.

The Skagit system is designed to be cast with a tip added to the front along with a leader or tippet. The tip is normally an 8- to 15-foot sinking-tip line but can

Shorter shooting tapers can be used on a wide variety of water and are the main advancement driving the increased interest in Spey fishing. Here I make a short cast to cover a narrow slot along the bank. NICK PIONESSA PHOTO

also be an intermediate or even a floating tip. Most Skagit heads are floating, but some are designed with intermediate or sinking sections to gain and maintain depth. Standard Skagit heads are best handled with rods in the 12- to 14-foot range, using a general rule of the head (exclusive of the tip) being approximately one and three-quarters to two times the rod length.

The Skagit head is a versatile and effective delivery system for a wide application of Spey fishing and allows anglers to effectively fish an array of water that wouldn't be possible with more traditional lines. The ability to deliver heavy tips and weighted flies in tight areas not only allows for attaining significant depths but also in targeting specific structure. Due to the short length and heavy mass that easily loads the rod deep for a cast, this style of head is considered one of the easier casting lines, leading to its popularity among anglers. And due to its versatility, Skagit heads can be used year-round in most Spey fishing situations.

While the Skagit head is an important part of my Spey arsenal, due to its mass, this style of line may not have the same smooth feel of a Scandi or longer head line. But often I find that matching the proper

grain weight and manufacturer with a particular rod can make all the difference when designing a system that is both versatile and enjoyable to cast. In addition, some line manufacturers are producing Skagit heads with a smoother casting feel.

Both Scandi and Skagit heads are available in shorter lengths than the standard discussed here. These lines are designed for rods of less than 12 feet, and the general rules for length of head to rod ratios as low as one and a quarter to two times the rod length. The short head concept is more popular in the Skagit design where micro heads down to 13 feet or less are offered by some manufacturers for short two-handers or one-hand Spey rods. The shortest of the micro heads can be Spey cast with almost any single-hand rod and truly expand the parameters of using Spey casting in situations where it would not have been considered in the past. The setup for the cast with a micro head is quite simple as compared to longer heads and can be used in the tightest casting situations.

It is fair to say that both the Scandi- and Skagit-style heads have some positives and a few negatives. Looking at the negatives, the long front taper of the Scandi

Skagit heads provide the ability to deliver sinking-tip lines and weighted flies in both small and larger water situations. The short head also results in a relatively short D loop—an advantage in tight casting situations. NICK PIONESSA PHOTO

Working a fly deep in the water column with a Skagit head and sinking-tip lines can have its rewards. This regal buck was positioned in a slot contained within a main pool requiring a tip to bring the fly to the proper depth.

does not handle heavy tips or flies, and the Skagit line can feel cumbersome or even clunky when cast. Over the years, some manufacturers have attempted to design hybrid heads to capture the smooth feel of a Scandi with the versatility of a Skagit. This hybrid design has been marketed under various names. While the concept is sound, the fact that it falls in between the two main styles of head design has led to confusion as to how a hybrid line fits into the mix. But a hybrid head properly matched to a favorite rod can provide for a pleasurable and effective fishing experience and in time more heads are most likely to be developed that fuse the positive attributes of each of these line styles.

Shooting tapers that don't identify as Scandi or Skagit are often designed for specific fishing situations. And while some may not have been designed as a hybrid line, most possess at least some of the positive elements of a Scandi or Skagit. Some of these shooting tapers are full floaters with the ability to handle a sinking-tip and others are designed with floating, intermediate, and sinking sections for fishing the fly deep. Heads with various sink rates or multi-density heads provide the ability to better maintain depth consistency throughout the swing and presentation.

A discussion of Scandi and Skagit shooting tapers wouldn't be complete without looking at grain weights. As stated earlier, the AAFTA Spey line weight standards need some updating as the shooting taper column does not line up well with the Scandi or Skagit grain weights required to balance or load a rod. As noted, a standard Skagit head matches well with a rod in the 12- to 14-foot range. The following is a general guide for rods in this length range with respect to Skagit head grain windows:

6-weight 420 to 480 grains
7-weight 480 to 540 grains
8-weight 520 to 600 grains
9-weight 580 to 680 grains

It is important to reiterate that this is just the head weight and does not include the weight of the tip looped to the front of the Skagit head. Also, the increments in which heads are offered vary by manufacturer and can be 25, 30, or even 40 grains between choices.

The concept of the grain weight window reflects the variations in rods, lines, and even casting style. Some casters feel more comfortable with a heavier head and others with one more on the lighter end of the range. Manufacturer charts can provide a very good guide for the recommendation for a specific rod, and a Spey clave or local fly shop where heads can be tried assists in the process of dialing in a rod / head combination. There are variations in Skagit head design from one manufacturer to the next that can also factor into finding the right setup.

To make things a bit more complex, the grain weight of a Scandi head that balances a rod is typically 25 to 50 grains less than a Skagit. The grain weight windows above for a Skagit head can be adjusted accordingly for a Scandi. And as with the Skagit head, the grain weight measurement is just the head and does not include any added poly leaders or tips. The reason that a Scandi needs less grains than a Skagit comes down to weight distribution. When a Spey cast is loaded for the forward stroke, line drapes down from the tip to the water's surface, creating the D loop. At this point it's the top or back of the head taper that provides most

Balancing the proper head with your rod and casting style is critical for both casting and fishing enjoyment. Here, a short head is matched to the intimate water of a perfect tailout. NICK PIONESSA PHOTO

A short head on a switch rod provides the ultimate in versatility in covering small to mid-sized waters. Vince Tobia makes a cast to drop the fly along the ledge on the far bank.

of the load. A Scandi has more of its weight concentrated to the rear of the head than a Skagit that is more evenly distributed. This allows a Scandi to provide a similar load with 25 to 50 less grains overall.

There is a school of thought that there shouldn't be a difference in grain weight from Scandi to Skagit for a given rod since adding weight disrupts the balance and makes it more difficult to complete touch-and-go casts when using lighter tips and flies with the Skagit head. But how a rod feels and casts with a certain line or head is often based on the caster's preference and the desired presentation. One caster may feel more comfortable with a heavier head and another with a lighter head of the same style for the same rod. Generally, a more experienced caster with a refined casting stroke tends toward a slightly lighter head.

This discussion of grain weights supports the idea that it may be more important to place the grain weight window for a line head on the rod than it is to have the line weight designation. Typically, a Scandi head is at the lowest end of the grain weight window, and it moves up from there to Skagit heads and then mid and long belly lines at the top end of the range.

SWITCH / ONE-HAND SPEY

Due to the shorter lengths of switch rods and those designed for one-hand Spey, lines used with this style of rod generally have shorter head sections in the 22- to 28-foot range with an integrated running line. Short Scandi and Skagit heads looped to a running line are also very popular combinations for a switch rod. There are short Skagit heads available under 20 feet in length and micro heads short as 11 or 12 feet. The shortest heads line up well with the shortest of switch rods or with one-hand Spey. The short heads can be used where there is no room for the D loop to pass behind the casting position and blur the line of classic Spey fishing.

To make the proper Scandi or Skagit head choice for a switch or one-hand Spey, it's important to note that the line designation for shorter rods is not consistent with that of longer rods. Shorter rods handle less grain weight for their line designation. While a 13-foot 6-weight rod may handle a Skagit head range of 420 to 480 grains, this is about the same window as an 11-foot 8-weight switch. When lining up a switch or one-hand Spey, it's important to consult the manufacturer's recommendation.

There are some switch lines available that have heads in the 40- to 50-foot range, reducing the need to strip as much line between casts. This style of line can be handled with switch rods at the longer end of their range. This type of switch line is usually a floater with an integrated running and is best for fishing up in the water column. It is typical for this style of line to have a long front taper.

A style of switch lines with an aggressive front taper typically marketed as a streamer line can be a very versatile delivery system for large flies, sinking-tips, or sinking leaders, or even a bulky indicator. This style of line typically is integrated with a running line and has a generous rear taper for a smoother casting feel than a Skagit head. The fact that this style of line can be used for such a wide range of applications makes it a great choice for the switch rod. The smooth connection of the integrated running line can be an advantage when stripping streamers to a point where the head passes through the rod tip.

TROUT SPEY

Trout Spey rods are similar in length to switch and one-hand Spey but scaled down to better match with the size of the quarry. Trout continues to be the most sought-after species with a fly rod, and trout Spey allows us to expand the array of successful techniques while enjoying the pleasure of Spey fishing.

Light two-handed rods with line designations of two through five are generally considered trout Spey rods. Lines marketed as trout Spey with head lengths of 20 to 25 feet or slightly more with long front tapers are a joy to cast on these light rods. This style is generally a floating line and may be available as just a head or an integrated line. The general trout Spey taper is best for handling small wet flies with mono leaders or light sinking leaders. Short Scandi heads can also be used for this purpose.

Short or micro-Skagit heads can be an important part of a trout Spey arsenal. It is more common to find a Skagit head as an integrated line in trout Spey sizes than in higher head weights. Short or micro-Skagit heads excel at delivering streamer patterns and sinking-tips or sinking leaders. The big, bushy weighted streamers used to entice trout of trophy proportions to attack require the mass in the head provided by a Skagit. And as consistent with switch rod lines, streamer lines in trout Spey sizes provide another option for delivering big bulky flies or turning over indicators. Streamer lines have a similar aggressive taper to a Skagit with a longer rear taper. This style of line is usually integrated so there is no loop in the way when stripping streamers.

It's important to pay close attention to manufacturer line recommendations with respect to trout Spey rods as there are wide variations from one company to the next in terms of line designation versus grain weights of the short heads used to balance the rods. Most 2- or 3-weights are in the 180 to 270 grain range for Scandi and Skagit style heads. There are some micro-Skagit heads available down to 150 grains.

OVERHEAD LINES

Shooting taper style lines with heads around 30 feet match up well with overhead two-hand casting. The head needs to carry enough weight to quickly load the rod with an absolute minimum of false casts. And when using techniques where the fly is stripped back inside the rod tip, the short, heavy head can be easily roll cast past the tip with minimal effort to begin the next cast.

Shooting taper style lines are available through most line manufacturers. This style line is typically 30 to 40 feet or so in length. In some lines, the head is all-sinking or could be a combination of floating, intermediate, and sink. There are wide variations of this type of line on the market. Some have a level head with a short rear taper, and others have an aggressive front taper with more rear taper to smooth out the turnover of the cast. When stripping the fly all the way back to the rod tip, I prefer a head shorter than 30 feet. I'll cut the head back to about 23 to 25 feet, but it must have enough grain weight in the head to load the rod. In this situation, I would use a head that in its full 30-foot length is too heavy for the rod and cut it back for a proper match.

Shooting tapers can also be easily constructed to customize for specific fishing situations. Homemade shooting tapers are made from connecting a non-tapered section of sinking line to a running line. The simplest approach for a homemade tip is to start by adding a loop at the front end of the running line if one doesn't already exist. Lash the line against itself to form the loop with tying thread and a bobbin, complete with a whip finish, adding a little superglue over the thread. A loop is then added to the tip using a

Success with one-hand Spey streamer fishing. On this day, a micro-Skagit head allowed me to efficiently cover a wide range of water types on a tight, bushy stream. NICK PIONESSA PHOTO

50-pound braided loop connector by inserting the back end of the tip into the hollow braid of the loop connector. The braid is then secured with a double nail knot and a touch UV knot sealer. The braided loop connector can be doubled up and a second nail knot added to increase strength and reduce any hinging effect during the cast. Another approach is to use a hollow braided running line by inserting the tip into the braid. A double nail knot and UV knot sealer completes the connection. Braided running line is discussed further in the next section of this chapter.

For fishing higher in the water column, a floating Skagit head can act as a shooting taper for overhead casting. The grain weight of the Skagit over its short length provides for a good overhead line. A monofilament or fluorocarbon leader can be attached directly to the head. Skagit heads that have an intermediate section or intermediate to sinking are useful for fishing lower in the water column.

RUNNING LINES

The running line or shooting-line (the term is used interchangeably) attaches the head of the line to the backing. Running line has no taper and is of a low diameter to reduce surface area and friction. The heavier head creates momentum when cast, and the running or shooting-line pulled free from the reel allows the head to shoot significant distances.

As defined earlier, a line with an integrated running line is a continuous fly line with a smooth transition. The running line section of an integrated fly line is almost always floating but can be an intermediate. For separate heads, the running line has a loop on the front. I also use a loop on the rear end to connect with the backing. The loop on the front end should be large enough to go over a coiled shooting taper for a quick, efficient change. There are three main choices for running line material to consider when rigging up a shooting taper system.

Coated running lines are the most popular choice. This style of line has a braided or monofilament core with a coating just like a conventional fly line. The coated running line is mostly floating, but intermediate options are also offered. The coating can be smooth or have some type of texture to further reduce friction allowing for longer casts. Most include a large, welded loop on the front end that may be marked with a contrasting color for easy identification of the transition from running line to head.

The popularity of the coated running line stems mainly from its general feel like a conventional line. It allows for an easy grip even in cold weather conditions, and most coated lines have low memory reducing tangles when casting. However, due to its diameter and surface area, coated lines may not produce the same distance as the other two options.

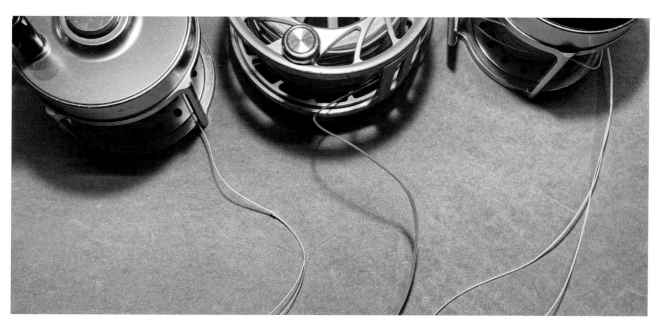

A selection of running lines—from left to right: flat monofilament, coated running line, and braid. Each style of running line has its positive attributes and negatives as the choice is typically made based on personal preference.

For pure distance, it is difficult to compete with a monofilament running line. The relatively thin diameter and slick nature of mono reduces surface area and friction, allowing the head to sail across the water. There are two styles of mono running line—flat and round. Flat running lines are typically a thin oval design but feels flat in the hands. Round running lines are typically made with hollow-core mono for better floating characteristics.

Mono running lines tend to maintain more memory than coated lines and represents one of the disadvantages of rigging with mono. However, a good stretch usually alleviates this issue. Also, due to the thin nature, mono running lines are more difficult to grip, especially in cold weather situations. Some anglers find the difficulties of handing mono to outweigh the extra distance gained.

Monofilament running line is normally packaged in large spools with no loops on either end. But an effective loop can be easily added with a double surgeon's knot. The front loop should be constructed large enough to fit over a coiled shooting taper. It's essential that the knot be tightened slow and evenly and then add significant tension to the tag end to completely seat the knot. Some UV knot glue adds extra security and helps smooth out the knot. A Bimini twist can also be used for maximum strength, although this creates a higher knot profile.

Braided line represents a third option for running line. Like coated lines, the braided line option has more feel than mono but is relatively low in diameter so that it shoots similar to mono. It also has very low memory. Braided line represents a combination of the best attributes of coated and mono running lines, making it my first choice in most situations. From a negative standpoint, some anglers dislike the noise that braided line makes as it shoots through the guides, and it can also be abrasive or even cause injury to fingers if mishandled. Also, being hollow, braided line absorbs or retains water, which causes it to become stiff when air temperatures are below the freezing mark. This hollow nature also brings more water into the guides of the rod when stripping back line and in freezing temperatures adds to the icing issue of the guides.

Like mono, braided line is marketed in spools so that a loop needs to be added at each end for a connection. Tying a knot with this material is impractical since it can slip, and it creates too high of a profile.

The hollow nature of braid facilitates an easy method to create a smooth, low-profile spliced loop by threading the material back on itself and finishing with a spot of super glue. To form the loop, the only tools needed are a pair of scissors and a homemade threading needle constructed by bending over a short length of single-strand wire. The first step is to remove about two feet of the core inside the braid. About 12 to 18 inches from the end, insert the homemade threading tool into the braided line toward the end, pushing the point in about two to three inches. Then push the end of the tool back through the braid. The end is placed inside the loop that is created with the tool outside the braid and pulled back through the original insertion point, leaving a tag end. The process is then repeated about two to three inches down on the braid by threading up to the original insertion point. The tag is placed in the loop of the threading tool and pulled back through the second insertion point. The loop can be slowly adjusted to the proper size before cutting the tag end. A drop of superglue where the tag was cut along with the braid tightening down on itself under tension keeps the loop secure.

When constructing a running line out of monofilament or braid, the length should be able to accommodate your longest cast. A length cut from 80 to 100 feet is common. Manufactured coated running lines typically have a length at or near 100 feet. All running line materials are available in a range of diameter and core break strength. In general terms, coated lines are typically available in diameters ranging from 0.025 inches to 0.040 inches, with core strength of 20 to 35 pound. Both mono and braid range in strength from 25 to 50 pound. For all the running line materials the lower diameter and strength options match best with the lighter heads and smaller fish encountered in Spey fishing for inland trout and other smaller resident species. Moving up the scale to heavier heads and larger fish, running lines in the middle and upper end of the range match best.

Leaders and Tips

The leader or tip is looped on to the front end of the head or integrated line. Almost all manufactured heads or lines have a welded loop at the front to facilitate a loop-to-loop connection. For heads or lines without a loop, one can be easily constructed by looping the line back on itself, lashing down with tying thread,

Matching the proper leader or tip to the fishing situation can have a significant impact on success. Zack Williams releasing a massive fresh Pacific Northwest steelhead. ZACK WILLIAMS PHOTO

and completing the knot with a whip finish. UV knot sealer or superglue completes the loop. Be sure that the thread bites into the coating of the line to eliminate slipping. Welded loops can also be added using kits produced by some line manufacturers. Leaders and tips can be broken into three main categories: monofilament or fluorocarbon leader, sinking or poly leaders, and sinking-tips.

MONOFILAMENT / FLUOROCARBON LEADERS

Monofilament or fluorocarbon leaders are mainly used when Spey fishing on or near the water's surface. This type of leader is usually tapered—either knotless or stepped down through a series of blood knots. The butt section of the leader should be thick and stiff enough to transfer the energy of the cast and turn over the fly. The diameter of the butt section varies depending on the grain weight of the head and size of the fly. Lighter heads are matched with lower diameter butt sections.

For constructing knotted leaders, a configuration of 60 percent butt section, 20 percent mid-section, and 20 percent tippet is a good guide for most Spey fishing situations when using a floating line and monofilament or fluorocarbon leader.

When fishing for large anadromous species, a case can be made for using a level diameter leader to reduce the chance of a failure in the terminal tackle. Extruded knotless leaders can have some variations in strength, and the knots of a knotted leader increase the opportunity for failure. While a level leader may not turn over as gracefully, it may bring the additional strength and confidence for landing big fish.

The length of the monofilament or fluorocarbon leader can vary. I have always preferred the leader length to be similar to the rod length as this seems to provide the proper tension for setting up the cast. The rear or butt section of the leader requires a loop for the connection to the line or head. Manufactured leaders typically have a loop, but for homemade leaders, a loop needs to be added. Either a perfection loop or surgeon's does the job. I prefer the perfection loop for its lower profile.

SINKING LEADERS

Sinking leaders are a versatile part of a complete Spey fishing system. Sinking leaders generally have a nylon core with a coating like a fly line that is impregnated with weight. This style of leader is tapered to facilitate a smooth turnover of the cast and designed with a low diameter to increase sink rate. Most sinking leaders have welded loops on the butt end and some at both ends. Lengths of leaders vary by manufacturer, from as short as five feet and up to 14 feet. The sink rates vary to meet fishing situations. An intermediate leader may sink at a rate of only one inch per second, and the heaviest options sink near seven inches per second, providing the ability to cover a wide range of the water column.

Sinking leaders can be matched with a variety of lines, including mid to longer belly lengths. But the most common use is to pair with a Scandi- or Skagit-style head. The low profile and taper of the leader allows it to easily be handled by the long front taper of a Scandi head. A Scandi head may struggle to turn over some of the longer and heavier sinking leaders. But a Skagit head can be used with a sinking leader when it is too heavy for a Scandi.

Sinking leaders excel when fishing smaller waters with short, light rods. When using switch or one-hand Spey, sinking leaders of 10 feet or less is the best match, and leaders up to 12 feet make sense with mid-length two-hand rods. Sinking leaders greater in length than 12 feet generally match best with long two-hand rods.

SINKING-TIP

A sinking-tip performs the same function as a sinking leader but has more mass. Sinking-tips are looped to the front end of a line or head to fish a fly down in the water column and can loosely be grouped into two categories—manufactured tips with welded loops that may or may not have a density compensated taper or homemade level tips cut to length from sinking material with loops added at both ends. Manufactured tips are available in various sink rate options from intermediate to eight inches per second and found in lengths from 10 to 15 feet.

The most common homemade tips are constructed of T-material with a tungsten compound coating that produces tremendous sink rates. This material is designated with a T- and the grains per foot of the material. In other words, T-8 weighs eight grains per foot, T-11 weighs 11 grains per foot, and so on. T-material can be used in a wide range of situations. The approximate sink rates of T-material are as follows:

T-8: 6 to 7 inches per second
T-11: 7 to 8 inches per second
T-14: 8 to 9 inches per second
T-17: 9 to 10 inches per second
T-20: 10 to 11 inches per second

When creating homemade tips, loops can be constructed using tying thread and UV glue as described earlier or by using manufactured welded loops made for this purpose. The manufactured loop has hollow heat-shrink tubing on one end that slides over the double-backed line and shrunk in place to create a secure loop.

Manufactured tips are commonly used with short-, mid-, and long-head lines that are designed for

Carrying a variety of lengths and sink rates of sinking leaders and tips provides the ability to make changes throughout the day as water and conditions dictate. Loops at both ends of the tip facilitate a quick change that can be completed in a few minutes. NICK PIONESSA PHOTO

Sinking leaders and sinking-tips looped on to the front of a head allow a fly to be fished in various levels of the water column. Nick Pionessa used a sinking leader and weighted fly to cover the rocky depths where this smallmouth was positioned.

interchangeable tips. This allows for coverage of various levels of the water column with the simple change of a tip. This style of line is normally sold as a package and the taper of the tip is designed to complete the full front taper of the head. The package of tip options may include a floating tip, intermediate, and two or three sink-rate sinking-tip lines. The line should be similar to cast with each of the tips although the heavier sink rate tips change the overall weight and feel. The interchangeable tip line is a great option when covering larger water and looking for a more traditional casting feel and experience but have the versatility to cover various depths.

Manufactured tips also match well with Skagit heads, and the 10- to 15-foot length of the tapered tip can smooth out the feel of casting this style head. Density compensation allows the end of the tip to sink as fast or faster than the butt section, providing an effective fishing tool for depth control and maintaining sensitivity. Manufactured tapered tips are available to purchase separately and generally vary in sink rate from three inches per second to eight inches per second. The tips may have a sink rate designation such as Type III (or 3) indicating a rate of three inches per second. Some tips can also be given a line-weight designation for matching with interchangeable tip lines. The grain weight of a Type III 9-weight tip is heavier than a Type III 7-weight tip that in turn can have a slight impact on how fast the tip sinks.

Level T-material tips are extremely versatile and allow a Spey fisher to sink a fly quickly and explore the dark depths of a river. T-material tips are generally constructed from lengths of 5 to 15 feet. The short lengths are used as mini tips in smaller waters or when fishing the fly higher in the water column. Long tips are associated with exploring depths on bigger waters. Ten to 12 feet is a common length for a T-material. When using a floating head, both the length of the tip and the grain weight per foot impact how deep the fly fishes. Eight feet of T-11 does not fish the fly as deep as 12 feet of the same T-11. And 12 feet of T-14 fishes the fly deeper than 12 feet of T-11.

Finding the right combination of length and sink rate is where homemade tip making can get complicated. There are advantages to maintaining a consistent length and carry a full range of sink rates.

Level T-material is effective for placing the fly deep and generally matches best with Skagit heads. This style of tip also allows for versatility in the type of water that can be effectively covered with Spey techniques.

There is little excuse for breaking of a fish when swinging a fly. Always be sure to use a tippet of sufficient strength. Here Keith Myott applies the appropriate pressure to quickly end the fight with a fall steelhead.

Adjustments can be made in finding the proper depth by swapping out the same length tip with different sink rates. This keeps one of the variables constant and maintains a consistent tip length to not disrupt casting rhythm. However, sometimes a small adjustment can be made by adding or subtracting a foot or two of the same sink rate tip. Due to the level nature and weight, T-material tips match best with the mass of a Skagit head, although some hybrid heads also handle lighter T-material.

Another tip option for Skagit heads that goes beyond a simple homemade version is the idea of a manufactured multi-density tip. This style of tip has two or three sink densities within its length with a smooth, seamless transition to each change in sink rate. Lines and products in fly fishing and especially Spey fishing change so regularly that it is impossible to name specific items in these pages without the risk of being quickly outdated. However, the multi-density tip idea was first produced by RIO Products and their MOW tips. These tips have become very popular and are as much a concept as a specific product with the moniker of a MOW tip becoming synonymous with multi-density sink rates.

MOW tips are designed with the fastest sink rate at the end that is connected to the leader or tippet. The tips may have a section of floating, intermediate, or multiple sink rates to provide both a smooth transition for casting and a graduated sink rate for managing depth control. Multi-density sinking-tips are typically available in lengths of 10 or 15 feet. A consistent length of the tip allows the head and tip combination to feel the same when a change in tip is made but based on configuration can make a significant difference in the depth that the fly is fished.

TIPPET

The terminal end of the rigging is where a battle can be won or lost. Paying close attention to this detail increases the odds of success while eliminating the possibility of heartbreak. The tippet is the last section of leader that is attached to the fly. In a long monofilament or fluorocarbon-tapered leader, the tippet is the last section of a knotted leader or the last couple feet

Dressing for the conditions is the key to enjoying the experience while staying engaged throughout the day. Joe Janiak intently fishes through a cold early winter day punctuated by a short snow squall.

of a manufactured extruded leader. For a long-level monofilament or fluorocarbon leader, the tippet and the body of the leader are essentially one in the same.

Sinking-tips and sinking leaders have a section of monofilament or fluorocarbon looped to the front of the tip with a length that can vary widely. The monofilament or fluorocarbon can be composed of one or two sections. My preference is to use two sections, with the rear piece being a few pounds of breaking strength greater than the terminal end or tippet. This allows stronger material to be used in the loop-to-loop as this connection tends to weaken with use over time. The tippet is then connected using a double surgeon's or blood knot.

The total length of the monofilament or fluorocarbon looped to the sinking-tip lines or sinking leader is impacted by various factors. I generally use a monofilament or fluorocarbon leader/tippet of two to four feet in length. The shorter end of the range is used in dirty water conditions or fishing in faster water so that

an unweighted fly remains close to the sink source, allowing the fly to sink at a similar rate as the tip. The longer end of the range is used in clear-water conditions. Longer leads can also be used when fishing an unweighted fly in softer water or with a weighted fly that sinks at the approximate rate as the tip. There are times where the leader/tippet can be extended from six to even nine feet. I have used this rig along with a heavily weighted fly and a heavy tip to get down quickly in fast pocket water as well as reaching significant depths in pools and slots.

The most important statement that can be said about the tippet is to never fish too light. Spey fishing often targets large fish when swinging a fly. Takes occur at a downstream angle when the fish may eat the fly and turn downriver with force. The tippet needs to be strong enough to withstand the initial grab and maintain its strength throughout a battle that could include contact with rocks and other underwater structures. Fish normally react from the impulse to chase and eat fleeing prey from the side or behind, and much of the time, active fish are not tippet shy. However, in very clear-water conditions, overall leader length and tippet size can make a difference. In clear water, it can pay to go lighter but always with enough strength to land the size fish that you expect to find in the water.

Whether to use monofilament or fluorocarbon for leader and tippet material can be a personal preference. There are a variety of good options for quality monofilament on the market today, but for many years, I have used Maxima as a tough and dependable connection to a heavy fish. I use both ultra-green and chameleon. While the chameleon has a brown appearance and looks as though it would more readily show in the water, it actually reflects less light than the ultra-green, making it stealthier. Due to the neutral buoyancy of monofilament, it is a good choice for surface fishing.

Fluorocarbon has a lower refractive index than monofilament so that it is more difficult to detect in the water. Fluorocarbon is a good choice in low, clear-water situations as it increases the stealth factor, and over the years, I have noticed a difference under these conditions. The specific gravity of fluorocarbon is greater than that of monofilament, allowing it to sink much faster than mono. This sinking ability matches well with the use of a sinking-tips. Also, because it is a harder material, fluorocarbon has superior abrasion resistance and can be a significant advantage when a big fish runs around rocks and boulders.

One disadvantage of fluorocarbon is that the hardness can make it slightly more difficult to tie a secure knot. The extra care required for a good fluorocarbon knot possibly makes mono a better choice for winter fishing with cold, numb hands. But when working with fluorocarbon or monofilament, be sure to fully lubricate the material throughout the knot-building process. This requires adding saliva or water multiple times through the various steps of the knot. Also, be sure to tighten the material slowly through completion. These steps allow the knot to properly set up and reduce friction that can build up heat and weaken the material.

Inspect the finished knot to be sure it is properly constructed and fully seated with no loose line. A knot that doesn't look good is probably weak and should be tied again. It only takes a few seconds to re-tie and eliminate the chance of losing a fish from a bad knot. Use pliers to pull strongly on the tag ends, and a pair of gloves can assist in grabbing the material to apply maximum pressure. Be proficient at the knots that you use most often. Practicing knots at home may seem like overkill, but practice always makes us better. And given that the knots in the leader or tippet are the weakest link in the system, we should take every step to make that link the strongest it can be.

Other

A pair of polarized sunglasses are a must when Spey casting and fishing. When performed improperly the Spey cast can result in the fly being on a collision course with your body. Glasses provide a line of defense for your eyes. Polarized lenses allow for identification of the nuances and structure in the water being fished or even spot fish holding in a pool or run. Glasses are as important as any other part of your Spey equipment.

It's also important to dress for success. Much has been written about layering for cold weather with a breathable shell to block wind and moisture. But possibly more important is the consideration of water temperatures and the layers under the waders. Cold water can quickly zap your heat if you are not properly prepared. Thermal layering underneath is essential to staying comfortable in the water. Boot foot waders or utilizing battery-operated socks can help keep your feet toasty warm.

3

SPEY CASTING

For someone not familiar with Spey casting, the most basic question may be how or why would such a cast be used? From a pure fishing perspective, a Spey cast allows for an efficient 90-degree change in direction with only a limited amount of line passing behind the casting position. Combined with the power gained by the use of two hands, great distances can be obtained, highlighting another advantage of this style of casting. The change of direction blends perfectly with the swing the fly approach, but various aspects of Spey can be used in other forms of fly fishing.

The attraction to Spey casting is not simply about fishing effectiveness. A Spey cast done right is a work of art—mechanical poetry in motion combining power with the delicate balance of timing. Proper Spey casting provides a feeling of being an artist expressing oneself through the world of angling with the rod as the brush and the line and water as the canvas. Every cast feels like a creation in itself that delivers an offering to the unknown.

Basic Spey casting isn't difficult to learn, especially today since shorter head lines have reduced the curve. Longer heads require more precise rod movement and timing to accomplish an effective cast. And while the curve has been shortened to learn the basics, Spey casters will spend nearly a lifetime in the pursuit of perfecting the craft. The endless combination of

Open water offers the opportunity to bomb out long casts to efficiently cover a big, wide pool. The breathtaking scenery of this Chilean river provides a perfect backdrop. JEFF BRIGHT PHOTO

rods, lines, and water types makes certain that there is always something else to try or new avenues to travel.

Science and the principles of physics are an integral part of fly casting and in full display when it comes to Spey casting. There are some basic standards and movements that are key to making an effective cast. Learning and refining the basics provide the building blocks for making each variation of the Spey cast.

For me, the challenge in Spey casting lies in making it all work when fishing. Wind, current speed, water level, and obstructions all impact the basic principles of the cast, requiring an understanding of this impact and making proper adjustments. Each cast can be a little different based on changes in the surroundings.

The objective of this chapter is to provide a full presentation of Spey casting by discussing and analyzing the key steps in consistently making effective casts. The chapter covers the various casts required to be a complete Spey angler as well as tips for troubleshooting and improving or taking your casting to the next level. From my perspective, the key to enjoyment and effectiveness as a modern Spey angler is reacting to conditions and the situation by employing the proper cast. There is information in this chapter to provide the basics for a beginner Spey caster as well as tips to improve a veteran angler's overall fishing experience and to fully appreciate all that Spey has to offer.

Setting Up for the Cast

In almost all physical and sporting activity, we tend to develop our own style. When watching a baseball game or golf tournament, it is fascinating to see the variations in the swing of the bat or club from one player to the next. Differences stem from an individual developing a style that best fits their physical and mental makeup. Spey casting is similar to these other sports. There are certain steps throughout the setup and completion of the forward stroke that need to be present for a successful cast. But we tend to develop our own style that fits.

Some variations in the setup and cast are influenced by the rod and rigging being used and are discussed throughout the chapter. The more traditional approach to Spey casting that utilizes a longer belly or double-taper line typically involves a fixed anchor point and wide, sweeping movements of the rod. This is contrasted with the style of casting associated with Scandi heads, consisting of a stationary anchor with a short,

efficient stroke placing emphasis on the bottom hand. A third style emerged to properly handle Skagit heads. The weighted flies and sinking-tips typically used with a Skagit head require a sustained or moving anchor to maintain the fly and line on the surface delivered with a more deliberate short stroke.

No matter what rigging or style of Spey casting is being utilized, there are some basic steps and principles required to be present with each successful cast. While I use a range of rods and lines over the course of a year, I'm not fixated on emulating a certain style of casting. However, the rod, line, leader/tip, and fly all factor into adjusting the setup and stroke to ensure that the basic principles of the cast can be maintained. I consider myself much more of an angler than a caster, and I have conditioned myself to adjust the casting approach to properly present the fly. A firm understanding of the basic steps of the cast form the basis for being flexible and adaptive.

A good starting point is to focus on hand position and the grip. For a medium to long two-handed rod, the hands will be positioned apart at about the width of your shoulders. A good starting approach is to let your arms hang at your side and use that distance apart as a starting position. Within that general guideline, the upper hand can be moved to find the most comfortable position and the point that allows the rod to balance when casting and fishing. Shorter handles on short two-handed and switch rods will result in the hands being positioned closer together when casting this style of rod. The physics of two-handed casting work best when the hands are positioned as far apart as possible while remaining comfortable.

A proper grip is critical for successful casting. Developing a feel for the grip for two-handed casting is commonly one of the first hurdles to clear for someone that is a proficient single-hand caster moving into two-hand Spey casting. A passive or loose grip with both hands allows the rod to move freely. To form the top or upper hand grip, I allow the handle to rest in the soft area of my palm between the thumb and forefinger. The thumb is loosely wrapped toward the top of the handle with the fingers also wrapped loosely underneath. The thumb points in the direction of the rod tip. For the bottom hand, I place the end of the lower handle so that it rests between the middle and ring finger. The thumb, index, and middle finger then wrap loosely around the bottom grip, with the ring and pinky resting off the end of the grip. Some casters simply form a ring with the thumb and index finger to control the bottom grip. As with hand position, the grip allows for some variation to fit the caster's comfort level. I think in terms of gripping the rod just enough that it doesn't fly out of my hands when making the cast, allowing the leverage of the rod with the movement of two hands and arms to do the work. The absence of a strong or power grip allows the rod to move smoothly and efficiently.

With Spey casting, there tends to be variations for different circumstances. Distance casting with long rods and heads can benefit from a stronger grip with the upper hand. Placing the thumb slightly more on top can provide for a firmer stop on the setup and additional power during the forward stroke.

While arguably not as important as hand position, foot positioning also plays into Spey casting. There seems to be much more variation and personal preference involved in foot placement. I tend to keep the foot on the side of my casting shoulder slightly back and the other foot slightly forward when casting shorter lines. This allows for a free transfer of weight during the setup to the forward cast. However, placing the feet fairly even or the casting shoulder foot slightly forward is also preferred by some casters. From a tactical standpoint, the casting shoulder foot forward can provide extra power when casting long heads and prevent over rotation on some casts. While out on the water, the terrain or fishing situation may dictate foot placement, and from a practical standpoint, there is an advantage to being able to work with feet in varying positions.

One of the more difficult aspects of learning to Spey cast with two hands is quite simply learning to truly use both hands. Those who have casted a single-hand rod for years generally have a tendency to overpower the rod when their dominant hand is on the upper grip. For an efficient stroke, the top hand pushes or simply guides while the bottom hand pulls toward the body to accelerate the tip and create line speed. There should be at least as much pull with the bottom hand as push with the upper. In fact, many casters advocate relying on as much as 80 percent bottom hand for the power of their froward stroke. It's important to reiterate that a successful two-handed Spey cast relies on the lever effect of the rod. The hands moving around the fulcrum or pivot point located between the hands is essential for power and line speed of the cast.

A loose or passive grip allows the rod to move and rotate freely while engaging both hands and reducing the tendency to overpower with the top hand.
NICK PIONESSA PHOTO

Effective use of the bottom hand can feel awkward at first and be a common area for troubleshooting and improving the cast.

For those new to Spey casting, it's important to understand some key terms to the mechanics of the cast. While it has already been mentioned earlier, a definition of the anchor point is essential. The anchor point is where the fly, leader, and, usually, the first foot

The key to a powerful forward stroke is for the hands to move around the pivot point, pulling with the lower hand while pushing and guiding with the upper hand. These photos show the bottom hand out as the D loop is formed and bottom hand pulled in as the cast is completed. NICK PIONESSA PHOTOS

The anchor should be placed at approximately a rod length away at a 45-degree angle in front of the casting position with the D loop formed by the drape of the line down to the anchor. NICK PIONESSA PHOTO

or two of the line meet the surface of the water to create tension that assists in loading the rod for the cast. With a floating line and a long leader, the anchor is formed by the fly, leader, and first few feet of the floating line on the water. Where it gets a bit confusing is when using a sinking-tip. However, consider a sinking-tip like a leader so that the anchor point is generally formed by the fly, short section of leader, the tip, and, typically, the first foot or two of the head.

The anchor point occurs at an approximate 45-degree angle to the front of the casting position off the casting shoulder about one rod length away. From a practical standpoint, the anchor point is more of a zone or area as opposed to an exact point. For safety purposes, it is essential that the full anchor point maintain a proper distance from the casting position as serious injury can occur if line and fly collide with any part of your body, especially the head and face. This is a good reason to always wear glasses when Spey casting. I ALWAYS make a visual of the anchor before completing the cast to be sure it is in a safe position. And if not, the cast is aborted. For casting effectiveness, it is critical that the anchor point, the fly, leader,

and line are all lined up and pointing in the direction of the cast. The cast will not be efficient or even possible when not lined up properly. Anchor point will be discussed more throughout this chapter.

The D loop describes the line draping from the tip of the rod to where it meets the water's surface at the anchor point as the rod represents the straight portion of a capital "D" and the line as the curved or rear section of the letter. In modern casting, the line draping from the tip typically consists of the head of the line plus a few feet of running line. The D is formed as the rod is swept back into position to set up the forward stroke. The acceleration of the sweep imparts energy to the line forming the curve. When significant energy is imparted during the sweep, the rear part of the D can take the look of a wedge or sideways V. There is some debate as to whether this extra energy aides in a better cast, but it is critical that enough energy be imparted so the drape of line be tight with no slack. In all styles of fly casting, slack represents inefficiency. The drape of the line combined with the tension of the water creates the load in the rod similar to the backcast when overhead casting.

Another basic element of the cast is rod angle. Earlier in this chapter, the concept of engaging the bottom hand was introduced as a key element in using both hands and taking full advantage of rod leverage. In setting up the D loop, the rod tip should stop and be pointing at an angle back behind the casting position. The angle may differ from one caster to the next but generally between the 1 and 2 o'clock position using a clock face for reference. While this rod positioning allows the tip to move through a sufficient distance to propel the line forward, it also places the bottom hand outward away from the body. This is where the bottom hand needs to be in order for full engagement during the forward stroke.

From the time I made my first feeble attempts to Spey cast, there have been some great books and videos produced specifically on the cast that have significantly reduced the learning curve. Various opinions and approaches exist as to the proper way to make a Spey cast. Instructors have different methods, and anglers develop certain approaches to understanding concepts in their own way. What is described throughout the chapter is how I have digested many instructional lessons and developed an approach that makes sense to me mentally and physically.

I learned Spey casting by thinking of it in terms of building blocks. A basic Spey cast used while fishing involves various well-timed movements to change directions and establish the anchor point before completing with the forward stoke. This final movement that propels the line forward is the one constant found in each of the various Spey casts.

The forward stoke or forward Spey is the first step in building the full repertoire of casts required for effective Spey casting. The forward Spey is also known as the switch cast. Perfecting the forward Spey or switch cast teaches how to establish the anchor with the proper rod position, set up the forward stroke with the proper position of the lower hand out away from the body, and deliver the cast forward using both upper and lower hand. The forward Spey also teaches the cadence and rhythm of Spey casting in general. Since the tension created by the fly, leader, and line touching the water is an integral part of any Spey cast, the forward Spey should be learned and practiced on water. But since there is no change of direction with this cast, it isn't necessary that it be moving water as a pond or lake will do just fine.

There are some similarities between the forward Spey and the roll cast. Both casts utilize water tension to assist with loading the rod to cast the line in a forward direction. However, the Spey cast is a much more active, dynamic motion that imparts energy in the setup forming the D loop and further loading the rod. This additional load, along with the resulting rod position between 1 and 2 o'clock, allows for more power and distance than the roll cast. The forward Spey can be used in most instances instead of the roll cast.

To begin the forward Spey, start with the head of the line beyond the tip. If casting on water with current, facing downriver will tighten the line. When casting on still water, a roll cast can be used to straighten the line. Start with the rod tip low to the water and no slack in the head. Slack results in wasted motion and energy during the setup and cast. For learning and practicing, I prefer a floating head with a leader of the approximate length of the rod. A floating Scandi head is good for learning and practicing. I also use a fly with the point cut off or a piece of yarn. The fly or yarn is key to properly establishing and locating the anchor point and is part of the resistance, creating water tension.

The forward Spey cast starts with a lift of the rod while pointing toward the end of the line. This is a constant theme as all Spey casts begin with a lift. The tip of the rod is lifted to about or just above head high, freeing the line from the water's surface and then in a continuous motion is swept off to the side with a flat movement of the rod. Some casters find that a slight dip in the tip as the sweep begins will allow for an easier setup. Use both hands in the lift by bending at the elbows. As the upper hand passes the shoulder, the rod is raised to the 2 o'clock position as it comes to an abrupt halt. The sweeping movement is made with acceleration as the rod travels at its fastest just prior to the abrupt stop—the same principle found in single-hand overhead casting. This motion causes the rod tip to move in an arc or crescent path, and at the stop, the rod is slightly angled away from the casting position. The upper hand should be about even with your cheek or shoulder and the lower hand out away from the body. Stopping the rod at the cheek or shoulder provides the best position in allowing the upper hand to move forward in a straight line, resulting in a tight casting loop. With the lower arm out and upper arm bent at the elbow, a triangle is formed by the rod going

The forward stroke or switch cast and all Spey casts begin with a lift. NICK PIONESSA PHOTO

The next step is to sweep the rod off to the side in a continuous flat movement arcing up slightly. NICK PIONESSA PHOTO

As the upper hand passes the shoulder, the rod is raised to the 2 o'clock position with upper hand back and lower hand out along with a slight rotation of the body. NICK PIONESSA PHOTO

Once the D loop is formed, the forward stroke begins by pulling with the lower hand while pushing and guiding with the upper hand in an accelerated movement. NICK PIONESSA PHOTO

The cast is completed with a firm stop at 10 o'clock. NICK PIONESSA PHOTO

from hand to hand. This represents the key positioning for the forward stroke.

An important part of the sweep into the 2 o'clock position is that this movement involves the body core. A slight rotation of the body through the hips allows the entire body and rod to do most of the work as the hands guide the rod through its path and add the final acceleration to form the D. When performed properly, the line releases from the water and the fly, leader, and first few feet of the line touch down in the anchor point area.

Right after touching down as the D loop is fully formed, the forward stroke begins with the bottom hand pulling toward the body and the top hand guiding and pushing forward. This motion should be made in an accelerating manner with a final strong movement at the end to complete the fulcrum with the hands. This creates an abrupt stop of the rod, creating line speed and propelling line. The rod should stop high—near the 10 o'clock position or between the 11 and 10 o'clock position. This stopping position, combined with moving the rod tip in a straight plane, creates a tight loop increasing distance and the ability to cut through the wind.

When the setup of the forward Spey is properly performed and the rod is fully loaded, the power of the forward stroke is felt deep into the butt of the rod, ensuring that the entire length is engaged and utilizing its complete leverage. At the completion of the forward stroke, the bottom hand ends up somewhere along the forearm or near the elbow of the upper hand. With shorter head lines, my finish tends to bring my hand into the lower mid-torso of my body. Pulling down slightly with the lower hand while pulling in loads the rod deeper and generates additional line speed.

When learning and practicing, a wading depth of calf to knee deep provides a good base with which to work. Increased depth impacts the setup of the cast, effectively reducing the length and leverage of the rod. Depth is addressed in more detail later in this chapter.

Two common issues can develop when learning or practicing the forward Spey. The first potential problem is that there is too much line on the water's surface so that the forward stroke is ineffective. Sufficient power can't be generated by the rod movement to overcome the line tension and lift the line off the water. This is referred to as too much stick and is a result of too much line on the water forming the anchor. When performing the forward Spey, too much stick can be the result of several errors:

- A weak lift that does not free enough line off the water before beginning the sweep.
- A pause between the lift and beginning the sweep that can cause slack to develop.
- The rod is swept too low, and the line continues to stay in contact with the water.
- The sweep is too weak to throw the line into the D loop.
- The rod stops beyond the 1 or 2 o'clock position when setting up the D loop.

The other common problem is not establishing or maintaining the anchor. In this situation, the line does not stay in contact with the water's surface, traveling behind the casting position similar to a standard backcast. This fails to establish the D loop and simply becomes overhead casting. Losing the anchor can be the result of several factors or errors:

- Using too short of a head for the rod.
- Not sweeping the rod off to the side but rather raising the rod too sharply, similar to a standard backcast.
- Sweeping the rod with too much power.

It takes some time to develop the proper angles and timing while committing the movements to muscle memory. I always focus on the positives and what is going right as opposed to what is going wrong. Making deliberate movements and slowing down always seems to help regulate the timing of a Spey cast. Allow the leverage of the rod to do the work.

Head length impacts the setup of the forward Spey. A long head line generally requires a slightly higher lift at the beginning of the setup to free the line. When using a long head line, try raising the rod tip above head height and a dip that allows the rod to follow along on a smooth arc during the sweep. The sweep needs to be strong and decisive to set the anchor and avoid too much stick. When using a short head line such as a Skagit, too high of a lift may free the line to a point where it is difficult or impossible to set the anchor. A Skagit head requires less of a lift and a slow, deliberate sweep.

Based on my own learning experience, I can't emphasize enough the importance of developing flat rod movements, proper timing and setup, use of both hands, and using the full leverage of the rod that can be gained from learning the forward Spey or switch cast. I use this cast to practice or regain my timing after prolonged periods of not casting.

Controlling Running Line

One of the key aspects of modern Spey casting is that great distance can be attained by casting the head with enough speed and force to pull the running line that has been stripped from the reel through the guides of the rod. Practicing the forward Spey provides the perfect time to work on shooting and managing running line. When performing the setup for all Spey casts, I pinch the running line off with the index finger of the top hand against the cork. When the rod stops after completing the forward stroke, the index finger is lifted, releasing the running line and shooting the head with the running line trailing.

When making relatively short casts, the momentum of the head will pull the running off the surface of the water. However, when making longer casts, the surface area of the running line resting on the water along with the pull of the current can cause enough tension or stick to prohibit all the running line from going through the guides and effectively shortening the cast. The solution to this issue is holding some or all of the running line off the water's surface.

The bottom hand is utilized in managing the running line. There are a few options when it comes to the actual process or technique. One approach uses the pinky finger that hangs off the bottom grip. Loops are formed by the stripping hand as line is retrieved for the next cast. The loops are maintained between the pinky and the ring finger of the lower hand while being formed. Once the running line is retrieved and loops are formed, the bottom hand takes its position on the lower grip with the pinky pointing up, so the loops stay in place or lightly touching the cork to pinch the loops. With the running line pinched off against the cork with the index finger or index and middle finger of the top hand, when the rod stops on the forward stroke, the running line is released by the top hand and the loops released from the bottom hand. Depending on how the loops are positioned in the bottom hand, there may be a need to loosen the grip of the lower hand to release the line. When forming the loops, the first should be the largest after five or six strips and then each additional loop should be smaller. Two or three total loops is generally sufficient.

Forming, maintaining, and releasing the loops may feel cumbersome at first. An approach that some casters may find easier to employ is by again forming loops in a similar manner as above but using the index or middle finger of the bottom hand to form the

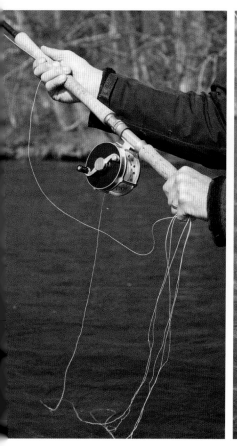

Forming loops with the running line can be cumbersome at first, but there is a method for running line management to fit each angler's comfort zone. Here loops of running line hang off the pinky finger of the lower hand (left). The running line is released by the top hand, and loops are pulled from the bottom hand as the rod is stopped on the forward stroke (middle). All the running line shoots smoothly without tangling (right). NICK PIONESSA PHOTOS

loops and, when the loop is formed, pinch the running line off against the bottom cork with the index finger. When the rod reaches its stop point on the forward stroke, the line is released by the index fingers on both the top and bottom hands, simplifying the approach. Managing running line typically loosens the grip and creates a smoother casting stroke.

A simple approach to managing the running that I frequently use doesn't entail forming loops while stripping in line. When all the running line has been stripped in, it hangs in a big loop in the current. By grabbing the long loop of line with the lower hand at the approximate midway point with the thumb and forefinger, the running line is then pinched against the lower cork during the setup and released by both the upper and lower hand as the rod is stopped on the forward stroke. This approach commonly removes most of the running line off the water's surface and what remains usually doesn't impact distance. However, this simple approach may not work best when

long lengths of running line are in use since it can be difficult to keep enough line off the water. For longer lengths, I use one of the methods previously described.

I always use the lower hand for managing running line. The loops can be maintained during the cast by the upper hand, but there is a much greater tendency for the loose loops to tangle around the rod or reel during the setup of the cast.

The Basic Casts

DOUBLE SPEY

Using the basic principles gained through practicing the forward Spey cast, the next step is in making a change of direction cast. The double Spey cast is a good place to start. The double Spey is used when casting off the right shoulder fishing on river right (this reference is from a rower's or paddler's perspective so that river right refers to the right bank while looking downriver) or when casting off the left shoulder on river left. When the fly has completed its swing and is in the hang down position, if more than just the head is being cast, the running line is stripped back so that the head and a couple feet of running line extend past the tip. The rod tip should be positioned close to the water's surface.

The objective of the setup of each Spey cast is the same—to establish the anchor with the fly, leader, and tip of the line pointed in the direction of the cast while forming a D loop to load the rod. The setup for the double Spey begins with a lift of the rod by bending at the elbows as the tip points skyward and the rod angled out. With the rod angled away from the casting position, draw a straight line across the horizon, moving the upper hand across the front of your body in an accelerated movement. When the upper arm has passed the front of your body, drop the rod tip so that the rod is low and parallel to the water's surface pointing upstream. Both arms are now extended across the body with elbows bent. The fly line or head lies lined up with the direction of the current and the fly is positioned in or near the anchor point zone.

The rod is now brought back across the body led by the upper hand and arm, ripping the line across and off the water. The rod movement is flat at first and then rising at a steady angled trajectory, starting as the rod tip passes in front of the body then accelerating into the 2 o'clock position with the upper hand about even with your head and the lower hand extended out. It is very important that the rod never dips during this movement. When raising and accelerating the rod and hands into the 2 o'clock position, the rod follows a curved path. I like to think about it as moving around the brim of my hat. At this point, the rod should be angled out slightly, and it is time to begin the forward stroke by pulling with the bottom hand and pushing the top while maintaining the hands and rod in a straight plane to deliver a straight-line cast. This is the same stroke as practiced with the forward Spey. But always get a visual of the anchor point before beginning the forward stroke to ensure it is safely in the anchor zone and lined up toward the target.

A small modification can be made in the initial phase of the setup to simplify the process when using a short head. In the starting position with the head pointing downstream and the rod tip low, raise the rod tip up straight while bending the elbows. Now, just flop the rod over so that it is pointing upriver by moving the upper hand in an upstream direction and the lower hand downstream. The hands simply switch positions, with the upper hand landing on top of the elbow of the lower arm. From this point, the cast can be completed as described above.

While I always attempt to focus on positive motions and thoughts when learning something new, it is critical to recognize failure points and what caused the problem. This knowledge base is not only of benefit when learning to cast but is very useful during challenging conditions when fishing. Let's look at a few common errors that can occur during the setup:

- The fly lands too far up on the initial phase—In other words, the fly is not in the anchor zone but even or upstream of the casting position. This places the cast on a dangerous collision course with your body. This is the result of using too much power when bringing the rod upstream of your body. From a safety standpoint, it is better to err on the side of being a little weak on the initial phase than too strong. If the fly is in front of or above your position, it is critical that the cast be aborted and the process started over.

- Improper rod angle during the initial phase—The angle of the rod while it is brought across the body in the initial phase should be somewhat steep so that the line lands fairly close to the body. Too far from the body results in a shallow D loop and less power. However, too close to the body can develop slack in the line during the second step of the setup.

- Not lowering the rod to parallel to the water at the end of the initial phase—It will be difficult to complete an effective sweep with the rod in this position. Starting the rod high as the second phase of the setup begins will typically cause the rod to dip during the sweep. The result is a weak D loop where the line on the water may not clear your body. Or starting too high without a dip will also create a weak D loop and typically cause a complete loss of the anchor point.

- Over-rotating on the setup—As the rod is raised and follows the brim of the hat, the rod tip must stay off to the side and well outside the elbow of the upper arm. Rotating too far during acceleration in an attempt to form a strong D loop can cause the line to travel on a dangerous collision path with the body.

- Anchor is not lined up—As the forward stroke begins the fly, line and leader should be in the anchor zone, lined up in the direction of the target. However, faults in the setup can cause a portion of

The double Spey begins with a lift to free the line. NICK PIONESSA PHOTO

The rod draws a line on the horizon as it is brought across the body and dropped down parallel to the water. The hands switch positions. The fly is now in the anchor zone, with the rod pointed upstream and angled slightly toward the bank.
NICK PIONESSA PHOTO

The rod is then brought back across the body in a flat motion or rising slightly in trajectory in an accelerated motion.
NICK PIONESSA PHOTO

As the rod passes the body, it continues to rise and is swept into the forward Spey position with the rod stopping near 2 o'clock and the upper hand near the shoulder or cheek. NICK PIONESSA PHOTO

Once a D loop is formed, the forward stroke begins by pulling with the lower hand while pushing and guiding with the upper hand in an accelerated movement. NICK PIONESSA PHOTO

The cast is completed with a firm stop at 10 o'clock. NICK PIONESSA PHOTO

the line to remain parallel to the current as opposed to lined up perpendicular to the current. This commonly occurs when the line remains above your position and doesn't comfortably clear the body as the rod is swept to a 2 o'clock position. Dipping the rod or maintaining too high of a rod position on the second phase as the rod moves across the body can be the main cause. So too can a weak sweep that lacks proper acceleration. Additionally, the situation can be caused when too much line and leader remain below the anchor zone after the initial phase of the cast. This will be more common with longer belly lines. To correct this situation, use slightly more acceleration and power as the rod moves across the body in the initial phase.

When performing the double Spey, ideally the fly lands in the anchor zone on the initial phase and stays in place as the line changes its direction by 90 degrees during the second phase, using the fly as the axis point. But many casts aren't ideal. The double Spey provides the opportunity to straighten out the line with the final acceleration and formation of the D. Provided everything is lined up toward the target just prior to the forward stroke, a strong cast is possible if everything else is set up properly.

When performing the double Spey with a short head line, such as a Skagit, slow and deliberate motion through the setup ensures that the anchor point stays intact while allowing for the line and tip to be in the proper plane and deeply loading the rod. The slower movement also creates a sustained or moving anchor as the point of contact with the water moves back slowly as the rod is brought to a 2 o'clock position. This allows a sinking-tip and weighted fly to remain at the surface as the forward stroke begins eliminating the possibility of too much water tension that can occur if the fly and tip sink.

The double Spey is considered a waterborne anchor cast since the fly remains in the anchor zone during the period between the first and second phase of the setup. While this cast can be used with nearly any setup, the waterborne nature of the anchor is what facilitates the idea of the sustained or moving anchor that excels when using a Skagit head, sinking-tip, and weighted fly.

As a general statement, slower, rhythmic movements work best in developing and establishing a good flow and understanding of the double Spey and the other Spey casts. If timing seems to be askew, slow it down to find a proper pace. Each phase or stage of the cast is an independent movement that is key to the completion of a successful cast and needs to be completely and properly performed or acknowledged. Shortcuts lead to poor casts. While there can be a slight pause between each step, seamlessly rolling from one phase into the next provides for an efficient casting style.

SNAP T / C SPEY

The snap T or C Spey (sometimes referred to as the circle Spey or circle C) is used when fishing on river left and casting off the right shoulder or river right casting off the left shoulder. The snap T or C Spey are essentially the same cast with the only differentiation being found in the initial movement of the first phase of the setup. The snap T involves a more direct, aggressive movement while the C Spey draws a softer line with the rod at the start. To have a full arsenal when on the water, a working understanding of this differentiation can be quite useful.

Focusing on the snap T movement is a good starting point. As with the double Spey, start with the rod tip low nearly touching the water with the rod and line in a straight line to the fly. Slowly raise the rod, bringing it back toward the body. As the rod nears vertical, the tip is pushed slightly toward the opposite bank, moving the rod and line from your body, and is briefly stopped. Then push the rod down with a quick, accelerated motion or snap in a downstream direction angling toward the near bank. The rod ends up in about the same position where it started the initial phase, with the tip close to the water and with the fly ending up in the anchor zone. The rod should be back in the start position slightly before the fly hits the water in the anchor zone.

The rod at the end of the first phase is in a similar position as at the end of the first phase of the double Spey. From here, the two casts are nearly identical. The rod is now brought back across the body led by the upper hand. The rod movement is flat at first and then rising at a steady angled trajectory starting as the rod tip passes in front of the body then accelerating into the 2 o'clock position. The rod is angled away from the body and the upper hand is about even with your head and lower hand extended out. It is very important that the rod never dips during this movement. The line should be pointing at the target and D loop formed. The forward stroke is completed with the push and guidance of the top hand and pull of the bottom.

The C Spey variation occurs at the end of the initial phase. At the beginning of the setup, the rod is raised to near vertical as described above with the tip angled toward the opposite bank. But now instead of pushing or snapping the rod down in an accelerated motion, the rod tip draws a backward C when casting on river left off the right shoulder (and a normal C when casting on river right off the left shoulder). It is critical to draw the entire C with an accelerated movement with the rod angled downriver in order to land the fly in the anchor zone and allow the rod to return to the starting position with the rod pointing downstream low to the water. The back edge of the C should be approximately even with the casting position. The cast is then completed in the same manner as the snap T described earlier. It is critical that the path of the rod tip clearly travels underneath the upper portion of the C when drawing the bottom part portion. Keeping the rod tip underneath ensures that it is out of the path of the line and fly before it hits the water in the anchor zone. A collision with a weighted fly and rod tip usually doesn't end well.

Let's look at a few of the common errors that can exist when setting up the snap T or C Spey:

- The fly does not land above the casting position in or near the anchor zone after the initial phase—This can occur when the rod hasn't been raised high enough to free the line or when either the snap is not made with proper acceleration or the C is drawn too shallow or incomplete.
- The fly lands too far upstream after the initial phase—This can occur when the angle of the rod is pointing across-stream or the rod tip travel past the casting position during the C. Too much acceleration at the beginning of the C can also be the cause.
- Not allowing the rod to return to the starting position at the end of the initial phase—As with the double Spey, it will be difficult to complete an effective sweep with the rod in this position. Starting the rod high as the second phase of the setup begins will typically cause the rod to dip during the sweep. The result is a weak D loop where the line on the water may not clear your body. Or starting too high without a dip will also create a weak D loop and typically cause a complete loss of the anchor point.

- Over-rotating on the setup—As the rod is raised and follows the brim of the hat, the rod tip must stay off to the side and well outside the elbow of the upper arm.
- Anchor is not lined up—As the forward stroke begins the fly, line and leader should be in the anchor zone lined up in the direction of the target. This can result from the fly and line landing too far upstream or when line remains above your position and doesn't clear the body as the rod is swept to the 2 o'clock position.

Like the double Spey, the snap T or C Spey uses a waterborne anchor. This allows for some ability to straighten out the leader, tip, and line to be pointed at the target as the D loop is formed. And like the double Spey, the snap T or C Spey provides for a sustained anchor and matches up well with a Skagit head heavy tip and/or weighted fly. Slow, deliberate movements during the setup best facilitate using this cast with a Skagit head. When performing the snap T or C Spey with a longer head and rod, a longer, powerful motion is required in the second phase as the rod is swept into the D loop. A longer head also requires a slight pause before beginning the forward stroke to allow the rod to fully load.

I tend to use the snap T approach when using lighter tips and flies but find that moving the rod over a greater area required by the C Spey movement works best with heavier tips and flies as well as it better keeps the rod tip out of the way. A collision between tip and weighted fly can easily result in a broken rod. The C Spey setup also results in the fly landing slightly higher upstream from the casting position than when using the snap T movement. This provides more of a safety net when fishing in faster currents where the fly and anchor point drift quickly toward the casting positions during the setup. Placing the fly further upstream allows you to maintain a proper rhythm of the cast and not rush the forward stroke.

If you become a fan of the snap T / C Spey, there is a way to utilize this movement off the downstream shoulder as well. The reverse snap T rotates the plane in which the cast occurs. I think of making this cast by drawing a capital D with the rod tip and the curved part of the letter toward the near bank. On river left, the D will be drawn backward. On the hang down, point the rod toward the main current in the river. Raise the rod tip to draw the straight line of the D and

The snap T begins with a lift to free the line. NICK PIONESSA PHOTO

The rod is pushed down with a quick, accelerated motion or snap in a downstream direction, angling toward the near bank. This places the fly upstream of the casting position in the anchor zone. NICK PIONESSA PHOTO

The rod is then brought back across the body in a flat motion or rising slightly in trajectory in an accelerated motion. NICK PIONESSA PHOTO

As the rod passes the body, it continues to rise and sweeps into the forward Spey position with the rod stopping near 2 o'clock and the upper hand near the shoulder or cheek. NICK PIONESSA PHOTO

Once the D loop is formed, the forward stroke begins by pulling with the lower hand while pushing and guiding with the upper hand in an accelerated movement. NICK PIONESSA PHOTO

The cast is completed with a firm stop at 10 o'clock. NICK PIONESSA PHOTO

continue into the curved portion toward the near bank with the rod returning to its original position prior to drawing the straight perpendicular line. Now the rod is swept into the forward Spey position in a similar manner as the standard snap T or C Spey.

On river right, the reverse snap T is performed with the right hand up and on river left with the left hand up. It can also be performed with the opposite hand up and casting across the body. Casting across the body is covered later in this chapter. The reverse snap T matches with shorter head lines.

SNAKE ROLL

Like the double Spey, the snake roll is used on river right with the right hand up and river left with the left hand up. The snake roll is a much simpler cast than the double Spey in that there are fewer steps in setting up the D loop. But in this simplicity, there is a need for proper timing to effectively execute. This is a cast that was originated by Simon Gawesworth while practicing casting on relatively still water. Simon's father provided the name of the snake roll.

Start the snake roll with the rod angled low and pointed downstream. Angle the rod slightly toward the near bank while raising the rod with minor acceleration to the point of being just higher than your head. Draw a lowercase "e" with the rod tip (or a backward "e," if your left hand is up) to pull the fly to the anchor zone. The "e" is finished by continuing with a tail that brings the rod to the 2 o'clock position angled away from your body. A continued acceleration throughout the setup creates a deep D loop and sufficiently loads the rod. The "e" movement should be elongated as if drawing the rod around an elongated object. And while a constant, smooth acceleration is required for the final setup, an overall slow, deliberate movement while drawing the elongated "e" assists in maintaining the proper timing. Avoid quick, short movements and think slow and rhythmic with a controlled acceleration into the 2 o'clock position. The rod tip should stay in the same plane while the "e" is drawn prior to moving to the 2 o'clock position. For longer head lines, angling the rod more steeply when drawing the "e" helps place more line in the air during the setup, resulting in an anchor closer to the casting position. More line in the air assists in developing a deeper D with stored energy.

The finish of the snake roll is different when compared to the double Spey or snap T / C Spey. With the snake roll, the fly, leader, and front of the fly line just splash or touch down briefly in the anchor zone as the forward stroke begins immediately to complete the cast. There is a brief period when the rod is moved into position for the forward stroke but pauses slightly to allow for the fly, leader, and front of the line to touch the surface. This contrasts to the previous casts where the fly remains in the water in or near the anchor zone during the entire setup. The splash or touch down creates just enough water tension to load the rod and requires the appropriate timing to follow through and complete the cast.

The snake roll lines up best with floating lines or when using lighter to moderate sink rate tips. It is a great cast when using Scandi or longer belly heads fished on or near the surface. It becomes more difficult when using Skagit heads with heavy tips or weighted flies. Heavy tips can create extra tension at the beginning of the cast when freeing the line and tip from the water. And heavy flies can disrupt the rhythm of the setup and create too much tension on the splash down, making one of the sustained anchor casts described earlier a better choice for heavy tips and flies. However, it is still possible to use this this cast with a short head and sinking-tip by using a slow setup and adding a slight movement of the hands toward the near bank to create a short, sustained anchor to smooth everything out.

Some of the errors you may encounter with the snake roll include:

- The end of the line doesn't clear the surface of the water—This can be a result of drawing too small of an "e" or not properly accelerating while drawing the "e."
- The line is not straight in the direction of the target at splash down—This can be the result of not maintaining the rod tip in the same plane while drawing the "e."
- The fly doesn't remain in the anchor and ends up behind the casting position—This can be caused by excessive speed or acceleration as the rod is brought to the 2 o'clock position.
- The line collides with your body on the forward stroke—This is caused by over-rotating the rod into a plane that overlaps the body. Be sure to maintain the rod in an angle away from the body when brought to the 2 o'clock position and that the line stays outside of the cast-side elbow.

The snake roll starts with the rod angled low and pointed downstream. NICK PIONESSA PHOTO

With the rod angled slightly toward the near bank, raise the rod with minor acceleration to the point of being just higher than your head. NICK PIONESSA PHOTO

A lowercase "e" is drawn with the rod tip (or a backward "e" if your left hand is up) to pull the fly to the anchor zone. NICK PIONESSA PHOTO

The "e" is finished by continuing with a tail that brings the rod to the 2 o'clock position with the bottom hand out and the top hand back near the shoulder or cheek. NICK PIONESSA PHOTO

Once a D loop is formed, the forward stroke begins by pulling with the lower hand while pushing and guiding with the upper hand in an accelerated movement. NICK PIONESSA PHOTO

The cast is completed with a firm stop at 10 o'clock. NICK PIONESSA PHOTO

SINGLE SPEY

The name of the cast implies a certain element of simplicity. The single Spey requires the least amount of movement to complete, but in this simplicity, proper timing and rod movement are required, making it possibly the most difficult of the casts to learn. However, once this cast can be made proficiently, it is very powerful and allows for a graceful and efficient coverage of the water. This cast is used on river left with the right hand up and river right with the left hand up.

The single Spey is an advancement of the switch cast or forward Spey where the single involves a more or less 90-degree change of direction. While all change of direction Spey casts utilize a degree of body and hip rotation resulting in a weight shift, the single Spey relies on this rotation in order to make the direction change. While foot placement may be more of a personal preference than with the other Spey casts, placing the right foot forward when casting off the right shoulder in performing the single seems to better align the cast and make a stronger delivery.

The single Spey starts with the rod tip low and pointing down the line. Lift the rod tip by bending the elbows so that the tip is about head high or slightly above. In a continuous motion, move the rod in a flat movement in front of the body into the 2 o'clock position. I have found it best to begin the rod movement with the arms until it approaches being in front of the casting position then allow the rotation of the body to take over and accelerate into the D loop while simply raising the hands into place. When performed properly, this movement breaks the line and fly free of the water and slashes or touches down in the anchor zone just after the rod is brought into the 2 o'clock position. As soon as there is splash down, the forward stroke is completed. Like the snake roll, the single Spey is a touch and go cast.

A variation that many casters, especially those new to the game, may find helpful is to utilize a slight dip after the lift. This is the only place in all the basic Spey casts where a dip in the rod still facilitates a proper cast. The dip in the path of the rod needs to occur immediately after the lift and just as the sweep begins. The dip should not be dramatic but rather the rod tip traces a rounded arcing path up the to 2 o'clock position. A smooth accelerating movement through the dip, sweep, and lift will allow the D loop to form and the line to straighten out.

The rotation of the body and hips will determine the direction and target of the cast. With less rotation, the cast is made somewhere between 45 and 90 degrees. By rotating the body more than 90 degrees, a cast can be made with the single Spey that angles upriver. The direction of the cast will follow where the chest and upper body are facing during the forward stroke. Once comfortable with the forward Spey or switch cast, it can be helpful to think of the single Spey as nearly the same cast, with the simple rotation of the body providing the change in direction.

The touch and go style of cast provided by the snake roll and single Spey offer a stealth advantage. The quick touch on the water's surface is considered less disruptive than ripping the line across the surface when performing a double Spey or snap T. For this reason, I try to utilize the touch and go casts when I feel that a less-intrusive approach will pay dividends.

While performing the snake roll with sinking-tips and weighted flies is somewhat cumbersome, I have found the single Spey to be a good option when using a short Skagit head, even when combined with heavier tips and weighted flies. To get the cast started, the lift is higher than with a floating line to clear the tip and fly from the water. There is a slight dip in the tip as the rod pulls the rod and line in front of the casting position and then a full rotation of the body with the arms raising into the D loop or forward Spey position. While moving into the forward Spey position, I make an additional modification to the cast. Instead of a true touch and go, allowing the body to continue a slight rotation and the arms continuing to move back after the fly and tip have touched down adds a sustained anchor element to the setup. This added motion keeps everything on the surface, eliminating the additional stick that could be created by a tip and weighted fly hitting the water during the standard single Spey motion.

Some of the errors you may encounter with the single Spey include:

- The anchor ends up above the anchor zone—This can be the result of using too much force during the sweep. It can also result from using too much arm in the setup as opposed to allowing the body to rotate rhythmically while performing the sweep. Also, when utilizing a dip in the sweep, the dip needs to be immediate. Dipping after the sweep has begun makes it difficult or impossible to land in the anchor zone.

The single Spey starts with the rod angled low and pointed downstream. NICK PIONESSA PHOTO

The rod tip is lifted by bending the elbows so that the tip is about head high or slightly above. NICK PIONESSA PHOTO

In a continuous motion, the rod is brought in a flat movement in front of the body. The rod movement begins with the arms until it approaches being in front of the casting position then the rotation of the body takes over and accelerates into the D loop while simply raising the hands into place. NICK PIONESSA PHOTO

The fly, leader, and tip of the line touches down just as the rod arrives in the 2 o'clock position. NICK PIONESSA PHOTO

Once the D loop is formed the forward stroke begins by pulling with the lower hand while pushing and guiding with the upper hand in an accelerated movement. NICK PIONESSA PHOTO

The cast is completed with a firm stop at 10 o'clock. NICK PIONESSA PHOTO

- The anchor ends up below the anchor zone—This is a dangerous situation as the collision with the body can occur if the cast is completed. This can be the result of not utilizing a high enough lift or enough force during the sweep. This can also occur when using a dip and the dip is performed too steeply.
- Line piles up—This can be the result of not accelerating into the 2 o'clock position and not fully rotating with the body. It can also be the result of a steep dip during the sweep.
- No power in the forward stroke—This can result from poor acceleration into the 2 o'clock position and from not rotating the body fully to the target. A lack of power can also result if the rod tip falls significantly past the 2 o'clock position, creating too much slack.

The spiral Spey cast combines the initial movement of the snake roll with the single Spey. The spiral Spey is essentially a modified single Spey, meaning it is used on river left with right hand up and river right with left hand up. While it adds more movement to the simplicity of a single Spey, the spiral Spey allows for less than perfect timing and is more forgiving.

To begin the spiral Spey, think in terms of making a snake roll cast to the near bank as opposed to out into the river. Begin by drawing a small "e" with a tail when fishing on the left bank with right hand up and a backward "e" on the right bank and left hand up. As the tail is completed, the head will all be in the air about head high. Instantaneously, a sweep of the rod begins by rotating the body so that it is square to the target and accelerating the hands into the forward Spey position, the D loop will form, and, as the fly, leader, and front portion of the line touches the water, the forward stroke begins immediately. It will take some practice to get the timing correct, but when performed properly, it is a powerful cast.

PERRY POKE

The Perry poke could be considered a separate cast, but I think of it more as an additional movement that can be added to any of the basic Spey casts. The Perry poke is performed after the setup of a standard cast and commonly used with upstream shoulder single Spey and snap T / C Spey casts. When used with the snap T / C Spey, the resulting cast is referred to as the wombat Spey cast.

The Perry poke is commonly used with sinking-tips. Heavier tips and weighted flies can create a challenge for positioning the anchor with the tip and head properly lined up when ready for the forward stroke. When in position to make the forward stroke, the Perry poke is performed by making a soft movement of the rod down parallel to the water, dumping the line to the surface while the fly, leader, and front portion of the head remains in or near the anchor zone. After the poke, everything should be more in line, and the rod is swept into position in a similar motion as the forward Spey, and the cast is completed.

The Perry poke can be quite useful when salvaging any cast where the setup results in a poor anchor position and is a good safety valve when the fly could possibly be on a collision course with your body. The poke allows the cast to continue without starting over and can be used in multiple succession until the anchor is properly and safely established with a straight line. The Perry poke can also be used to reposition the anchor, as discussed later in this chapter.

ADDITIONAL THOUGHTS

When performing any of the basic casts, the length of the head and rod has a direct impact on the length of the casting stroke and the overall energy that needs to be imparted to the line through the movement of the rod. Longer heads/rods require longer movements with more momentum. Stroke length is on full display during the forward stroke. During the forward delivery with a short head and rod, the stroke is more compact. The elbow of the upper hand remains bent at the conclusion of the stroke, creating a tighter casting loop and proper trajectory. With a longer head line and rod, the upper arm is more extended and can end up almost straight.

Making a change in head and rod length can be viewed from a standpoint other than the length of rod movement. As an accomplished tournament distance caster and Spey guide and instructor, Zack Williams, editor of *Swing the Fly*, has developed his own perspective on casting that can be described as anchor point centric. He explained his approach to making changes in lines and rods during a recent conversation.

"Spey casters often struggle when changing between different rods and lines. The timing and mechanics seem to change, and adjusting can be difficult. For me, the essence of all Spey casting is the anchor of the line on the water. If the anchor is pointing at the intended target and provides the proper amount of water tension

Casting longer heads to cover big water requires adjustments to the stroke when compared to casting shorter heads. Longer rod movements with more momentum allow the leverage of the rod to throw a longer head a great distance.

ZACK WILLIAMS PHOTO

(your leader and sinking-tip lying on the water, no more and no less) when beginning the forward stroke, it is guaranteed to be a fishable Spey cast. That's it.

"Often when we change and go to a new line and rod, we go through the same motions as with the previous setup and end up with poorer results. It can be frustrating. A change to a longer line often results in too much anchor, and a change to a shorter line often results in too little anchor.

"The fix can be quite simple. By watching the anchor placement, we can use our hand-eye coordination to adjust to the different line. Where are you typically placing the end of your line in the setup for your double Spey or snap T cast? For me, I always set the end of the line a rod length away from my body on the side I wish to cast on. Try to be as consistent as possible. If you change to a longer line or shorter line, all you need to do is adjust that first step of the cast so the end of the new line lands in that same spot. The rest of the cast should remain consistent.

"In my experience, when someone is struggling with an equipment change, anchor is almost always the root cause resulting in the caster changing everything else in their cast including speeding up and overpowering. This typically ends in frustration. Thankfully, it doesn't have to be that way."

An important adjustment for longer head lines is to finish the setup into the D loop with the hands high so that the upper hand is no longer even with the side of the head but slightly higher than the head. This positioning better allows for handling more line beyond the rod tip by reducing the amount of line on the water that can create too much stick. Making this change to a higher hand position for longer heads can take time to get used to if Spey casting was learned originally with a lower positioning.

When casting with a longer head, allowing the rod to drift slightly back and up after making an abrupt stop to set up the D loop creates a longer rod path for the forward stroke and controls the amount of line on the water. The longer stroke results in more line speed and overall power. Rod drift can be helpful even on mid-length and shorter heads for both power and aiming casts at a higher trajectory. Rod drift is performed by allowing the hands to move back and up slightly as the rod moves toward 2 o'clock. Timing is critical and can take some practice to get the feel. Be sure there is a complete stop to propel the line into the D and then a slight drift during the pause before beginning the forward stroke. But make sure the rod tip does not drop too far and cause too much line to be in contact with the water, making an efficient cast impossible.

Effective Spey casting requires feel and muscle memory. And it can be difficult to develop the proper timing by just going to the river and fishing. Dedicated practice is an integral part of becoming a proficient Spey caster and maintaining skills. The forward Spey or switch cast should be ingrained into muscle memory before beginning the setup for the change of direction casts. The forward Spey or switch can easily be practiced on still water while flowing water creates a realistic scenario for working on the change of direction casts. I find it best to practice with a floating head and a leader approximately the length of the rod using a piece of yarn instead of a fly. Be sure to practice good form as practicing poor form can work toward ingraining poor technique.

Change of direction can also be practiced on still water. I utilize a practice routine on a local pond using different casts in succession to simulate change in direction casts on a river. For example, I can perform a snap T and then rotate my body to the left and perform a double Spey. This approach can be used to practice all the casts. The pond lacks the current that straightens out the line and creates tension on the lift but provides a method for practice when a pond or lake is the most convenient water available. Regardless of your level of casting, practice is important for maintaining timing and feel as well as experimenting with various rod/line combinations and adjustments to the setup or casting stroke.

We don't often think about the fatigue imparted on the body while fishing until the day is over and the exhaustion is obvious. But when Spey fishing, I often notice the impact of fatigue on my casting as the day

Long head lines require greater movement combined with more momentum during the setup. A higher hand position in the D loop position reduces the amount of line on the water that can create too much stick to efficiently complete the cast. NICK PIONESSA PHOTO

Fatigue can have a significant impact on Spey casting efficiency. Keep your body fed and hydrated to go the duration and take breaks as necessary to rejuvenate. Focus on making smooth, repeatable casts that don't overly tax or stress your body.

wears on. I often feel that my casting is at its best for the first few hours and then drops off a little during the day similar to a baseball pitcher that loses speed off the fastball in the later innings. I think we all have a pitch count where fatigue takes over. I find that it can be as much mental as physical, and when my casting needs a reboot, it can make sense to take a short break or at least a deep breathe, refocus, slow down, and go back to the fundamentals.

But there is a physical element to this game as well. Keeping in shape allows your body to still work effectively in the later innings. I stress this in most of my writing, but hitting the gym and keeping the body fit has many benefits to fully enjoying the sport of fly fishing. This is certainly true for Spey casting since it is physically demanding on the entire body. Also, be sure to not short your body on nutrition and hydration during the day. It's important to drink water or other hydrating fluids, especially on cold days.

The largest impact of fatigue can be on safety. As we tire, there can be less concentration on wind direction or anchor placement. It is important to keep focus on these items throughout the day and not let your guard down. Also, as we fatigue later in the day it may make sense to shorten the cast if longer casts are failing to turn over properly on a consistent basis. From a fishing standpoint, it is always better to focus on the length of cast that can be made each time with consistency.

Making Adjustments

Spey casting is typically learned and practiced in a controlled setting. But that is often not the case when applying Spey casting to actual fishing situations. We need to adjust to conditions. This ability to adapt our casting for the many variables is part of the captivation for Spey and why this form of fishing can be so effective. Let's look at various adjustments required to meet changing conditions.

Water depth is a factor that impacts casting every time out. Spey casting tends to be easiest when standing in water that is no more than knee deep. Learning the Spey cast and practicing the casting stroke often occurs in water of this depth. But in the real world, we may wade much deeper to cover a pool entirely and allow the fly to hang in water that has enough depth where a fish feels comfortable chasing or holding. I can still remember some of my early struggles as I worked a pool from its shallow upper riffle to its much deeper bucket. My casting consistency improved as I understood how the depth impacted the dynamics of the cast.

Water depth effectively reduces the leverage advantage of a two-handed rod as the water's surface is now closer to the tip of the rod. And with more of us moving to shorter rods, the impact can be quite significant. One approach to gaining back some of the rod length when wading deep is to raise the hand position when setting up the D loop and the forward stroke. I also may choose a rod with greater length when anticipating wading deep all day long.

Wading to the upper thighs or even mid-section presents the biggest challenge. It becomes more difficult to clear line off the water's surface, resulting in more line stick during the setup—particularly when performing the double Spey or snap T/C Spey. The

line stick results in a week D loop and resulting poor cast. To clear more line from the water when ripping the line across the casting position to complete the D loop, keep the rod more angled and the tip pointed higher. Maintaining too flat of a rod movement when wading deep makes it very difficult to cleanly pull the line into a deep D loop. It may take some trial and error to determine the proper rod angle during setup as too great of an angle also results in insufficient tension to set up a sufficient D loop.

Current speed can also have a significant impact on the setup of a Spey cast. Moderate current speeds facilitate the cast by allowing the anchor point to stay well positioned, and the surface tension of a medium flow assists in keeping the line, tip, and fly on top eliminating excess line stick.

Faster current speeds create certain challenges. Setting an anchor point upstream of your casting position in a fast flow can cause the anchor to drift too close. In addition to creating a dangerous situation while making the forward stroke, the anchor point drifting toward

Wading deep changes the cast as the leverage advantage of a two-hander length is diminished. Raising the hands up while setting the anchor for the forward stroke assists in regaining some length. Here Mike Foley counteracts the water depth with a higher hand position.

Slower flows can cause a challenge in getting the next cast started when fishing with a sinking leader or sinking-tip. Roll casting into the setup can seamlessly begin the cast while maintaining a stealthy approach.

your position impacts rhythm while rushing the cast before it is fully developed. To counterbalance a faster flow, place the beginning of the anchor point further away from your position. Use the C Spey with an exaggerated movement where the rod is at least at even or past your body at the apex of the C motion, placing the fly slightly above the anchor zone. The faster current will then drift the fly into position during the setup.

Utilizing a single Spey cast in faster current speeds can also be a good approach. The touch and go nature of this cast allows for a quick setup and delivery with less time for the anchor point to drift into the casting position. However, it is always critical to locate the anchor point and fly, making sure it is in a safe position before completing any Spey cast. Another approach is to cast off the downstream shoulder. This will be discussed in conjunction with adjusting to wind direction.

Faster currents also have an impact on loose running line as the tension of the current holds the line from shooting. Utilizing the managing running line considerations discussed earlier in this chapter will be most beneficial in heavier, faster currents.

Slow water currents can also have an impact on the casting setup. When fishing with a sinking-tip and

weighted fly where the hang down ends in slow water, there may not be enough current pushing against the line to bring the tip and fly toward the surface. With the tip and fly deep in the water column, freeing the line to begin the next cast can be very difficult. But raising the rod and simply making a roll cast toward the fly brings everything to the surface and the setup so the next cast can begin. The Perry poke can also be useful in this situation when the slow current in conjunction with a sinking-tip line and/or weighted fly make it difficult to develop the cast with the standard setup.

Slow current flows can also impact the anchor point. The lack of surface tension of the slower flows allows a sinking-tip and fly to sink immediately during the setup. Focusing on a continuous anchor when using the double Spey or snap T/C Spey will be critical to form a proper D loop and avoid too much line stick on the forward stroke. With the touch and go nature of the single Spey or snake roll, the setup and casts are completed before the lack of surface tension can have a significant impact.

Windy conditions not only present certain challenges when Spey casting but also create a hazardous situation. A heavy wind or breeze blowing against the casting shoulder not only breaks down the energy of the D loop but creates the real possibility of the hook point making unfortunate contact with your flesh. Extreme care should be taken in windy conditions. Always wear protective eye lenses. A slight wind blowing against the casting shoulder can be counterbalanced by placing the anchor point slightly further away from your casting position. But heavier winds require moving the cast to the nondominant hand shoulder or off shoulder.

Casting from the off shoulder can be accomplished in two ways. The first is to switch hands so that the top hand now becomes the bottom and vice versa. For most anglers, this would result in the nondominant hand on the upper grip and the dominant hand on the lower. While this may sound and feel cumbersome, with some practice, a fluid motion can be obtained. The advantage of developing the habit of really engaging the bottom hand in the casting stroke allows for an easy transition to casting from the off shoulder.

The second approach is to maintain the hands in the same position with dominant hand up but to bring the rod across the body so that the cast is made off the downwind shoulder. This is often referred to as cack-handed casting. The definition of cack-handed is to handle things in an awkward or clumsy way. But some Spey casters feel that placing the nondominant hand up is more awkward than bringing the rod across the body. To cast cack-handed, the rod is positioned off the same side of the body as the lower hand with the arm of the top hand extending across to clear the rod past the shoulder and elbow of the lower hand. It can take some practice to feel comfortable extending the arm across the body.

When the cast setup is complete and D loop established, hand and rod position is similar or even mirrors when casting off the dominant shoulder. The upper hand should be near the cheek or side of the head, lower hand pushed out, and rod around 2 o'clock tilted off to the side. The wrist of the upper hand is rotated so the thumb is more or less on top the handle for power with the palm facing away and the lower hand fully engaged on the forward stroke. At first it may feel as though the cack-handed approach isn't as powerful as casting off the dominant shoulder, but with practice

Being able to cast off both shoulders is a must to handle on-shoulder winds and deal with casting challenges posed by obstructions and current flow. The cack-handed cast is set up with the upper arm across the body with upper hand back and facing away. NICK PIONESSA PHOTO

With a severe upriver wind on this productive Arctic river, there is no choice but to cast off the left shoulder. The angler places the left hand on the upper grip and right hand on the bottom to complete the cast. JEFF BRIGHT PHOTO

and proper rod alignment and hand engagement, very powerful casts can be completed.

Going with nondominant hand up or cack-handed is a personal preference. But being proficient at one or both is essential for effective and safe casting in a wide range of conditions and circumstances. I have gone back and forth over the years as to my preference and now utilize both approaches with a preference toward nondominant hand up. For myself, it seems that more consistent power is obtained with the nondominant hand up, particularly when using longer rods.

The completed cast for both of these approaches requires reversing the setup. For example, if you are fishing river left with the right hand up and a snap T cast but a downriver wind begins blowing onto your right shoulder, a double Spey can be used to set up the cast off the left shoulder. This setup applies whether casting with the left hand up or bringing the rod across the body with the right hand up.

Utilizing off-shoulder casts on the downriver side can also be a good strategy for faster currents when the flow is pushing toward your shoulder with the dominant hand up. Placing the anchor on the downriver side

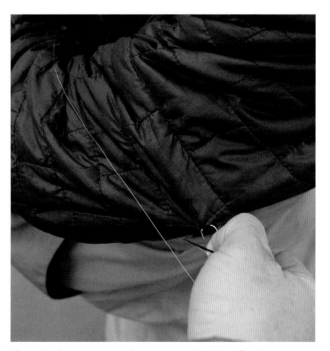

The wind can cause a dangerous situation for Spey casting; luckily this wayward hook only came in contact with clothing and not flesh. Be sure to have a casting plan for dealing with a wind direction toward the dominant shoulder. NICK PIONESSA PHOTO

pulls the fly and tip away, resulting in more comfortable and effective casts.

Since casts can readily be made off either shoulder, it gives Spey casting a decided advantage in windy conditions. Being able to fish in the type of extreme winds that keep others off the river provides the opportunity to have prime water all to yourself.

Winds can be tricky when on the water. Canyon walls or rows of trees have a tendency to funnel or swirl the winds. Always keep track of the wind direction because it can change throughout the day or as you change angles while working down a pool. On days when the wind is swirling, I think about the setup on each cast to make sure the wind has been properly considered.

Casting directly into the wind may not represent the same level of danger as a crosswind but can reduce distance and effectiveness. Maintaining a tight casting loop through an efficient forward stroke allows the line to pierce through the wind. The rod tip should draw a straight line that is parallel or slightly angled toward the water as it moves through the forward stroke. A heavy bottom hand movement assists in creating line speed supporting a tight casting loop. Changing the trajectory of the line so that it travels lower to the water keeps it beneath the main punch of the wind.

One of the main advantages of Spey casting is the ability to deliver casts in tight quarters without a backcast. Working around trees and logs along the near bank is made manageable by casting off each shoulder. Casts can even be made from underneath an overhanging tree by changing the casting plane so that the entire rod moves more parallel to the water's surface.

Spey casting while working along a high, brushy bank or a steep canyon wall can open up water that would be difficult or impossible to cover by any other means. Although shorter heads result in a shallower D, the standard Spey cast still requires some amount of line to go past your casting position to form the D loop. If you are backed right up to the obstruction because of the depth of the water along the bank, the D loop can become entangled in the bank during the cast setup.

To make the Spey cast work in these conditions, a modification can be made that essentially eliminates any line from going past the casting position. When

Delivering a fly on streams and rivers where the casting position is backed up against the brush and canyon walls is one of the greatest tactical advantages of Spey fishing. J. C. Clark uses a short two-hander and compact head to successfully negotiate a tight casting area.

The modified Perry poke starts by not fully completing the setup of the cast and forming a shallow D that barely passes the casting position. NICK PIONESSA PHOTO

A weak forward stroke is made pushing the end of the line and fly out 10 to 20 feet. NICK PIONESSA PHOTO

With the newly established anchor out in front, the D loop can be created without any line moving behind the casting position. NICK PIONESSA PHOTO

completing a cast under these circumstances, I utilize a slightly modified Perry poke. Instead of just dumping the line to the surface as with the standard poke, I use enough momentum to push the line out in front of me so that the fly, leader, and front portion of the line are out 10 to 20 feet in front of the normal anchor point. It is more like a weak forward stroke as opposed to simply dropping the rod with a normal poke. With letting the line at rest for only an instant, the rod is now swept into the setup for a forward stroke and stopped around the 12 o'clock position instead of 2 o'clock. The D loop is established from the new anchor point well in front of the normal positioning. This allows the end of the D loop to not extend past the casting position so that a cast can be completed with your back right up against the bank or canyon wall. The forward stroke is then completed by stopping the rod at 10 o'clock as opposed to 11 o'clock to allow the rod to move a long enough distance to complete the cast.

Over the years, the ability to make a cast in extremely confined areas has led to some of my most memorable successes. This is a cast I make repeatedly on one of my home rivers since high banks define the entire river edge. It is also a valuable tool on trips to British Columbia. One particularly long pool that runs along a high rock-lined cut bank comes to mind. The pool takes well over an hour to cover through its tailout. Depth drops off quickly with a very unstable bottom of round rocks and boulders. With little room to the rear because of the high bank, it is a challenge to fish to say the least. Most anglers were quick to pass on this water because of its difficulty, but making this adjustment to the cast has allowed me to have a handful of incredible experiences in this pool.

Single-Hand Spey

Contrary to common perception, Spey casting isn't just for two-handed rods as each of the basic Spey casts can be performed easily with a single hand. While some rods are manufactured specifically for one-hand Spey purposes, one-hand Spey casts can be made with just about any fly rod and have a wide range of fishing applications. The one-hand Spey game is a condensed version of full two-hand casting with a tighter setup while maintaining the ability to manage sinking-tips and heavier flies. This section looks at the nuances of single-hand Spey casts and discusses the various uses of this approach from a fishing perspective.

While single-hand Spey casting can be performed with just about any fly rod, for best performance, a length of 9 feet or greater is preferred. Lines and heads for effective one-hand Spey casting vary from short or micro-length Skagit and Scandi heads looped to a running line to longer integrated head lines allowing for more delicate presentations. Longer head lines with mass at the rear of the head that finish with a long progressing taper make for a very well-performing line for this style of casting. But longer belly lines result in a larger D loop and may not be as practical for tight casting situations. Regardless of head length, the shorter rod length places the anchor point closer to the casting position.

Skagit-style heads match best when casting streamer style or other larger flies or when using a sinking-tip or sinking leader. Scandi and longer head lines match best with smaller flies and fishing higher in the water column. Hybrid-style lines allow for a wider range of applications. Determining the proper weight head to match with the rod is always important in any type of casting but possibly even more so in one-hand casting since the weight grain range that lighter rods can handle is tighter than longer, heavier rods. Also, lining up a rod that is designed for single-hand overhead casting can be slightly more of a challenge since the rod manufacturer generally does not publish grain weight windows for Spey-style lines for these rods. Some trial and error may be needed.

Any Spey cast previously described that can be performed with two hands can also be accomplished by single-hand casting. The key to one-hand Spey is reducing the process down to fit the length of the rod and head with smooth, deliberate movements in setting up the cast. Touch and go casts work well with floating lines or heads and those with a light amount of weight added. Waterborne casts match well with Skagit-style heads and sinking leaders or tips along with larger weighted flies.

The movement of the cast setup is closely connected to the length of the head. Longer heads require more power to be applied to clear the line from the water and form a proper D loop. But short and micro heads require a slow, abridged version of the setup. Too powerful of a movement with an extremely short head pulls it from the water so that an anchor cannot be established or maintained. Utilizing a setup that is compact and tight to the body assists in properly setting

The setup for a single-hand Spey cast is nearly identical to using two hands. Nick Pionessa sweeps a one-hand Spey cast into the D loop position and ready to deliver the forward stroke.

up the anchor. With a short head, it's almost impossible to move too slowly while setting up the cast.

The obvious difference between one- and two-hand Spey casts is no bottom hand used during the single-hand version to establish a fulcrum of leverage. The forward stroke is like a forward overhead cast of a single-hand rod relying on firm, smooth acceleration to a definite stop creating line speed and a tight loop. The grip is also different. With two-hand casting, the upper hand grip is generally passive with the thumb resting off to the side acting more to guide the rod with the power provided by the push of the upper arm and heavy pull of the lower hand. Single-hand casting requires most or all the power to be generated with the rod hand. A firm or more powerful grip is required to effectively complete the casts. Moving the thumb to the top of the cork creates a stronger grip that assists in gaining power on the forward stroke.

The running line can be controlled with either the rod or line hand. Using the index finger or index and middle finger to pinch the running line off during the cast setup is the most common approach. The running line is pinched tight during the cast setup allowing the running line to shoot as the forward stroke finishes by lightly lifting the fingers to release the line. Proper timing of the release is critical to distance and fly turnover. Releasing the running line just prior to the definite stop of the rod produces the best results.

Controlling the running line with the off hand allows the forward stroke to feel more like a standard forward overhead cast. This approach allows the off or line hand to apply a haul on the forward stroke. But using the off hand to control running line takes some practice. There can be a tendency to develop loose line during the setup that reduces a cast of its power. The line hand needs to be engaged to follow along with the cast and gather any slack when needed. Adding a haul is also slightly more problematic than it may seem. Exact timing is critical. Since the forward stroke of a Spey cast loads the rod differently from a standard overhead cast, you don't get the same feel when hauling. Completing the haul just as the forward stroke completes and approaches the stop generates the best results. When the timing is correct, the haul can generate significant line speed and distance. However, when proper acceleration and power is applied to the cast

A one-hand Spey cast can be quite powerful. Accelerating the forward stroke into an abrupt stopping point assists in developing the line speed similar to a two-hand cast. NICK PIONESSA PHOTO

while maintaining the running line with the rod hand, good distance can also be achieved with an approach that is simpler to manage.

While the discussion of two-hand Spey casts provides the foundation for making each cast with a single hand, there are some nuances to one-hand casts, particularly when utilizing a short head.

The single Spey cast becomes quite simplified with a shorter head as the setup does not require the movement of much line. In order to establish a smooth anchor, the rod tip is lifted about head high to begin the cast. With the short head, the tip does not need to dip and maintains a consistent path until it reaches a point in front of the casting position. The body then rotates, and the rod sweeps up to form the D. While the single Spey works best with Scandi and similar style heads with a single-hand rod, the short head creates flexibility and Skagit-style mini heads can be easily controlled with a single Spey even when using a sinking leader or tip and weighted fly.

The snake roll is also easier to set up with a single-hand approach and short head. The rod tip is pointed more downstream during the initial setup while drawing the small "e" as opposed to angled to the sky when utilizing a longer head with a two-handed rod. And the loop portion of the "e" does not need to be as elongated. Both these steps will assist in establishing and maintaining the anchor. A slow, smooth motion is all that is required to establish the anchor. The single-hand snake roll can easily accommodate shorter Skagit heads as well.

When using either of the touch and go casts with a longer head, rod and body movements need to be elongated and with more power to move more line following similar principles for two-hand casting. Using a rod of longer than 9 feet will assist in casting longer head lines with a single hand.

Like two-hand casting, the double Spey and snap T / C Spey match best with Skagit-style head, sinking leaders and tips, and weighted flies. To begin the double Spey with a short head and single-hand rod, simply lift when the fly is in the hang down and flop the rod over by rolling the wrist so that the rod is pointing upstream low and parallel to the water. Now complete the setup by sweeping the rod with an accelerated motion at an upward angle into the D loop

Making a modified one-hand Spey cast by any means possible allows for enjoyable and efficient coverage on smaller streams. This may require making casts that deviate from what is historically considered Spey casting. NICK PIONESSA PHOTO

Here I deliver a one-hand Spey cast to the far bank with a micro head, sinking leader, and weighted fly. With the proper setup, this cast can be nearly effortless and extremely efficient as the fly is in the water a high percentage of your fishing time. NICK PIONESSA PHOTO

position. The cast is completed with an accelerating forward stroke.

The snap T or C Spey cast with a short head and single-hand rod requires a little extra caution. This cast lands the fly to your upstream side, and with a short head and rod, the anchor point will be close to the casting position, increasing the possibility of a collision. To begin the snap T or C Spey with a short head and single-hand rod, lift the tip on the hang down by pointing the rod more toward the opposite bank and then returning the rod so that it points directly downstream. This movement places the fly further upstream, providing more room to clear the body. The cast is completed by sweeping the rod with an accelerated motion at an upward angle into the D loop position and then making an accelerating forward stroke.

Very short or micro heads can nearly eliminate the need to be precise with the cast setup. Simply moving or flopping the fly and leader or tip into the anchor zone by any means and then sweeping the rod back to

form a D loop can result in an effective cast. While this may be hybrid casting at best, it allows for Spey movements to complete effective casts on small streams or in the tightest of situations. With a short head, it is quite simple to set up the forward Spey or switch with changing direction by simple body rotation.

Longer heads require less stripping between casts and are ideal for casting smaller flies while fishing on or near the surface. But longer heads require bigger, deeper D loops that can cause issues on smaller waters with various casting obstructions. It's possible to angle the cast to work around obstructions or to place the anchor farther than one rod length in front of the casting position. To meet the challenges of tight casting situations, it makes sense to always carry a short head when fishing with one-hand Spey.

Most rods designed for one-hand Spey and single-hand rods with uplocking reel seats have just enough extension of the butt to allow for a bottom hand to assist with the cast. The extra power gained by the bottom hand pulling in is useful when casting into the wind, trying to extend distance, or when the dominant hand becomes fatigued from a long day of casting. Two-hand assist differs from full two-hand casting. With two-hand assist, the bottom arm reaches across the body to pull the butt section toward the dominant shoulder during the forward stroke as opposed to pulling into the torso in two-hand casting. Adding the bottom hand with just a slight pull and completing the fulcrum can bring surprising power to the cast. The bottom hand can be part of the setup but works efficiently when just added to assist with the forward stroke.

Like two-hand casting and fishing, wind is a factor to consider when one-hand Spey fishing. Wind blowing onto the casting shoulder presents a potentially dangerous situation with an anchor point that is closer to the casting position than when two-hand casting. Since the rod hand controls almost all the rod movement in one-hand Spey, most anglers aren't comfortable or will not be casting effectively with their nondominant hand. The most common solution when the wind blows onto the dominant shoulder is to bring the rod across the body and cast off the other shoulder.

As discussed earlier in this chapter, the setup simply reverses. In other words, if fishing river right and casting with the right hand, a snake roll or double Spey is utilized in light or neutral winds. However, this switches to a single Spey or snap T / C Spey setup off the left nondominant shoulder. I have found that using the waterborne casts with either short or longer heads to be consistently easier to complete when one-hand casting off the nondominant shoulder. Slow movements are required to maintain the anchor. Due to the shorter length of the rod, the angle across the body tends to be sharper than with a longer two-hand rod. It becomes more of a challenge to maintain the rod tip in a straight plane for a straight-line cast. Be sure to extend the arm fully across the body to maintain a rod angle that is more perpendicular to the water's surface and rotate the wrist so that the thumb is on top of the grip for a powerful forward stroke.

Another option for casting off the nondominant shoulder is utilizing a two-hand assist cast with the nondominant hand up on the main cork of the rod. While this may feel more awkward than when casting a full two-hand with the nondominant hand up, adding the dominant hand to assist in guiding the rod through the setup and during the forward stroke makes the process much more comfortable.

While the focus of this book is Spey fishing, one-hand Spey movements can be utilized in almost any form of fly fishing. Once you become proficient at Spey casting, you will find yourself naturally blending in these movements to non-Spey fishing situations.

Since the forward Spey is a more dynamic movement and cast than a simple roll cast, it can be used in most roll cast situations, allowing for greater distance and power in windy conditions. It is also stealthier as the forward Spey clears the line from the water, creating less of a disturbance. The only disadvantage of the forward Spey is that line travels slightly farther behind the casting position during the D loop setup and could cause issues in tight casting situations. However, placing the anchor farther out can alleviate this situation.

I commonly use Spey movements when single-hand fishing dry flies for trout. When casting across river or down and across, the initial setup of the snake roll or single Spey allows me to get the line and fly into the air efficiently and stealthily to begin the next cast. Spey casting also allows me to deliver dry flies on tight, small stream situations where backcasting room is limited or nonexistent. Many of the small streams that I regularly fish require innovation to deliver the fly. When Spey casting a trout dry fly, it is best that it be a buoyant pattern as the cast doesn't allow the fly to dry itself as with traditional false casting.

Spey casting movements can easily be incorporated into nymph fishing presentations for trout and bass as well. Since placing a nymph in the proper spot for an effective drift often relies on a change in direction, blending in Spey movements can result in effortless casts that keep the fly in the water for a greater period.

4

PRESENTING THE FLY

In its basic form, Spey fishing and swinging the fly is quite simple. The line is cast across stream or on a slight angle down and the current pushes on the surface area of the line pulling the fly on or through the water imparting a lifelike motion. The fly can be fished at any level in the water column and at various speeds mostly within the control of the angler. It is this control and interaction with the fly that results in this style of fishing to be so captivating.

In my book *Reflections on the Water*, I examined the various stages of angling. These are levels that all maturing anglers go through over the years, and I understood there to be four such stages. The first is to catch a fish. Next is to catch many fish. The third stage is to catch the largest fish, and the fourth is to pursue and catch the most challenging fish. In the book, it is asserted that there is a fifth and final stage—to fish a fly well. And with Spey fishing, my objective is to

Almost every element of fly presentation is within the control of the angler. The key to success is often found in understanding and envisioning how the fly is presenting itself after each cast is completed. ZACK WILLIAMS PHOTO

make good presentations while trying to understand and envision what the fly is doing and how it looks in the water. Is it presenting itself in line with the intended objectives?

In its more advanced form, Spey fishing is a style of fishing that is both pleasing and rewarding, with the objective of truly enjoying the act of angling. How one fishes can replace how many, and the all-consuming act of fishing a fly properly creates its own satisfaction. When combined with persistence and confidence, success in terms of fish hooked and caught occurs at its own pace. Fish it well and success will follow.

This chapter focuses on the many aspects of swinging the fly well while examining how the presentation is controlled through rigging or active line management. Sometimes, the presentation of the fly is a personal choice such as choosing to fish a fly on the surface to experience the visual take as opposed to a potentially more successful approach in terms of numbers by fishing subsurface. And other times, the presentation is more about being as enticing or realistic as possible to attain the highest success in terms of hooking and landing fish.

Depth, speed, and angle of presentation are all within the control of the angler in most situations. There are often various combinations of rigging and line management available to meet a certain challenge. The proper combination is determined by a working knowledge of rigging and line management as well as experience. The objective of this chapter is to discuss the tools necessary to present the fly in its intended manner while making appropriate adjustments on the water. Spey casting may be the most enjoyable part of Spey fishing to some anglers, but it is a means to an end in terms of successful angling. It is what happens after the cast or in how the cast intertwines with the presentation that creates the entire picture of modern Spey.

Ultimately, the Spey and swing the fly approach plays on a fish's predatory instinct to chase and attack. The mindset or mood of a migratory fish as compared to a resident can factor into the anticipated response to a well-presented fly. There is some consistency in the trigger points for both migratory and resident fish, including the snap decision to hunt and pursue fleeing prey. The need for a migratory fish to feed depends

The basic swing has the rod tip pointed in the direction of the fly, allowing the push of the current to swing and swim the fly. The presentation can be altered and manipulated by rod position, casting angle, and line control. NICK PIONESSA PHOTO

Mid-length or longer belly floating heads work best when fishing the fly high in the water column. Here an angler uses a floating line to cover the clear-water flows of a beautiful Atlantic salmon river. JOE JANIAK PHOTO

on the circumstances, with the most prominent factor being the length of time spent in the river or stream. A leftover response from spending time as a juvenile in its natal waters may also impact the chasing instinct. But the need to eat, curiosity, competition, and territorial aggression all potentially impact whether a fish grabs your swung fly offering or not.

Depth

When it comes to presentation, depth control is a good place to start. When Spey fishing, the fly can be fished at any level in the water column, from riding on the surface to scraping the bottom and everywhere in between. Where to fish the fly is typically a combination of personal preference and tactical effectiveness being controlled by various rigging and line management strategies.

Fishing on the surface provides the extra excitement of witnessing the take of the fish. A floating line and monofilament or fluorocarbon leader the approximate length of the rod provide the basic rigging. The leader can be tapered or just a level length of material, provided it has enough backbone to turn over the fly and straighten out upon completion of the cast.

When fishing on the surface, some flies are buoyant enough that maintaining a surface presentation can be simply accomplished with an improved clinch or loop knot. However, other patterns that are lightly dressed may not stay on the surface without assistance. Enter the riffle hitch. The riffle hitch is an additional knot added after the fly is secured with a standard non-loop knot, such as the improved clinch. It is essentially two half hitches tied onto the front shank of the hook.

The tippet running from the second half hitch should be positioned so that it comes off the side of the fly. When the head or eye of the fly is pointing upstream, the tippet should run from the fly at the side angle toward the near or casting bank. With this positioning, the tippet, leader, and line act to pull and maintain the fly at the surface. This rigging even keeps a wet fly running in the surface film. The hitch works best with up-eye hooks and the farther the riffle hitch is positioned back, the more effective it is in keeping the fly up. This may require placing the hitch over the front materials of the fly. I leave extra room at the front of the fly for patterns to be used with a riffle hitch.

An alternative to the riffle hitch can be found by using a plastic tube fly for surface fishing. But instead

Getting to know the water can make a big difference. Learning the nuances and subtleties of the structure of a pool and where fish tend to hold goes a long way toward consistent success. NICK PIONESSA PHOTO

of simply inserting the tippet straight into the tube, a hole is created on the side or underneath the tube toward the head. The tippet is then inserted into the tube using this hole on the side. With the pressure being applied from the side, the fly is maintained on the surface when under tension in the same way as a riffle hitch on the hook. The specifics of resenting a dry fly while Spey fishing will be discussed in more detail later in this chapter.

A high percentage of Spey fishing techniques are performed below the water's surface. Placing the fly down in the water column is typically performed by using a sinking leader / sinking-tip or weighted fly or some combination of the two. Finding the proper combination to reach the desired depth relies on science, experience, trial and error, and line management. When using sinking leaders and sinking-tips, both sink rate and length of the tip will determine how deep the fly is fished in the water column. Sink rate of a leader or tip is measured when it is not under tension, providing a simple guide to how fast it sinks in a fishing situation.

Both current speed and surface tension have a direct impact on negating the ability of a leader or tip to reach the desired depth. Faster currents carry the leader or tip in a way that reduces the time it has to sink to a desired depth, effectively impacting the actual sink rate. Also, the hydraulics of some runs and pools create a heavy tension that works against the surface area of the leader or tip. Upswells caused by swirling currents can even push the tip toward the surface. Speed and surface tension also vary as when fishing down through a run, requiring adjustments.

When fishing below the surface, I begin with a plan for a desired depth to fish. Water temperature may dictate how far a fish will move for a fly, and water clarity may dictate the distance a fish will be able to see the fly. Both are key considerations when developing a strategy. Given that the current in a river or stream is less near or on the bottom, fishing the fly in the bottom third of the water column is typically a good starting point for many species that use the lower current to conserve energy. There is a certain degree of feel that goes into finding the right tip for a given situation. I carry a set of sinking leaders and tips to cover almost any situation that may be encountered, adjusting as necessary.

Becoming familiar with certain runs or pools on local waters will help dial in the proper tip to use. However, the proper tip may change with water level variations, impacting depth and current speed. I maintain notes on what tips work best on certain pools or sections of a river under certain water conditions. Most major waters have United States Geological Survey (USGS) gauges that provide a point of reference for water flow to be used when determining tip selection.

Attaining and maintaining the proper depth goes beyond leader or tip selection. While a weighted fly can add some complexity to casting, it is also a useful tool in depth control. A weighted fly has its greatest benefit when fishing fast-flowing water to assist in cutting through the surface tension. And a weighted fly can be essential for covering specific structure, particularly trout and bass Spey situations that require the fly to sink and fish almost immediately.

I often use a weighted fly to fine tune depth. While I prefer casting an unweighted fly, many modern Spey lines carry a weighted fly without any issues. Adding or subtracting a weighted fly or changing the weight of the fly directly impacts the potential fishing depth. Changing the weight of the fly is a tool for acute control. For example, as the depth and speed of a pool changes from top to bottom, a fly change represents a simple adjustment as compared to making a tip change. I often find myself using a weighted fly in the faster riffles at the head of a pool and moving to a less weighted pattern toward the tailout.

Another tool for maintaining depth is to utilize a head that partially or entirely sinks. This style of head allows the fly to reach a greater depth, but its greatest advantage is depth maintenance. A sinking head keeps the fly down better through the entire presentation, reducing the impact of the current raising the head and fly toward the end of the swing. This approach can provide a tactical advantage when pursuing fish that are less likely to rise to the fly as it swings out.

A more important control over depth can be attained through casting angle and mending. Casting slightly on an upstream angle allows the fly to sink faster and deeper than when casting on a downstream angle. But there are some other considerations with respect to casting angle. The use of the upstream angle can't be too abrupt or there won't be enough line extended across-stream to setup an effective swing. And the downstream angle can have a direct impact on speed. So simply casting on a downstream angle to reduce fly depth may speed the swing up to a point where it is less effective in certain situations.

Maintaining depth throughout the swing can be the key for fish that tend to hold and stay deep, like king salmon. I found this fish holding in a deep trench along the opposite bank, and keeping the fly in the strike zone was the key to getting a grab.

A slight downstream angle approach works best when covering structure where it is desirable to have the fly begin swimming as soon as it touches the water. When casting along log jams and boulders, it is best to rig so that the fly reaches the proper depth using this angle.

Mending after the cast is completed can have a similar impact as casting angle. A large upstream mend takes the tension off the fly and tip, allowing it to free fall until coming under tension. Mending is another tool for making depth adjustments while working a pool without the need to change tips or flies. Aggressive mending that results in multiple mends in succession is effective for allowing the fly to sink when covering pockets, slots, and other small areas where it is critical to sink the fly quickly.

Speed

Finding the proper speed of the swing often seems to be the trigger point for a fish to chase and grab or attack a fly. The path of the fly is created by the current pushing on the surface area of the fly line. Speed is controlled by simply manipulating the manner in which the current impacts the line.

Currents that slowly and uniformly taper to the side of the river being fished create an even and consistent swing path. In this situation, very little active line management is required to maintain a consistent swing speed. All that is needed is to cast, mend if required to gain depth, and simply hold on in anticipation of a grab. While it is relaxing to fish such ideal swing pools, the reality is most water requires more active participation.

When the current pushes on the line creating a downstream belly, the speed of the swing and the fly's movement increases. This can be exaggerated in water where the current flow remains strong or is at its strongest on the side of the river that is being fished. When swinging the fly, a low rod tip close to the water while pointing in the direction of the fly maintains sensitivity. Mending line by raising the tip and rolling it up and across stream reduces or eliminates the belly and slows the speed at which the fly is traveling. I attempt to mend the line in a manner that just moves the belly of the line without impacting the traveling path of the fly. This means mending the head of the line without impacting the leader or tip. Modern short

The wading can directly impact the swing path of the fly. Here the angler wades deep to eliminate the soft water on the inside of the main current allowing the head and running line to swing properly without adding aggressive downstream mends.

head lines create some challenges in mending due to longer sections of lower-diameter running line in play with longer casts. But mending can still be performed effectively. And while sinking or intermediate heads can excel at maintaining depth control, effective mending of a head that is below the water's surface becomes problematic.

An opposite mending requirement develops where a stronger current exists at the point where the fly lands but there is a distinct change to a very slow or almost nonexistent current on the fishing position side of the water. This scenario provides speed and presentation challenges as the fly and head travels faster than the running line or rear portion of the head. In extreme cases, it can be difficult to establish a proper swing. Performing a downstream mend places a belly in the line that effectively allows the running line to catch up and the fly to swing evenly in the current. The downstream mend should be sufficient to maintain the desired swing speed making additional mends necessary. Also, simply leading the fly and head by pointing the rod downriver and moving it slowly toward the bank may also keep the fly swimming in the slower water.

There are times when the challenge of a dramatic change in current speeds can simply be mitigated or eliminated by the wading position. Where possible, wading further into the water can place the fishing position closer to the main or faster current. This acts to reduce the soft or slow current in between allowing for more effective water coverage. However, this often comes with a tradeoff. Wading further out usually results in wading deeper. The depth creates casting challenges particularly when shorter rods are involved. Fishing this type of water requires finding the proper combination of wading distance and depth. Sometimes the inside water can be a deep eddy making it difficult or almost impossible to swing the fly properly.

Most of my mending is rather subtle by using a series of small, short mends. This enhances the ability of the fly to maintain a steady, seductive swing path while providing acute adjustments to the speed. When fishing currents that taper to a soft inside seam on the side of the river that is being fished, a downstream belly generally won't develop, but up and across mending can still be utilized to further slow the swing. Mending should be made with purpose. As full-time fly tyer and guide Nick Pionessa explains it, "mending is a literal term. As it applies to fly fishing it means to repair and should be used only to improve the presentation of the fly by reading the direction and force of the mend required."

Maintaining a slow or consistent speed is normally the objective. In fact, as the fly naturally speeds up when reaching an approximate 45-degree angle below the casting position, it seems to act as a trigger point for a fish to grab the fly. But there are also situations where a fast swing is desired as the best approach for certain species or conditions. To increase the speed of the swing, a downstream mend places additional belly in the line, pulling it through the current at an increased velocity.

Speed can also be controlled through rod position. Pointing the rod across river instead of at the fly changes the swing path and presentation. This position places the line at a more parallel angle to the current, reducing the impact of the push of the current on the line. With this rod angle, the fly isn't pulled across as quickly by the line but is held up as it works slowly

through the varying currents of the river. This approach has proven extremely effective for less aggressive fish, particularly under coldwater conditions.

Another approach to slowing down the fly can be found through acute line control at the beginning of the presentation. The cast is made across or even angling slightly upstream. As the fly begins to reach its desired depth, a gentle mend is made to place a portion of the line parallel to the current but not impacting the end of the fly line, leader, or fly. This subtle mend creates a slight "L" shape in the line, greatly reducing the push of the current on the line. This angle allows the fly to drift in a mostly broadside fashion and undulate in the current on a tight line in nearly a dead-drift manner. Additional subtle mends can be added to maintain the "L" shape while the rod is pointed in the direction of the fly. Flies that look lifelike under slight tension work best with this approach as well as patterns that represent injured or damaged prey.

As the fly reaches an approximate 45-degree angle, the current will catch up and begin to push the line while swinging the fly. Pointing the rod directly

Pointing the rod toward the opposite bank changes the angle of the line and slows the speed of the fly. The angle or "L" in the line formed by an upstream mend maintains the fly at a broadside angle throughout the initial phase of the swing. NICK PIONESSA PHOTO

Fly speed is one of the most controllable factors regarding presentation and can be the most important for enticing a strike. Working the fly extra slow in cold water resulted in the grab from this big brown trout.

downstream maintains the broadside angle while reducing the tension and push of the fly line, maintaining a slower presentation until the very end of the swing. The broadside presentation can be effective at all levels of the water column depending on factors such as species and water temperature.

The concept of the slow broadside approach has evolved from a salmon fishing technique referred to as the greased line presentation developed and made popular by Arthur Wood in the early 1900s. In this approach, Wood sought to present the fly in a slow broadside manner near the surface under the premise that salmon on his home waters preferred to rise from their resting lie to take close to the surface during periods of warmer water temperatures. The name of the technique refers to the effort involved in maintaining a fly line from this era made of hair or silk to float on the surface. Drying and greasing the lines with Mucilin, lanolin, or even animal fat was required to keep the line from sinking.

There has been much discussion as to the intricacies of Wood's method of fishing the fly in a near dead-drift fashion while maintaining a proper amount of tension to hook a fish on the take in a manner that allows the fish to mostly hook itself. This technique was the topic of a 1933 book by Jock Scott titled *Greased Line Fishing for Salmon*. The book was later reprinted in the 1980s with an introduction by Bill McMillan.

Angling the cast at a more upstream direction can further encourage a very slow dead-drift presentation. After the cast, a slight upstream mend can be added to assist in sinking the fly and the rod tip is held high similar to a high-stick nymphing approach. As the fly reaches a 45-degree angle, the rod can be pointed at the fly to complete the presentation with a faster swing or point downstream to maintain a slower swimming motion. Utilizing this approach with a weighted fly can be very productive in colder water or for fish that are less likely to chase.

Another approach for slowing the speed of the fly can be found by purposeful rigging. A weighted fly combined with a monofilament or fluorocarbon leader of the approximate length of the rod allows for a slower swing than when a sinking-tip or sinking leader is utilized. The smaller surface area of the monofilament or fluorocarbon reacts less to the current, allowing it to cut through more efficiently, resulting in a slower presentation, particularly on the inside

Lower water temperatures in the early morning after a cold night may require fishing the fly down in the water column. Colder water also typically requires fishing the fly at a slower speed.

of the swing path. This rig can also be used to more effectively dead drift a fly near and around specific structure. Rigging with a weighted fly and long leader has its greatest benefit in low, clear-water, and/or cold-water conditions.

Sinking-tip Control

Speed and depth control are much more visible and obvious when using a floating line than a sinking leader or sinking-tip rig. The clues to properly controlling presentation are on or near the surface. But many modern Spey techniques involve fishing the fly down in the water column using an integrated sinking-tip or the more popular approach of looping a sinking leader or sinking-tip to the front of a floating head.

Adding a sinking leader or tip allows for presenting the fly to a much greater audience of fish up and down the water column. Some anglers argue that this increased ability of modern Spey to reach more fish throughout the year has hurt the ability to bring migratory and resident fish to the surface when the proper conditions exist. However, the use of sinking leaders and tips has become an integral piece of the modern

Spey approach and an important part of a complete tool kit that can still include the use of floating lines when the situation dictates.

Properly fishing a sinking-tip requires a certain degree of finesse and thought while constantly considering the impact of sink rates, casting angle, and water speed and depth. There is an art form to properly managing a tip in order for the fly to fish in the desired and effective manner and includes proper rigging, casting technique, and line control.

The first step in fishing a tip is determining the desired level in the water column to place the fly considering key factors such as the species, fish activity, and water temperatures. Water temperature is one of the key factors as colder water generally keeps fish lower in the water column. Determining the proper tip typically includes some trial and error, but maintaining a small repertoire of tips to meet a range of situations assists in narrowing the choices. Sinking leaders and tips from intermediate sink to 3 inches per second work well for maintaining the fly higher in the column and shallow water situations. I rely on 5 to 7 inches per second for placing the fly down in medium to larger waters with moderate depths and currents. For getting down in the deepest, heaviest water using tips of 8 to 10 inches per second of sink rate is typically required. These tips are commonly constructed of T material although some 8 inch per second density compensated tapered tips also work well when fishing deeper.

Simple sink rate of the tip isn't the only consideration regarding depth. The length of the tip attached to a floating head is an additional factor as a longer tip of a similar sink rate will fish deeper than a shorter tip. My preference is to maintain a constant length on most of my tips and leaders so that a difference in sink rate is the only factor to consider when gauging the impact of a tip or leader change. I generally use 10-foot tips on smaller to medium-size waters and up to 15-foot tips on larger rivers. However, when it comes to the faster sinking level materials such as T-14 and T-17, I do use a variable length approach for controlling depth by carrying sections from 10 to 15 feet in length.

There are many variables that impact the anticipated sink rate of a tip or leader, including water volume or surface tension, inaccuracies in manufacturers' indicated sink rate, style of fly, and even water temperature. And while the head itself has some impact on sink rate, it can have a marked impact on fly depth. The thinner diameter of a Scandi head allows the fly to gain a deeper depth than if the same tip or sinking leader is fished on a Skagit head. Also, Skagit heads with an intermediate or sinking section allow a fly to gain a greater depth. There is a certain amount of trial and error involved in determining the proper tip for a situation. I have a few "go-to" tips and then tend to adjust as needed. I also tend to fish lighter rather than too heavy. I dislike hanging up on the bottom as it disrupts fishing rhythm and the presentation of the fly. My preference is to rig lighter and then make casting, tip adjustments, or fly adjustments to fine tune the depth.

A more scientific approach to tip selection is also possible through mathematical calculations. Pacific Northwest steelheaders Tom Keelin and Bob Pauli have developed a calculation and standard to aid in selecting the proper tip for a given situation based on hours of controlled research. Under this system, the building block for determining the proper tip is to establish what length of a particular tip material is required to sink an unweighted fly to a depth of 1 foot at the end of the swing or at the hang down with a current speed of 3 miles per hour. This system provides valuable information on comparing one tip with another. Details of this research and online calculation models are available on their website at www.flyfishingresearch.net.

Once a tip has been selected, properly controlling the swing allows the tip to perform its intended use. This isn't simply sinking and swimming the fly but presenting it in a manner that will receive interest from a fish and entice a take. Presentation is determined by understanding what the fly is doing under the water and interacting with the variations in current flow and speed. Nearly all presentations will benefit from a straight-line cast that allows the line to completely straighten out to the fly. The fly begins to fish almost immediately after hitting the water. As discussed earlier, a weighted fly can aid in getting the fly to depth faster and increasing the time that the fly is in the fish's zone of view.

In most cases, fishing a swung fly with a sinking leader or sinking-tip involves getting the fly to begin swimming right after it has reached the preferred depth. And sometimes this is immediately after hitting the water. A cast that flops to the side is a detriment since the initial portion of the swing is required simply to straighten everything out while losing the proper presentation angle. Actually, a fair amount of the swing can be wasted as the fly travels directly up- or downstream in a somewhat unnatural manner before it straightens to more of a broadside angle. A cast that flops to the side at the end is commonly caused by the rod tip not moving in a straight plane during the forward stroke.

Overpowering the forward stroke to a point where the line straightens with force and then reverberates as the running line tightens quickly can also cause unwanted slack in the line at the end of the cast. Controlling the forward stroke with just enough power to complete the cast and straighten out the line eliminates the slack. Finding the proper balance requires adjustments throughout a day of fishing. Also, completing the cast at too sharp of an upstream angle can cause slack and the fly to move unnaturally at the beginning. It can also cause the tip or sinking leader to sink too fast and hang up on the bottom. Be sure that any casts aimed upstream are at only a slight angle up and the line is near perpendicular to the current as it passes in front of the casting position.

There is a challenge in finding the right sinking leader or tip for water that has various speeds and an uneven bottom. Erring on the side of fishing too light is always preferred to fishing too deep and repeatedly hanging up the fly on the bottom.

Once a desired cast has been made, mending may be required to sink the fly or it can be allowed to swing almost immediately. I generally prefer one big mend to allow the fly and tip or sinking leader to free fall and attain the desired depth. And instead of making a mend after the line lands on the water, a reach mend can be placed into the forward cast, allowing the line to land upriver of the fly. The reach mend is a line movement that occurs during the cast and is accomplished by pointing the rod upriver after the forward stroke has completed its abrupt stop at 11 o'clock.

A significant part of the modern Spey movement has been the versatility created by Skagit heads opening a wider range of water types and greater depths to Spey fishing. Fishing with a Skagit head provides for its own style of fishing. While a Skagit head can be used in almost any Spey fishing situation, this style of head excels at placing weighted flies at significant depths and overall versatility. A Skagit head with a sinking-tip and weighted fly is commonly fished in a three-step fashion. For reaching the greatest depth,

the first step is to make a cast across or slightly up and across. The second is the setup. For greatest depth, make an upstream mend or reach mend and finish with the rod high. Slowly lower the rod, introducing the running line caused by the high rod tip into drift. This maintains a loose connection to the fly at first, allowing the tip and fly to drop in the water column the entire time. The third and final step occurs as the rod is lowered completely and the fly begins a broadside presentation swimming into the hang down.

I prefer maintaining a broadside angle to the fish as this provides a complete view of the fly and has resulted in more grabs and takes over the years from most fish species. A very subtle upstream mend right after the cast or after the initial mend to gain depth places the middle portion of the head upstream but allows approximately the last five feet of the head and tip to remain mostly perpendicular to the current. This slight mend creates a similar result as the greased line presentation discussed earlier but deeper in the water column and allows the fly to swim at an enticing speed from the beginning of the presentation. The broadside angle is maintained with a low rod tip pointing in the direction of the fly or slightly ahead of the fly until it nears the end of the swing and begins to take more of an upstream angle. As discussed, a rod angle that points to the opposite bank and slows the swing will place the fly at more of an upstream angle throughout the presentation.

During the swing, reading the currents and manipulating the line through mending or simple line placement allows the fly to maintain a desired path. Water that tapers somewhat evenly from a faster outside current to a soft inside current may require very few if any line adjustments throughout the swing. This type of water usually provides enough current on the inside to elevate the line and tip so that the fly stays off the bottom in the hang down position when wading knee to thigh deep. However, it's quite common to fish water that doesn't have such smooth transitions in current variations. The true challenge in properly fishing a tip is to read the situation and make the adjustment to fish the fly at the desired depth and speed without hanging up on the bottom.

A common situation is when the line is cast across a faster current into slower water flow. The faster current quickly forms a belly in the line, pulling the fly quickly out of the slower water. Fish will often hold in this slower seam on the far side of the faster water. Presenting the fly in the slower water requires slowing it down and making the offering accessible to the fish. Adding a succession of mends as the swing begins can eliminate the belly, allowing the fly to spend more time in the slower water before swimming through.

Significantly slower current on the inside also poses a challenge when swinging the fly as the main current carries the tip and fly faster than the line close to your fishing position. A downstream mend or adjustment of the line is required to allow for a smooth continuous swing of the fly. As the fly swings into the slower water of the inside current, the fast sink rate tip that may be required to sink the fly in the heavy main flow may not allow for the fly to hang below the fishing position. However, raising the rod tip as the fly moves into the soft water may provide enough elevation to keep the fly fishing into the slow current. Stripping the

Mending by lifting the rod and repositioning the line is often the key to attaining the proper speed and depth. When required, active line management allows the fly to move on a desired path. NICK PIONESSA PHOTO

Swirling, uneven currents can cause frustration when swinging and presenting the fly. Reading the flows and pulses of water can dictate the angle of the cast and required mends for an enticing presentation. NICK PIONESSA PHOTO

line as it moves into the slower water can also keep it from hanging up in slower currents.

Swirling- and pulsing-type currents may offer the largest challenge when fishing a sinking-tip or sinking leader. One of my home rivers has taught me many lessons on fishing a tip through swirling uneven flows. And while some of this type of water can occur as the result of power generation on the river, strange uneven currents occur naturally on steelhead, salmon, and trout rivers. The key to fishing this type of water is patience and continually reading the visible signs to determine the occurrence of the variations in the current. Swirling and pulsing water may require both upstream mends to sink the fly and downstream mends to maintain an even swing while the fly swims broadside to the current. It may also require understanding the timing of the pulses and making the cast at a point that maximizes the swing of the fly.

Many anglers find this type of uneven, swirling water to be frustrating to fish. But learning to fish uneven currents can teach valuable techniques to be used on a range of water types. I recall a memorable large steelhead caught from a deep, dark, swirling tailout on a British Columbia river. I was casting from water that had virtually no current into a flow that pulsed on an irregular interval. The pool required a long cast to catch the main current with an upstream mend to sink the fly into the deep, dark water and then a downstream mend to create enough belly to pull and swing the fly. Receiving a big grab midway through the swing was incredibly rewarding.

Typically, the sinking leader or sinking-tip is set up for a current speed and depth at the beginning of the pool. As current speed and overall depth changes, it's important to identify the factors and make adjustments discussed above. Less experienced Spey casters and anglers tend to struggle with the consistency of the cast. Variations in the length of the cast or angle can have a significant impact on how the current pushes the line and allows the fly to swing. A faulty shorter cast or one that is angled higher than the others may not fish the fly properly, resulting in a hang up on the bottom during the swing or at the hang down. It's important to recognize instances where the current isn't providing the proper push on the line and make adjustment before a hang up occurs.

The key to successfully fishing a swung fly on a tip or sinking leader is to stay connected with the fly and truly understand how it is presenting itself. The swing can be varied in so many ways by casting angle, fishing angle, and mending. Each cast should have its own plan as to the preferred approach for the given water, conditions, and mood of the fish. I always envision how the fly is fishing, making sure that it is swimming in a desired and enticing manner. Properly swinging the fly involves active management. And while some water requires less thought and line manipulation, swinging the fly on a tip should always be done with mindfulness as opposed to simply making a cast and holding on.

When fishing a sinking leader or tip, I normally wade to at least knee to thigh deep for the hang down position to be most effective. It is best to have the

depth below your fishing position to be sufficient for a fish to feel comfortable holding in or following the fly into as the swing concludes. Fishing the fly carefully through the hang down is an important component of the swing approach as many fish are hooked at the end or when the fly is stripped back. But wading thigh deep may not always be the preferred approach. When you are the first person through the pool for the day or fishing water that has been rested for a long period, fish may position in shallow water. Taking a stealthy approach while wading calf deep with a lighter tip can payoff. Here a good approach can be to make one pass fishing shallow and then another wading deeper.

Allowing the fly to keep fishing and swimming into the hang down is a key step for complete water coverage when fishing a swung fly. The fly in the hang down gives the appearance of bait simply holding in the current and can entice fish to strike that have followed the fly or that are positioned in the soft inside seam. When there is a consistent current below the fishing position,

While it's fun to swing the fly, don't ever give up too soon on the hang down. I can distinctly remember this fish grabbing after the fly had swung to a full stop just hanging in the current.

the flow should be enough to keep the tip off the bottom and the fly simply hanging in the current. When the current below the casting position is soft, additional rod and line manipulation may be required to maintain the hang down. When soft water exists in the hang down, placing a large mend toward the near bank allows the fly to swim as the bow in the line created by the mend straightens out. Another effective approach for dealing with softer inside currents is to simply point the rod out toward the opposite bank as the fly approaches the hang down position. This pushes the line out more into the current, elevating the line and tip and keeping the fly swimming off the bottom in the current with an enticing action. The tip pointed out approach can be an essential move for maximizing the effectiveness of the hang down presentation. These two moves can be combined to create extra action on the fly by first mending toward the bank and then pointing the rod out. This creates a serpentine swim path for the fly at the end of the swing.

Don't be too quick to pull the fly out of the hang down. After allowing the fly to hang in the current, making a couple short strips before retrieving line for the next cast can be the trigger for a fish that is simply looking at the fly with latent interest.

Swinging and Waking Dry Flies

Many anglers would agree that witnessing the take of the fly is one of the most exhilarating experiences in fly fishing. Some of the same elements of line and fly control that exist for fishing subsurface are present when swinging or waking a dry fly. But to fish the fly in an enticing manner, specific elements of line control are needed for the ideal surface presentation.

This section looks at the approach for combining Spey fishing with swinging or waking a fly on the surface for migratory and resident fish. Waking a fly for migratory fish is generally aimed at representing a disturbance on the surface, possibly playing on a fish's leftover instinct for feeding on the top during its formative years before moving from its natal waters. Surface fishing for residents typically involves representing natural food sources occurring on a specific river or stream.

Scandi heads and mid or long belly heads or integrated lines are most useful when swinging or waking dry flies. Longer works well with surface fishing since the floating properties of the head or line allow for an easier release from the tension of the water to begin the next cast than when using a sinking leader or sinking-tip line. This allows intermediate or even beginning casters to efficiently use Scandi or longer heads.

Longer rods will typically be required to handle a longer head. But the longer rod also has its advantages for line control when covering big water with a waking fly. The monofilament or fluorocarbon leader length approximates the length of the rod with enough strength in the butt to turn the fly over and straighten out the leader. Surface fishing with floating lines lends itself perfectly to touch and go casting, increasing the efficiency and stealth of the approach.

Most dry flies used for waking are buoyant and tied with spun deer hair or foam to keep the fly at the surface. However, when a buoyant pattern is fished on a tight line, the water tension can push the fly down below the water's surface. A properly applied riffle hitch allows both buoyant and lightly dressed patterns to fish at the surface when under tension. Using a tube fly with an underneath or side exit for the tippet is another good option for surface fishing.

The term waking refers to the slight disturbance or "wake" that the fly makes as it is fished under tension across the surface. This can also be referred to as skating a fly. The disturbance of the fly and resulting wake is designed to bring a fish up to investigate and hopefully eat. The wake also provides a visual for the angler to track the fly, watching for a take or other disruption on the surface that could indicate that a fish is showing some interest.

The cast to wake a fly is made at a slightly downstream angle. The tension of the tippet pulling off to the side keeps the fly on the surface while cutting a visible V. The rod tip is held high, much higher than when fishing a subsurface fly. This position removes line from the surface and provides the ability for acute line control and maintaining the proper speed of the fly. Finding the proper tension and speed for the water being fished is the key to this presentation. When there is not sufficient tension, the fly fails to move enough to form a V, and too much tension forces it to plow into the water dragging the fly below the surface.

Rod position controls everything. Water with a slow to moderate speed, a consistent current across its width, and a smooth surface is easy to fish with a waking fly. A rod angled up and above parallel to the water should be sufficient in creating a visible V and allow

Fairly shallow water with an even flow and structure to provide both a break in the current and security makes for a perfect spot to wake a fly.

the fly to travel at an enticing speed. Faster, uneven currents may require a higher rod tip to remove the impact of the variations in the water's surface.

Fly control is also attained by the direction the rod tip is pointing. The normal starting position slightly favors the inside bank as opposed to pointing directly at the fly. To start the fly waking in slower currents, the rod tip may need to draw more toward the near bank to create sufficient tension. Often, at the end of the swing, this position toward the bank allows the fly to move and wake even as it enters the hang down position. Pointing slightly to the outside of the fly may be required to slow its speed if judged to be moving across the surface too rapidly or reduce the tension if the fly is plowing under the water's surface.

What I enjoy most about fishing a waking fly is the active nature of the presentation. How the rod is managed controls speed, angle, and whether the fly will even wake at all. Some water is just perfect, requiring little manipulation to get a nice V. Other water requires

some effort by finding the proper combination of rod angle with relation to both the water's surface and the position of the fly. Additional action can be added to the fly by moving and twitching the rod tip to provide a variation to the standard waking approach.

Starting and maintaining the wake throughout the presentation can be challenging and sometimes frustrating. When having trouble with establishing a waking fly, especially in slower water, lift the rod tip higher and lead the fly by moving the tip toward the near bank in an exaggerated fashion. This movement can create just enough tension to establish a V. It's possible that the rod tip can be dropped during the presentation once the V has been established.

Faster water can also pose issues in getting the fly to wake. Lifting the rod tip high and pointing at the direction of the fly reduces some of the tension that can drag the fly under. In faster water, the rod tip follows the fly as opposed to leading. Faster water with heavy chop can be somewhat problematic as the small

Witnessing a fish poking its head through the water's surface to engulf a waking fly is one the most exhilarating experiences in Spey fishing.

Sometimes it takes a few seconds before enough side tension is exerted on the fly to begin waking. It can take some training of the eye to consistently make a visual and see the fly through the entire presentation. Focus on looking for the disturbance on the surface and use flies with multiple colors to aid in the detection process. Black, white, and orange tend to show up best, but variations in the lighting can cause one color to show better than another. When the water's surface looks light gray and oily, black tends to show best. White and orange show well on dark waters. Carry a variety of colors and experiment.

It goes without saying that being able to see your fly is important not only for witnessing the heart-stopping experience of a large head poking through the surface to engulf the fly but also to watch for any activity that may show that a fish is interested but didn't grab. Migratory fish are often a bit clumsy or even playful when it comes to waking flies. Sometimes a fish will roll or push water up around the fly. Other times, it may look to have grabbed the fly without taking it down. While the focus should be on the fly, keep your range wide to look for activity behind and around the wake. You may also find that bombing out long casts may make it difficult to see the fly when it is far away. In that case, shorten up for control and visibility.

While it can be both exciting and disappointing when a fish shows for the fly but doesn't take, all is not lost. Sometimes that same fish will show for the fly again on a subsequent cast or, better yet, grab the fly and take it down. When a fish shows, I'll typically make the same cast immediately with the same fly. If the fish doesn't take or show, I typically go to a smaller fly, usually a riffle-hitched wet fly or a low-profile dry that rides in the surface film. The time it takes to change fly rests the fish for a few minutes. If that doesn't bring the fish back, I'll step back a few steps provided there is nobody fishing behind me and rest the fish for another 15 minutes before working through again with either the original fly or a low-profile pattern. Over the years, this repertoire of techniques has been successful in bringing a percentage of fish back to the surface. But it doesn't always work, possibly because an individual fish isn't aggressive enough or can't easily be fooled. You can also experiment with angle and speed. Be sure to always let the fly swing all the way out and sit in the hang down for

waves douse and drown the fly. It may be difficult to wake in faster flows but wading as close to the area being fished reduces the line on the water, making a more effective surface presentation. When all else fails with respect to keeping the fly at the surface, move the riffle hitch back farther so there is more side pressure on the fly even if it is tied into the materials of the fly. Some of the new fly designs that rely on closed cell foam are quite buoyant and tend to stay on the surface quite well.

Afternoons on autumn days after water temperatures have had a chance to rise can be the optimum time to fish a fly on the surface for steelhead. Here an angler observes a waking fly working over a boulder run in the waning light of the day.

a few seconds as I have caught several fish that follow and eat the fly as it stops.

Where legal, using a two-fly rig with one waking on top and a wet fly following below provides a two-pronged approach that works well for fish that don't quite commit to the surface. The trailing fly can be added using an improved clinch knot and separate tippet tied to the bend of the dry fly and then tied to the eye of the wet fly. This approach has a greater application to trout but can also be a strategy for migratory fish.

When a large migratory fish finally takes a waking fly, the hook set requires an element of calm and patience. The best-case scenario is allowing the fish to take the fly down and turn so that the hook is set on the weight of the fish. But sometimes, the fish doesn't take and turn so that the weight of the fish isn't apparent. In either situation, it is critical to give the fish time to take the fly down. This may be easier said than done as the common reaction is to set immediately on the visible sign of the fish. But setting too quickly literally pulls the fly right out of the fish's mouth due to the rear attack angle of a waking fly—snatching defeat from victory.

Having the restraint to wait a second or two on the hook may take some experience and a couple fouled attempts. But Spey fishing is about remaining cool and rhythmic through the cast, presentation, and even the hook set. Think in terms of reacting to a take of a waking fly by observing, waiting a second, and then smoothly raise and sweep the rod to the near bank. This approach results in a high percentage of hooked fish.

Swinging representations of land-based creatures, such as mice, juvenile rats, frogs, or baby birds, is a variation of the waking fly approach that can be an effective, enjoyable, and exciting approach when fishing for resident trout and bass. The idea is to present a helpless, land-based animal that has wound up in the river by accident or choice.

The presentation begins with a similar cast angled downstream, as with a waking fly. Rod angle controls the speed of the fly. But there are a couple differences in this approach. First, the patterns used to represent mice or frogs are quite buoyant and won't need the aid of a riffle hitch to maintain a position on the surface. Secondly, action should be added to the fly to give the impression of swimming and struggling on the surface. Quickly moving the rod tip from side to

side transmits shock waves in the line causing the fly to wiggle while swinging on the surface to draw the attention of a would-be predator.

The Swing Approach

If I had to describe the objective of Spey fishing in its simplest terms, it would be effective water coverage. Each pool or run represents an opportunity to show your fly to holding fish, and performed properly, Spey fishing shows the fly to as many fish as possible. The process typically begins by starting at the top of a pool or run. In Spey fishing, it is always considered proper etiquette to start above other anglers and never below. This approach works well on rivers where all anglers understand the prevailing etiquette. On some rivers it is even the regulation or law to begin at the head. But most waters see a range of angling techniques that present competing objectives. More on that subject later in this chapter.

The key is to cover a run or pool in a grid-like fashion by performing quality repeatable casts. In other words, making a cast of length and angle that can be performed consistently within your abilities. Trying to reach out longer casts that are only successful a percentage of the time lack the rhythm and stealth required to be successful with the Spey approach. It is preferred to shorten the cast to a distance that is comfortable and cover the run or pool at that length. If more length to the cast is desired or required for additional success, it is best to work on the technique and timing during practice sessions before going to the river to fish.

The water coverage part of swinging the fly is dependent on a continual movement through the pool by consistently stepping down after each cast. The movement down may be a short one or two steps or a longer pace of three or four. I typically make my steps down as I retrieve running line for the next cast. But taking the steps down immediately after completing the cast is a tool for sinking the fly deeper as tension is taken off the line during the steps downstream. The amount of distance between each cast depends on a number of factors. Water clarity is usually the most dominant factor. Lower visibility caused by stained water calls for less distance between casts to maximize the number of fish that may see the fly. When the water is significantly off-color, I may try a couple casts from each position attempting to fish one deeper

The lack of visibility caused by dirty water conditions requires a slow approach to covering a run or pool. Short steps after each cast create better odds that any fish present in the run or pool will see the fly. NICK PIONESSA PHOTO

than the other to cover more of the water column. Clearer water calls for more distance between casts under the assumption that a fish will have the ability to see and move farther laterally or up in the water column to intercept the swing. Too short of a distance in clear water can actually be a detriment. You want the fish to see the fly at just the right distance to catch its attention and close enough that it can easily catch up for the capture. In clear water, too short of a distance between each cast can result in the fish seeing the fly multiple times before it is close enough to chase, thereby eliminating the surprise element of first seeing the fly.

I may also utilize a shorter step process in colder water and for heavily pressured, less aggressive fish to provide additional accessibility to fly. And I may move faster when prospecting for aggressive fish or when my fishing time is limited or running out. I also tend to move slower when covering specific structure. Often more than one cast from each position at different angles or speeds is required to completely cover the potential holding area. Making additional casts

from each position in water with swirling or irregular currents can also be key to attaining a complete coverage. But always make sure you are not holding up other anglers behind you when taking a methodical approach to the rotation as this could be viewed as improper etiquette.

Another reason for a more methodical approach is when a fish shows interest in the presentation without actually taking the fly or getting hooked. When fishing subsurface, its common to feel a tap or a lazy pull on the fly or a fish may follow the fly for a significant distance while continually tapping. Other times, the pull may be quite dramatic, leaving you wondering how the fish didn't get hooked. The sensation of a grab can also be caused by a fish positioned closely behind the fly discharging water through its gills to feed but the taught nature of the line prevents the fly from being sucked into its mouth. While a tap or pull can be a frustrating occurrence, it is evidence there is an active fish present that can possibly be fooled and caught.

After receiving a pull from a fish with no hookup, my feet are planted so that the same water can be covered with the same pattern. If that doesn't yield success, I'll try another fly pattern, usually smaller in size. Etiquette becomes a consideration at this point. If there are other anglers in the rotation, it is deemed good manners to keep moving. But if there are no other anglers, I may take a couple steps upriver and try the original pattern again since the fish may have repositioned after the initial grab. If that still doesn't work, I'll wait a few minutes to allow things to settle and fish down through the water again. There have been times where I hooked a fish below the point of the original grab, indicating that the same fish may have backed down in the current after its initial interest.

Occasionally, the fish will pull a second or even third time. At this point, I continue with the same pattern but change the speed through mending or casting angle. While it seems that the chance of hooking the fish goes down with each cast, I remember one particular steelhead that pulled or grabbed the fly on six consecutive casts before hooking it on the seventh attempt.

When a fish is encountered that doesn't return to the fly, a mental note should be made of its position. If another pass is made through that pool, be sure to work that area thoroughly as a rested fish often moves to the fly again.

Finding Water

Finding good swing water can be a challenge in itself on some rivers. Having an entire pool to work through is the preferred situation as you can develop a rhythm and can cover all the holding water that the pool contains at your own pace. On rivers that receive less fishing pressure, open pools are typically not difficult to find. Based on the private management approach of some rivers worldwide, there may be a limit on the total number of anglers on a river or sections of the river. The fee for prime private sections or beats on some waters can be quite pricey. Open public water on popular rivers can require some strategy.

Finding good swing runs and pools on public water usually requires a plan. It doesn't have to be an elaborate plan but rather some thinking outside of the box. I typically take a contrarian approach, using the movements and habits of others to an advantage.

It makes sense to take a more methodical approach to covering a run or pool during coldwater periods. Here Jay Newell slowly works a pool on a chilly late November day.

Boats and rafts provide the option to explore and separate from fishing pressure while adding an adventuresome aspect to the day.

Possibly the most consistent manner for finding open water on most rivers is to simply take a hike. Good water can be found near popular access points, but odds are someone will already be there casting a line. I select starting points on sections of the river with the most limited access. Hiking far enough almost always works. But it can be tiring, especially when covering terrain with limited trails. Be prepared. Pack in plenty of fluids and a meal or energy snacks to keep the body fueled for the hike back out. One other trick for fishing with a friend and two cars is to walk from one access point to another. It's basically a walking float trip.

On rivers that are large enough, floating from one point to another can work very well to spread anglers out. Drift boats, rafts, pontoons, and even kayaks all have a place to take anglers from point A to point B. On intimate waters, care is needed to respect other anglers. I always float behind others and never through someone's water. When walk and wade fishing a river that has a fair amount of float boat traffic, I focus on the water above the boat launch in the morning and water below in the afternoon and evening to avoid the distraction caused by watercraft floating over or near the water being fished. Where feasible, jet boats can provide the ultimate vehicle for finding prime water.

There are a few obvious steps for finding your own water, such as avoiding the weekend when possible. Inclement weather always reduces the number of anglers on the water. With today's clothing and outer wear, it is possible to stay reasonably comfortable in even the most miserable conditions. Some of my most memorable days have occurred on dark, dreary, inclement days where only the hardy showed up to the river. There is a feeling of accomplishment in meeting the weather head on. Immersion into the elements is both energizing and revitalizing.

There are other factors that tend to keep anglers away as well. High water can be intimidating. But if

Inclement weather keeps anglers off the water. Dressing properly for the conditions is essential for enjoyment and possibly finding memorable experiences that others may miss. NICK PIONESSA PHOTO

the river maintains some of its general character and has at least a foot of visibility, there is a chance. After all, covering a lot of water is one of the advantages of swinging the fly. The one factor that really seems to deter other anglers is heavy winds. But armed with a two-hander and the ability to cast off each shoulder, heavy winds can be handled quite easily. Selecting areas in the lea of a gorge wall or stand of forest can take the edge off of gusty conditions. On a recent Alaska trip to swing for king salmon, we were faced with a day-long onslaught of 40 to 60 mile per hour winds. But casting off each shoulder and keeping the rod low while fishing saved the day and even resulted in some hook ups.

Another approach for finding good water on popular rivers is to work the shoulder periods—the time just before and just after prime time. This may mean less fish opportunities and inclement weather, but having more water to yourself is a worthy tradeoff.

Timing during the day can have a significant impact on fishing pressure. The early bird gets the worm mentality on many rivers with high angling effort experiences the highest pressure from first light through noontime. Angling pressure can lighten significantly in the afternoon. I have long used this strategy for both finding my favorite pools wide open and success in term of encountering aggressive fish. I truly enjoy venturing deeper down the trail as I pass anglers on their way out for the day. A headlamp aids in finding my way back in the darkness.

The obvious, popular pools always seem to hold fish as well as attracting anglers. And Spey anglers are constantly in search of that perfect pool. But sometimes fish are in the off spots—small pockets, fast runs, and even shallow riffles. High angling pressure pushes fish into heavier water. Switch rods or two-handers are great for distance casting but are also effective tools for creative presentations that allow for controlling depth and speed even in confined areas. More on this in the next chapter.

One of the many things that fly fishing has taught me is to not get caught in a rut. Nothing is automatic.

Every day on the water is unique. Keep an open mind as to the best strategy for each day to find both water and fish. Going against the grain is often part of that equation. And finding open water isn't merely about the esthetics of being able to cover a pool or run at your own pace, but it can be the best way to find fresh, aggressive fish that have received less fishing pressure than other holding water. In terms of Spey fishing, finding aggressive fish can make all the difference.

There are times when it will be impossible to find open water and sharing it with other anglers will be necessary. This is typically not a problem on rivers where a rotation ethic exists. Here all anglers start at the top and methodically work through the pool or run. However, for many rivers, it is common to find anglers using a variety of fishing equipment and techniques, including remaining stationary or even

working upriver. Normally it is easy enough to work around other anglers, and it may even be an opportunity to carefully educate an angler on the benefits of rotation even when not Spey fishing.

There are situations when I'll actually choose to fish water with other anglers. There are pools and runs that are such a pleasure to fish or contain elements that attract and hold fish on a reliable basis that makes sharing water the best approach. An Atlantic salmon trip to Quebec's Gaspe Peninsula sticks out in my mind. It was fairly early in the run with limited numbers of fish spread out over many miles of river. By midweek of the trip, it became clear that fish were being caught in two or three of the main pools with very few or any salmon being found in numerous others. We took the strategy of getting into the rotation line in the productive pools even if we had to wait our

Be sure to not wade too deep on the first pass through a pool in the morning. Fish will often be located resting in the soft inside currents. Tim Gelinas uses a short rod to remain close to the bank for a stealthy first pass of a productive pool.

When fishing behind other anglers, mix it up with different flies and presentations to find the right combination. This provides a good opportunity to experiment and often results in finding a new productive fly pattern or presentation strategy. NICK PIONESSA PHOTO

turn to step in at the head. It was a strategy that ended up working out well for both my brother Jerry and me as we both landed our biggest salmon in one of the most popular pools on the river.

When fishing behind other anglers in a rotation, try to take a contrary approach to the other anglers ahead of you. When fishing with a partner, ask about their rigging and fly using this information to vary your approach. When following anglers that you don't know, observe what you can, and try to do something different. I'll attempt to vary the size, color, or design of the fly. But more important may be the depth and speed. Since there are so many tools available for varying the depth and speed, don't be afraid to try something entirely new or even unique when compared to the other anglers fishing the run or pool.

5

TACTICAL SPEY FISHING

As a Spey angler, I think and dream about finding that perfect pool. At the head of the pool where the current flows in, the depth is thin, but the surface is broken enough to keep fish hidden. Moving down, the water turns darker and slower, and the current that is strong in the middle softens as a tapered inside seam offers a perfect resting spot for a fish while creating little need to mend the line.

There are visible swirling disturbances on the surface indicating rocks and contour changes, offering ideal holding structure. The pool fishes deep into the tail as the bottom rises to meet the next heavy riffle downriver. A few boulders nearly poke through the surface creating a slightly irregular current and respite for a traveling fish.

To fully utilize all that Spey has to offer, it's important to focus on the many tactical advantages to this approach, even on smaller waters. An angler explores some intimate Pacific Northwest water for fresh-run steelhead. JEFF BRIGHT PHOTO

The perfect pool may take an hour or two to completely work through all its nuances. You can get lost in its vastness while imagining what exists below the surface. The pool allows you to bomb out long casts to cover its width while adjusting the casting stroke for the changes in wading depth. The rhythmic cadence of cast, step, and cast can put you in a zen-like state that is only disturbed by the heavy take of an aggressive fish. But this type of water may not readily exist on some rivers or may be one of the more popular pools making it difficult to get in the rotation. Developing a more tactical approach can be effective, challenging, and satisfying.

Non-typical Holding Areas

Fishing the water between and around the main pools and runs in a river can yield many benefits, including avoiding fishing pressure on popular rivers and finding aggressive migratory or resident fish looking to attack a swinging fly.

Two-hand and one-handed rods combined with Spey casting are tools of versatility. While these rods allow you to swing a fly using effortless casts and acute line control, there is also the advantage of creativity. Rigged with the proper line, tip, and fly, myriad water can be explored while fishing the fly on a tight line. Skagit-style lines have opened the possibility of covering just about any type of water with Spey techniques. Taking a contrarian view to a river allows you to see it in a different light and exposes opportunities that might not otherwise be obvious. There is often an advantage to leading and not following.

Pocket water created by boulders, rock formations, drop-offs, or submerged logs should never be overlooked. This type of water can regularly hold migratory fish while resting on their journey upriver or resident fish holding or looking for food. Pockets can be found within a typical run or pool, as a series of pockets in fast currents, or in less-defined water between the main pools. Pocket water is often covered by anglers using high-stick techniques, but using a tight line and swinging fly can result in aggressive grabs with the proper presentation.

Pockets provide good holding areas because the structure creating this type of water is blocking the main current, allowing a fish to use less energy. The

Fishing a wide variety of possible holding spots aside from obvious pools and runs can produce surprising results. NICK PIONESSA PHOTO

The soft water of the pocket created by a large boulder is a perfect resting spot or feeding spot in streams and rivers of all sizes. The soft flows created by the boulder extend downstream and also include the area just in front of the boulder.
NICK PIONESSA PHOTO

soft water of a pocket also tends to attract bait fish and other living creatures. It is important to note that fish can be positioned in front of the structure, creating the pocket as well as behind. A large boulder causes the current to split around it, leaving soft holding water directly in front. Making sure the fly shows itself to both the front and behind the structure will maximize the coverage.

The presentation challenge when fishing pocket water exists in placing the fly at the proper level and controlling the line for it to swing through the target area. How deep the fly should be presented often depends on water temperature, but it is always important to be rigged in a way that places the fly deep enough for attracting a fish's attention. A weighted fly can assist in reaching the proper depth to break through the heavy surface tension often found around pocket water, especially when attempting to cover water in front of a large boulder. A tippet section longer than 3 to 4 can assist in depth control.

While I prefer to reach the desired depth through the sink rate of a sinking leader or sinking-tip and

weight of the fly, there are times when it may be practical, where allowed by regulations, to add some weight directly to the leader as well by using wrap-on strips or split shot above the tippet knot. This flies in the face of tradition but is a last resort strategy for acute depth control when fishing a fly near specific structure. Adding weight to the leader is a strategy that best matches when using a floating line, long mono-filament or fluorocarbon leader, and weighted fly. The weight on the leader assists with getting the fly deeper and more quickly when needed for short, controlled swings in heavy pockets or near structure.

Line control is the key to fishing pocket water. In big pockets where the fly needs to sink quickly, aggressive mending will be important. Taking the tension off the line allows the fly to free-fall for a short period. In some situations, one big upstream mend will be enough to set up the swing, but greater depths and current flow may require a series of mends. Stack mending refers to making repeated short mends to create maximum slack and depth to set up the swing. Stack mending can require a fair amount of effort but pay dividends when fishing around large boulders. Treat the head almost as dead drifting with an indicator until the fly reaches the desired depth and is in the proper position to begin swimming.

The water in front of the obstruction causing the pocket will normally have a relatively uniform flow but care is needed to ensure the fly and sinking-tip don't swing into the obstruction and become snagged. The water behind the boulder or other item creating the pocket requires a more calculated approach. As the current flows around the obstruction, it creates soft water directly downriver with a more forceful current on the outer edges of the pocket. The first casts that allow the fly to swing into the pocket are made while positioned above the obstruction. Swinging through water with abrupt changes in the flow can be challenging. Make the cast so that it lands on the far side of the pocket, mend as necessary to get depth, and allow the fly to swing through. To get a good swing, line manipulation may be required throughout the entire presentation. Mending the line upstream might be required

to slow the fly down by removing a belly in the line. After the mend, maintaining a rod angle that points to the opposite bank continues to slow the swing and keep the fly in the pocket water for an extended time. If you are close enough to the pocket, lift the rod tip to take some of the line off the water to help control the swing. In most situations, presentation is enhanced by wading as close as possible to the pocket without making fish aware of your presence and maintaining a safe wading position. Downstream mends might be required if the water behind the obstruction is dead or placid where a belly is used to pull on the line and swing the fly through. Making more than one cast from each position by changing the angle or approach to managing the line makes sure the water has been covered thoroughly.

Fishing the fly up in the water column around and behind pockets can be a productive approach for migratory steelhead and salmon as well as resident trout. A fly fished on a floating line and long leader on or just below the surface can trigger a quick response

Fish can hold in any spot where there is a sense of security; using a tactical approach that allows the fly to swim through off beat areas can be surprisingly productive. NICK PIONESSA PHOTO

Ledges can often be determined by a change in water color, allowing for an acute coverage of this important structural element. However, in darker water, ledges may be determined through more of a trial-and-error approach or previous knowledge of where the structure is located. NICK PIONESSA PHOTO

in clear-water conditions. Speed can be controlled by the angle of the cast and rod positioning. A faster swing by casting across and allowing for a downstream belly is a preferred approach when fishing near the surface.

The fast, shallow water found between main pools is constantly overlooked. On some of the more heavily pressured rivers in my home Great Lakes region, migratory fish may take to heavy cover to avoid anglers. Resident trout and bass may also move into heavy water to feed on aquatic life. Over the years, I have consistently found fish in water that by simple observation looked much too fast and heavy to hold fish. However, the current is always heaviest on the surface, and structure along the bottom creates just enough soft water for fish to hold.

Look for areas or spots that appear darker to indicate a drop in the bottom and possibly offering softer water. Also, focus on any other types of structure such as rocks and boulders that can break the main current flow. A weighted fly along with a sinking-tip work best in quickly achieving the proper depth for fish

positioned near the bottom. An upstream mend immediately after completing the cast will allow the fly an opportunity to sink. In fast water, there is a tendency for the fly line to develop a big downstream belly as the heavy current works on the surface area of the fly line, causing a fast swing. Making continual upstream mends that reposition the line to eliminate the belly while not impeding the swing allows the fly to maintain a consistent speed.

For resident trout feeding on aquatic insects, it's not as important to place the fly deep, as a wet fly or nymph pattern up in the water column may represent an emergent stage. But maintaining a slower speed is still important for the fly to look natural.

Ledges in slate or bedrock are a type of structure that tends to attract and hold fish. Ledges can be found on many rivers, and a few come to mind that are primarily composed of this type of bottom structure. For aggressive fish, simply swinging a fly high in the water column or on the surface over the ledge may be enough to entice a take. But for fish clinging more

Slack is developed by an upstream mend and rod held high. The slack is then placed into the setup by lowering the rod, allowing the tip and fly to sink under limited tension while gaining maximum depth. Raising and lowering the rod can also be useful when fishing near uneven bottom structure. NICK PIONESSA PHOTOS

closely to the security of structure, placing the fly down in the water column along the ledge will be the key to a successful presentation.

It is important to determine where the ledge begins, recognizing that it is not always straight but commonly has various cuts and uneven angles. The ledge normally shows up as a change in the color of the water. Simply casting to the ledge may not place the fly at the proper depth. A weighted fly assists in allowing the presentation to drop along the ledge. An effective approach to ledge water is by making a long cast that lands in the shallow water across the ledge and immediately raising the rod tip high to pull the line and fly back until it can drop into the deeper water. There's now slack in the line that allows for this drop along the ledge. Some additional upstream mending may be required for deep ledges. Once the fly comes under tension, it begins to draw away from the deepest part of the ledge water, creating a very effective presentation. Reaching out with the rod tip to point at an across-stream angle assists in slowing the swing slightly to allow the fly to stay along the ledge for a longer period.

Identifying the specifics of ledge structure can take some trial and error in recognizing the quality of the structure from a fish-holding perspective. Low water conditions provide a perfect opportunity to see into the water and get a better understanding of the ledges in a pool. Low summer flows are often a great time to do a little scouting in gaining a greater understanding of specific ledge structure. Be sure to make some notes.

A deep narrow slot or trench can be similar to ledge water without the steep edge. The key to covering this type of water is punching the fly through the surface currents, attaining the desired depth, and controlling the speed of the swing. A weighted fly assists in cutting the surface tension of the current and taking the fly to the desired depth. Slightly overpowering the forward stroke allows the fly to hit the water and begin sinking before the line. Fishing narrow slots or trenches is an ideal situation for lengthening the monofilament or fluorocarbon between the tip and fly to between 6 and 9 feet to allow it to dig deeper than the tip. This type of water is also a good situation for rigging with a long monofilament or fluorocarbon leader on a floating head with a very heavy fly.

When fishing a narrow slot or any type of water that doesn't allow for a full cast and standard swing, I think in terms of the setup and swing to be two distinct steps by first getting the fly into position before it begins swimming under tension. First angle the cast slightly upstream and add an exaggerated upstream mend by reaching out with the rod and pulling the line upstream, placing slack in the line and allowing the fly and sinking-tip to free-fall. The rod starts at a higher angle and then lowered as the slack begins to tighten. Additional stack mends can be added to the setup for extra depth or simply place more running line beyond the tip by moving the rod tip back and forth. Making the step down after the cast also assists in sinking the fly deeper. As the fly reaches the desired depth downstream from the fishing position, lower the rod tip pointing at the fly, bringing it under tension and swimming broadside to the current. Pointing toward the opposite bank can control the swing.

A key to fishing a narrow slot and other non-typical lies is understanding that the presentation may consist of a rather short swing distance. The fly typically twists, turns, and undulates in the current during the setup and beginning of the swing. The presentation may be better considered a tight line approach than a true swing. Be sure to get the line tight after the setup is complete to establish contact with the fly and identify if it hits the bottom or is grabbed by a fish.

Boulder fields or uneven bottom structure require special consideration. This type of water may look like a standard run or pool on the surface, but underneath, various sized boulders or dramatic changes in the bedrock that defines the bottom can impact how this water should be approached. Disturbances on the surface represent clues as to the presence of boulders strewn throughout a run. And changes in water color can indicate abrupt depth variations in slate or bedrock. Low water periods represent a good time to scout boulder fields and bedrock bottoms to uncover their nuances. Becoming familiar with the water both by fishing and observation goes a long way toward properly presenting the fly.

Approaching this water with a standard swing may result in hanging up on the boulders or high spots and not getting deep enough in the holding areas. To be successful, it's important to pick apart the water, making each cast unique and with meaning. Subtle adjustments to depth and speed may be required from cast to cast while working through the pool. Casting angle and the presence or absence of mending can impact depth. But simply adjusting rod angle up and down during the

When fishing boulder fields, be sure to fish around and behind every potential holding spot. This approach can require a patient and methodical approach. NICK PIONESSA PHOTO

setup and swing can provide the acute depth control required to fish uneven bottoms. For example, raise the rod tip as the fly, tip, and head pass over a boulder or high spot and drop the tip to allow the fly to sink behind the boulder or pocket caused by distinct change in the bottom. Rod angle can be a very useful tool for changing depth and impacting presentation.

It's best to not get into a rut of always fishing a pool or run from the obvious softer inside current side. There are some pools and runs where the off side or heavier current side should be explored as well. Even though fishing from the off side can cause wading and casting challenges of being backed up to the bank, the depth of the water along with a narrow soft edge along the bank can hold fish that may not be reachable from any other position. Shorter rods and heads are ideal for the tighter obstructed casting scenarios that fishing the off side typically requires. The flow of the off side is heavier, requiring a rigging and casting angle to get the fly to the desired depth quickly and maintaining that depth through the hang down.

Another scenario where fishing the off side can be productive is at the head of a fairly narrow run or pool where a cast can be made across the water. Fish can sit in the softer inside water at the top of a run or pool where it is difficult to present an enticing swing from an inside position. Take a position above where it is anticipated that the first fish would be holding. Make the cast across into the softer water, allowing it to reach a desired depth with the aid of an upstream mend and then allow a small belly to develop in the head to pull the fly through the soft water.

While I generally consider a tailout as part of the final section of a typical pool, the tail end of a run or pool often deserves special attention so that an opportunity is not overlooked. And some tailout water is commonly avoided by other anglers. Tailouts can extend quite a distance to reach the next set of downstream riffles. But even in shallow, fast tailout water, migratory and resident fish can be found when there is some structure to break the main current. Always be sure to fish a tailout all the way through, even as the current begins to pick up speed. Focus on all soft water caused by boulders and changes in the bottom.

Some tailouts are deep and slow before rising to meet the next riffle. Slow tailouts can look so uninviting from a swing perspective that it is easy to walk or float right by. But the lack of flow offers ideal resting water for both migratory fish and residents, especially when the current immediately below the tailout is fast and heavy. Fishing a slow tailout usually requires reducing the sink rate of the sinking-tip and fishing an unweighted fly. Angling the cast downriver may be required to keep the fly from digging too deep. You may also need to throw some downriver mends into the line to keep the fly moving. In extremely slow flows, it may be necessary to slowly strip the fly or use an overhand retrieve to keep it swimming. Even with the fly moving very slowly, I have experienced explosive takes in slow tailout water.

Don't overlook any potential spot that can hold a fish. Think in terms of any type of break in the current where a migratory fish could rest or where a resident can set up to feed. A few years ago, on a trip to British Columbia, I hooked the largest steelhead of the trip in a small piece of water that took about five short casts to cover. The holding water was simply a soft edge along a significant stretch of heavy riffles. The soft edge was created by the contour of the bank, and I hooked the fish while barely standing in the water. This holding spot made sense since resting areas in this section were at a minimum.

Some non-typical lies are even difficult to classify. Sections of river come to mind that are a combination of pockets, slots, ledges, boulder fields, and mini tailouts. Working the fly in an unconventional manner by varying each cast length and angle to fit the water and swimming it through any dark, soft areas can be

Runs filled with boulders provide a multitude of holding areas. This fresh buck was positioned at the bottom of a long series of boulders in a soft flow just above a fast riffle.

Slow tailout water may require a downstream mend or even stripping the fly to keep it moving and off the bottom. Adding action to the fly in slow or soft water can keep the presentation alive and result in surprising takes.

A Spey cast doesn't need to be long to be effective. At the heart of modern Spey fishing is the ability to present a fly to a wide range of structure and holding areas. Nick Pionessa delivers an accurate cast designed to cover a deeper trench along the far bank.

both challenging and rewarding. In areas that feature uneven bottom and structure, strong wading skills are important for positioning and safety.

The key to utilizing more than obvious runs and pools lies in observation and creativity. Offbeat holding water requires a plan that includes trial and error. But with the short head lines available today combined with myriad two-handed and single-hand Spey rods, flies can be delivered to and controlled in a wide range of water types. Complacency and routine can really work against us as anglers. Maintain a fresh perspective on both familiar and new waters to determine all the opportunities that a river has to offer.

Being observant also includes acute changes to fishing conditions. Water levels and clarity can vary during the day possibly requiring adjustments to rigging and fly selection. The one variable that is present on most days is the change in lighting and how it impacts the water being fished. Direct sunlight shining on a pool or run at angle that places the sun into the fish's eye is a negative factor for most fish species. Shade caused by a gorge wall or a stand of trees can make a significant difference on fish activity. I go to great lengths to find even the smallest amount of shade on sunny days and attempt to use the knowledge gained from past outings to know when to make a move to a certain pool that begins to shade sooner than others.

Tactical Casting

When covering open water with room for an unobstructed D loop, the cast becomes somewhat repetitive while adjusting for water depth, current speed, and wind. Not all casting situations are wide open on smaller waters. Using Spey techniques may require more creativity. Shorter head lines provide the most versatility when meeting the challenges of tighter casting situations.

The first step in tactical casting is understanding that not every cast needs to be long to be effective. Accurate short casts that turn over and present the fly to specific structure are required on both small and larger waters. Shorter casts require less energy to be applied on the forward stroke to allow for a straight-line cast that doesn't develop shockwaves from too much power. You must be able to throw a changeup that takes into consideration the distance and the

Micro Skagit heads excel in smaller water fishing situations. Here I use a micro head and short sinking leader to cover a soft run of a small creek in search of lake-run brown trout. NICK PIONESSA PHOTO

amount of tension of the line and leader at the anchor point. A smooth acceleration that fully engages the tip of the rod allows a short cast to turn over and fish as soon as it hits the water.

Occasionally, a cast needs to fit in under overhanging brush or tree. A standard Spey cast that aims at the horizon will land the fly squarely on a branch. However, tilting the rod forward so that it stops at a lower point allows the line to travel just a few feet off the water's surface. Engaging the rod tip to create a tight casting loop allows the fly to fit in under most overhanging brush and branches.

For tight overhangs, it is possible to tilt the rod well off to the side. This allows the rod to work in a plane more parallel to the surface to deliver the fly just above the water and fit it in to tight overhangs. This approach also compresses the D loop and can be useful when backed up to overhanging brush off both shoulders. However, compressing the D loop is problematic as it causes much more stick on the water and works against the general principle of the standard Spey cast

that sweeps the rod high during the setup. While it is an unconventional approach, an effective cast can be made with the rod tilted to the side with a low, powerful sweeping motion that rolls directly into the low forward stroke. This can only be accomplished with shorter head lines.

Micro Skagit heads facilitate versatile casting on a wide range of waters. Given that the D loop space required is negligible, this style of line is perfect for tight situations and creative casting. The micro head also short cuts the full setup, allowing for easy single Spey casts off each shoulder. It is simple to get the micro head into the forward Spey position from almost any angle, creating a versatile fishing tool for both swinging and stripping a fly. While the micro heads won't cover great distances, the only real limitation is an angler's imagination.

To this point, all discussion of casting has assumed wading in the water or fishing along the bank. However, Spey casting and fishing can be effective from a boat when it is impossible or impractical to reach holding water by wading. Provided there is a stable fishing platform or area, casting from a boat can be performed quite easily since the entire length of the rod is in use as opposed to being limited by wading depth. And with a spot in the boat for stripped running line to lay without any obstructions to catch on, line management is easier as well.

The standard position for Spey casting from a boat is to fish from the bow with the vessel pointed downriver or from the stern with the bow positioned upriver. This positioning works best with casts that anchor on the downstream side of the casting position—in other words, the double Spey or snake roll.

When utilizing the double Spey from the boat, slow and deliberate movements combine well when standing up high in the boat. And maintaining a low, flat rod movement while sweeping into the forward Spey position assists in maintaining the anchor and developing a deep D loop. The snake roll should also be performed slowly with a smooth acceleration into the forward Spey position. Be sure to maintain an elongated movement when drawing the small "e" to establish a proper anchor and D loop.

Using the double Spey or snake roll assumes a neutral or downriver wind. And since wind is part of fishing, there are times when there will be the need to deal with upriver breezes and gusts. Moving to the stern when the bow is pointed downriver or pointing the bow upriver then allows for a snap T / C Spey or single Spey. Slow, deliberate rod movement are most efficient when setting up these casts from the boat. There is some urgency to complete the snap T / C Spey, so that the anchor point and fly does not drift into the path of the boat. Also, depending on how the boat is anchored, the upriver cast most likely needs to accommodate an anchor line or chain. When setting up any cast from a boat, it is normally helpful to set the anchor slightly further away than when wading. This reduces the possibility of the fly and line colliding with the boat.

It is possible for two anglers to Spey fish from a boat at the same time, provided the boat is both large and stable enough. The downriver angler can use a double Spey or snake roll and the angler on the upriver end of the boat uses a snap T or single Spey. Both anglers can safely Spey cast in the absence of a significant upriver

Post-spawn brown trout can be active feeders aggressively chasing and attacking a swinging or swimming fly.

or downriver wind. Wind blowing up or down the river may require one of the anglers to cast overhead to avoid a collision with the boat and body.

It is also possible to Spey cast from a boat where instead of the D loop being formed off the bow or stern, it is formed off the shoulder that is toward the middle of the boat. In this situation, establishing the anchor point further out into the river than normal and forming a shallow D loop allows for completion of the cast where the fly doesn't contact the boat. Angling the cast downriver also provides more room for the D loop. The key to making this cast lies in applying extra power on the forward stroke to make up for the less rod load caused by a shallow D loop. A Perry poke can also be used to place the anchor further from the boat.

When fishing from a boat, a systematic approach to water coverage replaces the cast and step of wading. An effective approach is to make increasing length casts at each station or boat position. The casts start short and increase at a consistent distance until the width of the run or pool is covered or until the longest length to the caster's ability has been made. Then the anchor is lifted, allowing the boat to drift down to the approximate point covered by the last cast. The process of short to long cast begins again along with moving the boat until the run or pool is covered.

Dead Drift

Utilizing Spey casts along with longer rods provides a tactical advantage for dead-drifting flies. The efficiency gained by maintaining the fly on or in the water for a longer period along with increased line control created by rod length adds to overall effectiveness.

The dead-drift approach can be applied to both surface and subsurface presentations. Surface fishing with dead-drifted dry flies generally involves prospecting the water for trout and salmon but can also be used to target actively feeding fish. Dead drifting subsurface flies involves prospecting water of various depths with flies that represent aquatic insects, eggs deposited by other fish, and stunned or injured bait floating helplessly in the water. Dead drifting below the surface can be productive in water that is too fast, deep, or narrow for an effective swing approach or when presenting to fish that are not in an aggressive enough mood to chase a fly. This can also be a good approach for fish that are keyed in on a consistent food source delivered free floating with the current.

Let's first look at how dead drifting dry flies can be aided through the Spey casting approach. The advantage of Spey casting for working the surface lies in its efficiency. Without a backcast or series of backcasts as in traditional fly casting, the fly can be placed back on the surface in less time with less effort. And when prospecting and covering water blindly on the surface, it can simply be a numbers game with the more time the fly floats on the surface the more chance an active fish will see it floating down the river.

A floating Scandi-style head with a leader the approximate length of the rod is a preferred rig for dry-fly prospecting. However, on larger water where longer casts are preferred or required, a longer belly floater adds to the efficiency by reducing or eliminating the need to strip line.

The drift path of a dead-drifted fly is generally quite short. A long tippet section on the leader can assist in developing slight curves or slack to encourage a longer free-floating drift. When fishing faster, uneven flows, pulling back slightly on the tip of the rod after the forward stroke is complete places shockwaves in the line and leader to assist in developing some slack. This prevents the current from pulling the line, leader, and then fly in an unnatural motion immediately after hitting the water. Pulling back on the tip can impact accuracy and may take some practice to develop the proper rod movement to create the desired amount of slack.

Direction of the cast and presentation also have a direct impact on the quality of the dead drift. A cast that is angled slightly up and across with some slack provides for a good drift angle. This should allow for a drift of a few feet from above the casting position to just below that point. However, a cast that is positioned at too much of an upstream angle has a tendency for the line to be pulled by the current and quickly cause it to drag—the enemy of the dead drift.

I prefer an across or across and slightly downstream angle to best manage a dead drift and reduce drag. This angle places the line slightly above the fly, creating less opportunity for the current flow to pull the leader below the fly. Pointing the rod upstream after the full stop on the forward stroke places the line at more of an upstream position that positively impacts the dead drift of the fly. This move is essentially a reach mend while the line is in the air on the forward stroke. The timing can take some practice but is very effective in creating a dead drift.

Spotting a target sitting in a likely taking spot greatly increases the chances of a topwater hookup. Here a large Atlantic salmon holds in the clear water of a pool, providing a prime opportunity to fish a dry fly. JOE JANIAK PHOTO

When prospecting with a dry fly, relative accuracy is the key to adequately covering potential holding spots. However, when casting to a specific fish or structure, pinpoint accuracy becomes essential. When presenting a dry to a visible fish or to a known holding area, placing it in a specific window on the surface or wrinkle in the current may be the only way to raise the fish. Once the desired length is determined and proper amount of line removed from the reel, repeating the length of the cast is simply a function of providing enough power to the forward stroke to cast the head and any running so that the fly turns over properly. The line can then be lengthened or shortened by pulling more from the reel or by reeling up line to cover multiple distances when prospecting the water. Or sufficient line can be pulled from the reel to cover the longest distance and adjusting the power of the forward stroke is used for distance control.

Touch and go casts match up perfectly when using a floating line, a long leader, and a dead-drifted fly. The change in direction when dead-drift dry-fly fishing is typically much less than 90 degrees, and both the single Spey and snake roll set up easily even when the fly doesn't swing out entirely. Since the direction change can be quite short when casting a dry, the single Spey becomes more of a hybrid switch cast. And the snake roll is typically initiated by pointing the rod at an approximate 45-degree angle across current as opposed to downstream. The setup of the snake roll is now performed by forming the D loop so that it is lined up with the direction of the forward stroke. Both the single Spey and snake roll allow for flexibility in the direction of the setup and D loop while the line is in the air determined by the direction of the rod and body alignment during the D loop formation.

The touch and go casts also add to the stealth factor of the surface presentation as compared to the use of the double Spey or snap T / C Spey that involve ripping the line across the surface, causing extra disturbance. Dry flies used with Spey casting need to be constructed with buoyancy in mind. The lack of traditional back-casting doesn't allow the fly to shake off the water and dry out between casts. Materials that repel water and keep the fly riding high cast after cast are preferred.

Using touch and go casts allows for a stealthier approach with less disturbance on the water to complete the cast. The stealth factor can be a significant advantage when fishing placid water. NICK PIONESSA PHOTO

Occasionally there are opportunities to utilize Spey casting to present a dry fly to visible fish feeding on the surface. The advantage of Spey casting in this situation can be the extra distance gained over single-hand casting on big rivers or fishing areas with limited backcasting room. Spey casting to visibly feeding fish matches best with faster current or water with more of a broken surface. When using this approach on more placid surfaces, it is important to keep the disturbance caused by the anchor at a minimum.

Dead drifting flies while Spey casting isn't limited to the surface. In fact, dead drifting subsurface flies represents one of the most effective methods for catching trout and other species in rivers and streams. While dead drifting a fly may seem to fly in the face of all Spey casting and fishing traditions, the length of short two-handed rods and switch rods provides for the ideal dead-drifting tool. Short Spey movements can be used to set up the cast. These movements can also be applied when dead drifting with a long single-hand rod.

Dead drifting a subsurface fly with the current matches best with a floating line or head that has a long, fine front taper. A monofilament or fluorocarbon leader the approximate length of the rod or slightly longer is paired with the floating line or head. A lower diameter allows the fly to sink faster and provides less surface area for the currents to push and pull to negatively impact the drift. The leader requires a strong enough butt section to complete and turnover the cast with a weighted fly or possibly weight added to the leader. The strength of the butt section is impacted by the size and weight of the fly.

There are two basic approaches to subsurface dead drifting a fly with a two-handed or switch rod. The tight line technique utilizes an entire leader constructed of low-diameter material. The butt section of the leader is constructed of a highly visible fluorescent color for following the drift and assist in indicating when a fish has taken the fly. The length of a two-hander or switch creates a good tool for line control and maintaining contact with the fly. The basic approach involves making a Spey cast up and across stream to the intended target and allowing the fly to drift below the casting position. The rod starts low at the completion of the cast, is raised during the drift to remove line from the surface to aid in eliminating drag, and then lowered at the completion of the drift. The fly can be allowed to swing out slightly at the end. Any stop or hesitation that is sensed through sight or feel is met with a sharp upward hook set.

The second setup relies on a low-diameter tippet to place the fly to the desired depth and drift drag-free. For this approach, the entire leader is approximately the length of the rod but constructed of a heavy, stiff butt section and a long section of low-diameter tippet. Near the junction of the butt and tippet section is placed a high-riding indicator of poly yarn. The basic concept is for the tippet to drop off the butt section at a right angle allowing for a very efficient dead-drift system. The length of the tippet should approximate the desired depth to fish the fly. A simple approach for setting up the right-angle presentation is to first attach the indicator to the butt section using a loop or improved clinch knot. The tippet is then attached directly to

the butt section so that the connecting knot is at a 90-degree angle. The tippet is attached using a tippet ring or loop at the end of the butt section. The weight of the fly sinks it to the desired depth. The right-angle dead-drift approach is visual, using the indicator for clues that a fish has grabbed the fly. An advantage for the right-angle approach is that it can be used on a wide range of water and situations. It is an effective approach for short cast situations but excels in covering bigger water where longer casts are required. By mending the line so that it doesn't pull the indicator faster than the current, long drag-fee drifts are possible even on big, placid pools. Additional line can be fed into the drift to extend its length downstream.

The cast for dead drifting a subsurface fly generally angles upstream while finishing the drift slightly down from the casting position. Like dead drifting a dry, the body and casting movements should be rotated slightly to accommodate this casting angle. Typically, casts with the tight line approach are quite short, and carefully working upstream provides a stealthier approach than working downstream. Casts for the right-angle approach can be longer and more across stream than

A dead-drift approach on the surface or beneath is very effective in representing insect life flowing freely in the currents of a river or stream that make up a significant part of a trout's diet.

up. For lighter rigs and short distances, simple touch and go casts work fine. However, when casting heavier flies and possibly weight added to the leader along with an indicator, the double Spey and snap T / C Spey casts make for a smoother approach. A slower forward stroke allows the rig to turn over while avoiding tangling.

Flies utilized when subsurface dead drifting typically incorporate weight on the fly allowing it to sink to the desired depth. Nymphs, crayfish, or baitfish patterns tied to represent dead or injured bait are commonly used with this approach. Patterns tied with a lower profile sink more efficiently than big bulky patterns. Dead drifting baitfish patterns can be surprisingly effective for both predator and migratory fish. In situations where additional weight is required to sink the fly to the desired depth, shot or wrap-on weight can be added to the tippet knot.

Setting the Hook

Hooking a fish that has taken a fly on the swing seems like a fairly simple process. And often, a fish quite literally hooks itself against the tension of the line.

But hooking a fish while swinging the fly has a few different schools of thought. Given that each take is unique based on such factors as the angle of the fly, speed of the swing, and aggressiveness of the fish, each approach has advantages. The hook set can also be impacted by the species of fish in pursuit.

The conventional wisdom is to not lift or strike until feeling the weight of the fish. In other words, don't react to plucks and pulls but only when you feel that the fish has firmly grabbed the fly. Hookup percentages are enhanced when there is some ability for the fish to take and turn on the fly before there is any forceful movement in the rod. If the line is too taught, the fish can grab but not get a firm grasp of the fly before being pulled out by too much tension.

There are a few techniques used to make sure you feed the fish that has grabbed the fly. My favorite is an approach that was shown to me by British Columbia steelhead guide Mark McAnally many years ago. Using either a click and pawl drag or a light setting on a disk drag, when a fish grabs the fly, it is allowed to take a few clicks of drag directly off the reel without

Hooking a fish after it has grabbed the fly can take experience while utilizing various approaches. Joe Janiak maintains a deep bend in the rod during the final stages of a battle with a winter steelhead. NICK PIONESSA PHOTO

Waiting for the pull—I prefer to be patient when a fish grabs, allowing it to take line off the reel before pulling back with a sweep of the rod. This approach takes discipline and commitment but in the end results in a higher percentage of landed fish. NICK PIONESSA PHOTO

moving the rod. The tension of the drag is enough to bury the hook but light enough so the fish can firmly grab the fly. Only after line has been taken from the reel is the rod lifted and swept to the side toward the near bank. I have found this approach to be incredibly effective as it teaches patience and eliminates the urge to set with an itchy trigger finger. This technique also results in mostly quality hookups and a very high landing percentage.

I prefer a click and pawl drag for this technique to keep a constant with respect to drag tension. When using a disk drag, it's best to use a reel with definitive drag settings so that you can use a consistent tension from day to day. It is extremely important to find the right drag setting as too much won't allow the fish to pull line and too little won't create enough tension to hook the fish or could cause a backlash if the fish grabs and takes off.

A similar approach involves holding a small loop of loose line between the reel and where it is pinched off

on the cork. This works in a similar fashion as the light drag setting. When a fish grabs, the loop is allowed to slip through where it is pinched off under light tension. This allows the fish to take and turn on the fly before raising and sweeping the rod to the near bank for the hook set. While the loop method is an effective and popular method for gaining a quality hookup, it is more complex than the light drag approach. Adding the extra step of releasing the loop opens this process to more operator error and more practice to become proficient.

Simply extending the arm when a fish takes can provide enough soft line for the fish to turn on the fly. Typically, there is a slight bend in the elbow during the swing. Straightening out the arm when a fish takes and rotating the shoulder slightly toward the fly creates a similar result as when line is released with the loop method. Once the line comes tight, the set is completed by raising and sweeping the rod. This approach reduces some of the potential for error when compared to releasing a loop of line. However, it still takes some reaction and increases the possibility of failure.

I prefer the extended-arm method when fish aren't aggressive or turning on the fly when grabbing. This can be common in coldwater conditions. Often, I use the extended-arm approach in conjunction with the lighter drag approach when a fish grabs but doesn't take line from the reel. Not taking drag can also occur when a smaller fish has eaten the fly.

While aggressive takes with the fish turning on the fly tend to be quite common when swinging, occasionally a fish just grabs and holds or even lunges forward as it eats. This is common for coldwater situations, fish that see heavy fishing pressure, or certain species like smallmouth bass. In these situations, the feeling of a tug, light pull, or a forceful tap may be a fish eating the fly and not turning or possibly moving toward you. My personal approach is to err on the side of feeling the weight of the fish. But I occasionally feel that being more aggressive is warranted.

For a more aggressive approach to setting the hook, a direct rod movement is most effective. Pulling the rod straight back sharply with line pinched off against the cork provides the equivalent of a strip set. A direct set or strip set motion is much more effective for burying the hook than rod movement. The rod simply has too much cushion when used for hook setting and produces much less force at the point of impact than a direct pull of the line. Since the tippet used with a swung fly is normally stout, there should be no concerns about a break off with the direct set method. However, there could be some exceptions to this, such as swinging small soft-hackle flies to trout where lighter tippets may be required. In this situation, engaging the rod to cushion the grab and protect the tippet may be essential.

While the direct set can run the risk of setting too early, it can also result in a hookup that may not have occurred without this approach. While I don't want to train myself to strike too early, direct setting is a good tool to have in the box and has served me well on some occasions, most notably when swinging for smallmouth bass. Another advantage of the direct set is if the hook doesn't connect with the fish, the fly is only pulled a very short distance away, providing another opportunity to chase and eat. However, a rod set can

The direct set method is the most effective approach for a fish that takes the fly but doesn't turn or swim away after eating. This situation is quite common when fishing for smallmouth bass. NICK PIONESSA PHOTO

The hookup and excitement of the battle is the ultimate reward of our pursuit. Nick Pionessa keeps a low rod angle while hoping to stay connected as an energetic fish tears through the water's surface.

pull the fly away by a great distance, most likely out of the sight line of the fish. The key to effective hook setting lies in consistency. Relying on a main approach and applying it in most situations while making some adjustments for the situation is more effective than attempting to be too reactionary to each grab.

Setting the hook when the fly is visible or not under tension requires more of an active approach. As discussed in the previous chapter, setting the hook when waking or fishing a riffle-hitched fly may take some patience to ensure that indeed the fish has firmly taken the fly. In a perfect situation, the fish eats the visible fly, takes it down, turns practically hooking itself, and a firm hookup is completed by sweeping the rod toward the near bank. But it's not that simple. A fish will generally not hold the fly forever. An active approach by pulling back or sweeping the rod when evidence points to the fish firmly having the fly before actually feeling its weight can be required. The key lies in having close visual contact with the fly not only

to ensure that it is working properly but to immediately detect the take of a fish no matter how obvious or subtle. Action should be taken once it appears the fish firmly has the fly. While the weight of the fish may be simultaneously felt, acting on a sixth sense that indicates the fish has the fly in its mouth can complete the hookup before the fly is dropped or spit out.

Dead drifting flies whether on the surfaces or below clearly requires a more active hook set. A dead-drift hook set typically involves raising or sweeping the rod. Since there will be an element of slack in the line during the presentation, the rod raise assists in picking up line to come tight to the fish. As discussed earlier, setting with the rod does not create as much force as a direct pull or a strip but represents the most practical manner for tightening the line and creating enough force. Moving the rod toward the near bank while raising the rod provides the best angle for a quality set.

When fishing a dead-drifted dry fly for salmon, trout, or any other species, the hook set movement

A low rod angle allows for greater control of a big fish and is an effective approach for leading a fish into the net. Here I put the finishing touches on a tense battle with a steelhead.

should be made based on the appearance that the fish has eaten the fly and closed its mouth. The weight of the fish will typically not be felt with a dead-drifted surface fly. Being able to clearly see the fly is the key to witnessing the take that initiates decisive action. High-riding, visible patterns make the task of continually locating and observing the fly a much easier task.

When dead drifting subsurface, clues that a fish has taken the fly can be strictly visual or visual and feel. Strike indicators or fluorescent butt sections of a leader assist in assuring the drift of the fly is proper as well as determining when a fish has eaten the fly impeding its drift. When the indicator or colored butt section no longer moves with the current or is even pulled under the surface, quick action is required to connect with the fish before it drops the fly. Any indication, no matter how subtle, should be met with a decisive hook set. If too much weight is used and the fly hangs on the bottom with any regularity, adjustments are required to keep the fly positioned to drift freely. When using a tight line nymphing approach, the take of a fish may

be telegraphed by feel as well. The stoppage of the drift and the subtle feel of the weight of the fish can be experienced before visualizing the stoppage of the drift. Sometimes, a take will be felt as a slight tap. A hook set movement should be made anytime these sensations are felt through the rod.

Landing the Fish

Once a fish is successfully hooked, it's time to enjoy and focus on the battle. My preference is to maintain a low rod angle with a deep bend throughout the length of the rod during the fight. The lower angle provides greater control and tends to keep a fish from going airborne and providing the increased opportunity to throw the hook. The low rod angle also allows you to apply side pressure and use the full leverage of a longer rod in tiring a fish as quickly as possible. The low rod angle is especially useful when ending the fight with a large fish.

A high rod angle combined with the length of a two-handed rod gives a fish extra leverage to wrench the hook out of its mouth and makes it more likely for the fish to jump or thrash at the surface, only increasing the chance of a lost connection. The weight of a heavy sinking-tip seems to increase the possibility of a thrown hook with a high rod angle. But a high rod angle has its place in the toolkit. When fighting a fish near and around boulders, ledges, sunken logs, and other obstructions, a high rod angle results in a vertical line angle, reducing the opportunity for a large fish to hopelessly wrap line, tip, and/or leader around an immoveable object.

I suppose one could be too pragmatic when it comes to the proper approach of fighting an energetic fish hooked on a two-handed rod. The low rod angle that assists in keeping a fish under control potentially robs you of the experience of a big fish tearing through the water's surface while putting on an exhilarating aerial show.

I was reminded of this by Spey expert Tom Larimer one day after posting my thoughts on social media with respect to maintaining a low rod angle throughout the battle to increase the percentage of landed fish. Tom relayed a story of fishing with mutual friend and legendary steelhead guide Adam Tavender. Adam asked Tom why he was fighting a particularly energetic steelhead with his rod positioned low. After Tom explained that the positioning maintained control and kept the fish from jumping, Adam pondered and took a long draw from his pipe and asked, "Isn't the fun in hooking a steelhead to feel completely out of control and to watch them jump?" This was a question that Tom could only respond to by saying "Good point!" And it provides yet another example that Spey is about personal preferences and self-expression. There is no one right way but choices to be made to allow us to most enjoy the journey.

The most enjoyable fights with a big energetic fish are those that occur in an open pool where the fish has room to run and jump. You can sit back and enjoy the

There are some fish that were just meant to be landed where everything during the entire encounter goes right. I'll always remember how everything fell into place to land this big buck on a British Columbia river.

Maintaining a deep bend in the rod throughout the fight is the key to staying attached to a fish when using barbless hooks.

show while taking in line when the fish allows. But the most memorable experiences occur in tight situations where allowing a fish to run too much can result in certain doom.

In tight areas where there is little room for a fish to run, I always rig with extra strength tippet and utilize enough drag to make it difficult for the fish to pull line from the reel. If a fish is attempting to run into a snag such as a long jam or attempting to leave the pool where chasing the fish is impossible, you are left with no other choice but to be aggressive and make a stand. Keep the rod low and try to get as much of a side angle as possible. As soon as the fish's head turns in your direction, take up line immediately to keep the fish free of the obstruction or in the pool.

I frequently fish pools and tailouts where there is no chance of following the fish if it were to leave the pool. And despite using heavy tippets and a strong drag system, the angle of the fight may not allow for side pressure. Forcibly pulling a big fish back upriver can be very difficult. Once a downstream run of a

fish has been denied leaving the pool by taking a firm stand, I attempt to lighten up on the pressure ever so slightly. A fish tends to fight away from the pressure. But when the pressure applied is reduced slightly, the fish typically calms down. Enough pressure needs to remain to stay tight to the fish, but as it settles down, the fish can slowly be directed upriver where the fight can be concluded in the main part of the pool. My brother Jerry and I refer to this technique as "walking the dog." It is remarkable how a fish can simply be walked and led around after it is calm. It is a technique that we use regularly on the forceful currents of the Niagara River and directly resulted in landing one of my largest Atlantic salmon and West Coast steelhead.

One other use for taking the pressure off during a fight is when a fish has broken away by running helplessly downriver aided by the current. With a fish's desire to run away from the pressure, it keeps going while it feels the weight and tension of the fly line in the current. However, where possible if slack can be introduced, the fish can be tricked into thinking it is free. Reducing the drag or moving fast enough down-river to develop slack may give the fish the feeling it is safe to pull into a softer current or eddy, providing the opportunity to catch up to its position. You must be careful when reducing drag to not overrun the reel, and slacking the fish runs the risk of the hook falling out, especially when using barbless hooks. But this is another tool to utilize that can save the day.

It is common during the fight with a big powerful fish even where there is room to follow down the river to be faced with the decision to hold your ground or let the fish run. Sometimes it is more of a reaction than a decision. There are many factors that quickly need to be considered. Using a tight drag and fighting a fish in tight quarters has some advantages, provided you have a solid hookup, good knots, strong enough tippet, a reel with sufficient drag, and a stout enough rod. Keeping the fish close reduces the opportunity for a negative outcome with the many dangers that exist for a runaway fish. Keep the rod low with the tip near or in the water so that the fish fights against the tension of the line in the water as well as the drag of the reel. Take line when possible. The decision to fight a fish without letting it run should include an assessment of whether there is a soft break in the current where the fish can be landed or netted.

The decision to let a fish run also needs careful consideration. Are there obstructions that a fly line could easily wrap around? How difficult is the terrain, and do you have the energy to keep up with the fish? Is the current too fast or are there no good breaks in the current that allow for landing a fish? When a boat is available, it opens another option for chasing.

When fishing areas that I know will provide a challenge for landing a fish, I have a plan even before a hookup. Assessing the positive and negative factors allows for quicker decision-making and more commitment to the perceived best course of action.

The use of a net or cradle with a soft catch-and-release bag is the best way to conclude a fight. This allows for the careful handling of the fish as it can stay in the water away from rocks. I prefer a net as it is easier to operate and can conclude the fight in a more efficient manner. A net or cradle allows the fish to remain in the water while camera gear is readied. The fish can be gently lifted for a photo or better yet remain in the water while photos are taken. Some regulations now require keeping a captured fish in the water the entire time through release.

It isn't always practical to carry a net. But a big fish can still be carefully landed by yourself without one. Look for deeper soft edges in the current. Raising the rod as the fish tires in close typically places the fish on its side in position to grasp the wrist of its tail. The rod hand can then be slid under the body of the fish as the rod rides up the inner forearm. This approach takes some practice but is a safe approach to landing a fish with no net. A fish that is to be released should never be beached or allowed to flop on the rocks. Studies have shown that head trauma caused by banging on the rocks is responsible for post-release mortality. Also, be careful to not place too steep of a bend in the rod when landing a fish. In other words, maintain an angle so that bend remains through the rod and not just the tip area. This can easily lead to a broken rod tip.

Barbless flies or those with the barb pinched to a point where there is a bump or a nub allow for an easier release of a fish. Barbless hooks are required on many rivers. Barbless hooks allow for better penetration than those with a barb. But with no barb, the hook can fall out and become unattached if slack develops during the fight. When using barbless hooks, maintain a substantial bow in the rod to prevent slack and lean into the fish when it jumps. By keeping the fish tight, I feel that the landing percentage of fish hooked with a barbless fly is quite comparable to a hook with a barb.

6

SPECIFIC STRATEGIES

The previous chapters focused on the generalities of rigging, casting, presentation, and structure to employ Spey casting and fishing techniques to a wide range of opportunities. This chapter looks more specifically at the various fish species that are typically targeted with Spey techniques and other species where the advancement of Spey equipment has expanded the options for this style of fishing. The objective of this chapter is to take a more in-depth look at how to approach certain fish while identifying opportunities to expand your horizons with respect to the effective and enjoyable use of Spey fishing.

Steelhead

I'll start with steelhead since this is the fish that has most inspired my interest in Spey fishing. Steelhead are migratory rainbow trout native to the Pacific Coast but transplanted to the Great Lakes region and South America. Debate has existed as to whether the term steelhead refers only to anadromous migration or includes migration entirely within a freshwater system such as the Great Lakes. To me, the debate is moot, and the migration factor seems to be the key ingredient to creating a steelhead. And based on my direct experience, fish in the Great Lakes behave similarly to their West Coast ancestors.

But I would be remiss in not reporting that as of this writing many if not most of the significant steelhead fisheries on the Pacific Coast face serious

Fishing a dark slot on a Norway salmon river. Even backed right up to a rock wall, effective casts can be made with the proper combination of rod and line. JEFF BRIGHT PHOTO

Native steelhead exist in beautiful places and wild rivers that attract anglers to the entire experience as well as the untamed character of a very special fish. Here Matt Chabot lays out a smooth cast to some good-looking steelhead water.

challenges while others have already been lost. Habitat destruction, dams, climate change, escapement issues, and commercial fishing practices are adding up to challenging factors for survival. A sad fact of human inability to place a high enough value on such a special resource. Much is being done to turn the tide and there are some positive signs. But on some river systems, if significant action is not taken soon, native wild runs could be forever lost. Now is the time to get involved in any way possible.

I believe it is the spirit of the steelhead that attracts so many anglers to its pursuit. While a steelhead is the same species of resident rainbow trout native to Pacific drainages, it is the migratory urge of a steelhead to roam in search of higher protein levels that makes it strong, tough, and greatly admired. And it is this migratory urge that allows this fish to grow to impressive sizes. While the broad average may be 6 to 10 pounds, steelhead up to and exceeding 20 pounds can be caught on some rives.

Studies show that the migratory urge is not simply genetic. Rivers that host both resident and migratory rainbow have shown that steelhead parents can produce resident offspring and resident parents can produce migratory steelhead offspring. Studies also show that steelhead crossbreed with resident fish. In the end, it seems to be a desire to find a richer diet as fueling the migratory urge.

Steelhead generally thrive in beautiful places that attract anglers not only for the fish but for the entire experience. Steelhead can grab a fly with authority and provide an exciting display when hooked, highlighted by reel-screaming runs and aerial displays. And based on the run timing of specific rivers, steelhead availability in their natal drainages is nearly year-long. It is very important to develop a specific understanding of the run timing of the rivers and drainages that you intend to target for steelhead.

This ability of a steelhead to find comfort and security in a wide range of holding waters provides an opportunity to approach the river with a degree of creativity. Most of the main pools and runs are obvious but finding fish holding in secondary holding waters is rewarding.

Dependent on water temperature, steelhead can be taken on the fly in all levels of the water column, providing the opportunity to use a wide variety of rigging and techniques when pursuing with a swung fly. Summer run fish or winter runs that enter their natal waters in late summer or early fall are the best candidates for fishing with a floating line on or just under the surface. Water temperatures of mid 40s and above provide the best opportunity for fishing up in the water column even though I have had some surface activity on water with temperatures near or below 40. Rivers with natural reproduction and returning adults that fed on insects on the surface as juveniles seem to provide the best opportunity for fishing up in the water column. In the Great Lakes, spring fish that linger in the rivers until water temperatures become too high can also react well to a fly fished on the surface.

Working the fly down in the water column is never a bad a strategy for steelhead. Sinking leaders and sinking-tips are part of nearly every steelheader's rigging options. Arguably, the common use of sinking leaders and tips has had a negative impact on the ability to bring steelhead to a fly fished on a floating line. But the effectiveness of this approach can't be denied and is the approach that makes most sense as water temperatures drop. While I really enjoy seeing a steelhead show for a surface fly, the heavy grab of an aggressive fish on a sinking-tip is not far behind.

The varied places where steelhead exist combined with the techniques that can be employed lend themselves to a plethora of rod and rigging choices. Big rivers with the opportunity for surface fishing can call for mid to longer belly lines to efficiently deliver the fly. Mid belly exchangeable tip lines can also be valuable on larger rivers. Scandi heads have their place for fishing on the surface or delivering the fly below with sinking leaders. But Skagit-style heads are the choice for serious depth work being able to carry sinking tips and weighted flies to fish in about any type of water.

The swung fly plays well on a steelhead's instinct to chase. A slow but steady swing speed seems to work best for steelhead. I think in terms of making the fly accessible to the fish controlling speed through line manipulation. The movement entices the fish, but too fast of a swing seems to lose their attention. But there are no hard-and-fast rules as a faster speed can be used as a trigger in clear-water conditions. When fishing a sinking-tip, I attempt to place the fly in the lower portion of the water column while avoiding any consistent contact with the bottom. Coldwater conditions call for an extra-slow swing to correspond with a steelhead's lowered metabolism.

Steelhead transplanted to the Great Lakes nearly 150 years ago have created a robust fishery that includes beautiful rivers supporting wild fish as well as others maintained through hatchery programs. NICK PIONESSA PHOTO

Atlantic Salmon

Atlantic salmon could easily be the lead story in this chapter due to this species' direct connection to the creation and development of Spey. After all, this style of casting and fishing is named after an Atlantic salmon river. Atlantic salmon are indigenous to the northern reaches of the Atlantic Ocean and migrate to rivers along the northern rim in North America, Europe, and Iceland. There were once native populations of Atlantic salmon in Lake Ontario that were extirpated by overfishing, habitat destruction, and horrible resource management in the late 1800s. Restoration efforts have been in place for years with limited success, and Atlantic salmon have been transplanted to small pockets in the Great Lakes. Atlantic salmon also occur naturally in a non-anadromous form referred to as landlocked salmon. These populations were apparently trapped in freshwater drainages that once flowed to the ocean by receding glaciers. Landlocked salmon grow to a much smaller size than their anadromous relatives but can provide fun action on a lighter rod.

Anadromous Atlantic salmon can grow to a significant size. While the average of an adult returning fish is 8 to 12 pounds in many rivers, some reach the 20- to 40-pound range with a few exceptional individuals growing even larger. Size expectation varies widely by river system, with some rivers being renowned for their larger salmon. It is the Atlantic salmon's size, leaping ability, fishing challenge, and regal appearance that give it the reputation of the king of freshwater fishes. Like the steelhead, Atlantic salmon face challenges within their native range as historic run levels have been diminished by overfishing, compromised habitat, and ocean conditions impacting survival. In fact, runs that once existed in the northeast United States currently hang on by a thread. But thanks to work largely spearheaded and performed by salmon conservation groups, some improvements have been made, including removal of dams and a large-scale buyout of commercial fishing operations. These steps have led to a stabilization and modest improvements to run sizes in some rivers along the Canadian maritime provinces, Greenland, and Europe. But sadly, declines continue on many rivers, and the future of this magnificent fish is uncertain.

Based on my experience, one of the main differences between steelhead and Atlantic salmon fishing success is in the coverage of holding water. Steelhead generally take up a wide range of positions when migrating or holding in a river while Atlantic salmon tend to take up more specific locations. Flow and structure seem to drive salmon holding water selection as moderate current that is not too fast and not too slow tends to be the sweet spot. This often positions salmon toward the head or tail of a run or pool in normal flows. The prime lies may shift in various water levels as increased flows could push fish more to the body of the pool and low water can push salmon to the very head to be able to find the sufficient flow. Being more tactical in locating prime holding lies as opposed to covering large expanses of water is an important step to success in the Atlantic salmon game.

Holding position location on Atlantic salmon rivers also includes fish showing a preference for one pool over another. In other words, it is common for fish to be located in a few specific pools or runs while others are devoid. Cumulated knowledge of the historically best holding lies given a certain water level is useful information on a year-to-year basis. Atlantic salmon that are best positioned to take a fly are typically in depths of 2 to 6 feet. In clear-water rivers and conditions, salmon are commonly found toward the deeper end of that range.

Atlantic salmon generally migrate to their natal waters in late spring and throughout the summer then spawn in the late summer and fall. This run timing places salmon in the rivers when water temperatures are conducive to moving a fair distance to take a well-presented fly. Atlantic salmon are typically quite surface-oriented, and on many rivers, it is common to fish a high percentage of the time with a floating line approach. And on larger rivers, fishing for salmon provides a great opportunity to use a longer belly line.

Bringing a large salmon to the surface to suck in a high-riding dry fly is arguably the pinnacle of the sport. A leftover instinct from spending years as juveniles feeding at the surface in natal waters seems to have adult salmon looking up while resting during their return migration. While fishing a dry fly on one of my first Atlantic salmon trips, I remember small juvenile salmon rushing to the surface in attack mode as soon as the large spun deer-hair pattern slapped

The splendor of a fresh-run Atlantic salmon considered by many as the top prize to be encountered when Spey fishing and the highest-ranking freshwater gamefish. JOE JANIAK PHOTO

The battle with a large Atlantic salmon reaches its conclusion. The desire to fool and catch Atlantic salmon was the driving force behind the concept of Spey casting and as a species will always be linked to the beginnings of this style of fishing. JOE JANIAK PHOTO

down on the water. This same surface trigger appears to be carried into adulthood. Dead drifting large patterns such as a bomber or similar flies that float well on the surface is a preferred method on many salmon rivers. Dead-drifted flies can be used to target visible salmon that have been spotted in clear water or blindly prospecting likely holds. Accurate casts are critical to the mission of landing the fly 2 to 3 feet above a salmon holding spot. Touch and go casts provide for an effortless and efficient way to present a dry fly for salmon. Waking a dry fly or riffle hitching a wet can also be a productive approach for salmon, allowing for greater water coverage.

The wet fly swing utilizing a floating line or a sinking line, tip, or leader, where allowed by regulation, is the most popular approach to Atlantic salmon fishing. There is a rich tradition and history behind Atlantic salmon wet flies. These beautiful creations have created a cult following on their own that often seems to represent the face of salmon fishing. A combination of traditional patterns and modern tying techniques are currently used today.

Successfully swinging wet flies for Atlantic salmon typically involves adding more speed to the fly than for other species. While making the fly accessible to the fish can be the best approach for species such as steelhead, Atlantic salmon seem to react best to a fly that moves with more urgency triggering a response to not let it get away. Speed can be gained by angling the cast downstream or placing a downstream belly in the line. Fly speed should be controlled under the consideration of temperature as colder water typically results in fish that are less aggressive. A faster fly speed also applies when waking a fly on the surface or using the riffle hitch for Atlantic salmon.

Pacific Salmon

There are five Pacific salmon species indigenous to North America—king or Chinook salmon (*Oncorhynchus tshawytscha*), coho (*Oncorhynchus kisutch*), chum (*Oncorhynchus keta*), sockeye (*Oncorhynchus nerka*), and pink (*Oncorhynchus gorbuscha*). These species also provide abundant runs throughout Russia and the entire Pacific rim. The cherry salmon (*Oncorhynchus masou*) is a sixth species found only in the western Pacific.

The significant difference between Pacific salmon as compared to steelhead or Atlantic salmon is that all six species make one run when sexually mature and die after spawning. The post-spawn decaying carcasses then provide rich nutrients to the natal river systems to support future generations. In contrast, steelhead and Atlantic salmon can spawn multiple times and the

health of their runs is dependent on a mix of repeat spawners. However, the rigor of spawning can cause some mortality in steelhead and Atlantic salmon as well.

Of the North American Pacific salmon species, the king, coho, and chum provide the best sport on a swung fly. Sockeyes tend to be the least desirable from a swinging-fly perspective. A sockeye is mainly a filter feeder dieting mostly on plankton caught by gill rakers as water is taken and expelled through the gills. With this feeding style, sockeye do not have the instinct to chase and kill so there is little interest to eat a swung fly after entering its natal waters. Pink and cherry salmon are on the smaller side and generally

An angler swings for chum salmon on a glassy pool of an Alaskan river. Chum salmon can travel and congregate in large schools. When you find one there are usually many more.

The sheer power of the king or Chinook salmon is unmatched in freshwater and is a highly sought-after fish along the Pacific Coast. Locating rivers and areas that allow you to intercept fish fresh from the ocean provides the best sport.

average around 4 to 5 pounds. When matched with light rods, pinks can provide good sport chasing and grabbing an assortment of flies.

The average size of coho and chum vary by river system, and 8 to 12 pounds for both species is a reasonable estimate of the average. However, individuals exceeding this average are caught on a regular basis. King salmon are by far the largest, although they can vary in size dramatically by drainage. A reasonable average for king salmon is 15 to 20 pounds, but individuals greatly exceeding this weight are possible on nearly every river where runs exist. In fact, kings up to nearly 100 pounds have been caught by sportfishing in Alaska.

Since all Pacific salmon die after the spawn, their approach to migration is different from steelhead and Atlantic salmon. There is a great sense of urgency to move and arrive at preferred spawning areas. From an angling standpoint, timing can be everything when swinging for Pacific salmon as fish are consistently on the move and the best angling targets are fish fresh into the river system. Pacific salmon runs have sadly been reduced in rivers along the lower United States and parts of British Columbia for similar reasons as steelhead. However, sections of the Canadian Coast

and much of Alaska continue to experience abundant salmon runs. It is quite clear that all migratory runs are fragile and face continued multiple threats and challenges. Diligence will be required to protect this valuable resource into the future.

Pacific salmon runs generally begin in late spring and continue through the summer with variations in timing between river systems and due to seasonal weather patterns. Some rivers receive spring-oriented runs that occur mid-spring. Of the Pacific salmon targeted by Spey fishing, kings typically show first in river systems that host this species. And due to their size, king salmon illicit a significant following of anglers on an annual basis. Skagit heads and modern Spey techniques have really opened up the opportunities for pursuing kings on a fly in a wider range of water.

The first step in successfully pursuing kings on the swing is fishing water that is manageable with a Spey rod and low enough in a river system to encounter fresh, silver fish. When hooked, the power of a king fresh from the ocean is incredible—being attached to a freight train comes to mind. An exhilarating battle can involve aerial displays, out of control runs, and the show of sheer strength.

King salmon have earned their name. As the largest of the Pacific salmon, it is truly king of the river. This stature allows king salmon to take up the preferred lies that include the gut of a pool, the drop in a gravel bar, or the seam where softer currents meet the main flow of a river. But kings can also feel at home in heavier runs and tailouts. Off-color water can spread kings into a wider range of holding areas while clear conditions may result in the fish moving to deeper pools and runs. The movements of the tide typically impact the timing of fish being drawn into the river, and it is common for kings to travel in groups.

Skagit heads rigged with heavy tips and big, bright, flashy weighted flies are required to fish the type of water where kings typically hold. Large flies are the norm for fresh fish and water with some color or stain. Smaller patterns can be more productive in clear-water conditions. Stout, short rods are also best matched with kings to offset their power. Placing the fly deep and swinging in a broadside manner is key to successful king fishing. Utilizing depth control techniques of angling the cast across or slightly up, utilizing an upstream mend as well as introducing slack during the setup, and stepping down as the fly is sinking all

assist in the fly digging deep enough to cover preferred king lies.

Fishing kings on the swing involves plenty of challenges from proper run timing to getting a fish to grab a fly that is now more interested in propagation than feeding. But when the stars align, the grab and pull of a big king is incomparable. Allowing a king to eat the fly and turn before sweeping and raising the rod provides the best opportunity for a solid hookup. Powerful head shakes typically begin the fight and then hold on. Encountering a king on the two-hand rod never gets old. A powerful drag system is required when fighting kings in a wide range of water. A large fish headed downriver can pull line from even the tightest drag setting. Keeping a king in proximity to your position can be critical for a good outcome by going toe to toe while risking broken equipment. But in some situations, it is inevitable that there will be a chase by foot or boat to catch up.

King salmon have been transplanted to the Great Lakes and South America. In the Great Lakes, the run timing is typically late summer into early fall, and there is some limited opportunity to swing or fish a tight line for fresh-run fish on some rivers. The average size of

While not as highly prized as other Pacific salmon, the chum can provide fun and fast action when Spey fishing.

Great Lakes kings is estimated at 15 to 25 pounds. The South American kings can grow to an incredible size, with fish of 30 to 40 pounds considered typical.

Chum salmon typically arrive just after or during the king migration. And while this species is not revered in the same manner as the other Pacific salmon, chum can provide great sport when swinging a fly. Solid grabs and a heavy fight can be expected, and if fortunate to encounter a school on its way up the river, the action can be fast and furious. Schools of chums are typically found in softer flows out of the main current. Fresh-run fish take on a grayish-olive hue across its deep body with faint blotchy streaks that tend to grow darker as the fish moves upriver. Bright flies with a lot of movement fished on a sinking-tip work well for chums, and there is occasionally the opportunity to bring fish to the top with a mouse or similar floating pattern that creates a disturbance on the surface.

Coho arrive next on rivers that host this species. Mid to late summer is the best timing for encountering coho, although this can vary on many rivers. Coho salmon provide outstanding Spey fishing opportunity. Aggressive grabs and acrobatic runs make the coho a favorite of many anglers. Fresh-run fish have a beautiful silvery appearance similar to a fresh steelhead, then take on a reddish hue after living in the river for a time. Brightly colored flashy flies fished on a sinking-tip or floating line can be very effective. Coho are the most surface-oriented of the Pacific salmon, and waking a mouse pattern or gurgler can be quite productive for pooled-up fish.

Migratory Trout and Char

Brown trout have become well distributed throughout the world, adapting to a wide range of environments. Where there is access to open water, brown trout can become migratory, satisfying the urge to find a protein-rich diet. The famous runs of sea-run browns in the Patagonia region of South America may be the most widely known migratory fishery. Sea-runs can also be found in Iceland and parts of Europe. The Patagonia region grows some of the largest migratory browns, as fish over 20 pounds are caught with some regularity and fish of 30 pounds are possible.

There are also many freshwater instances of migratory brown trout running from lakes or impoundments

Brown trout migrating from freshwater lakes or saltwater provide the best opportunity to catch trophy-sized trout on a swung fly.

into tributaries. The Great Lakes fishery may be the best example, with brown trout up to 10 pounds readily available to be caught on a swung fly and fish up to 20 pounds being a possibility on some rivers. Other opportunities exist on some rivers where dams create unique feeding opportunities for brown trout to grow at a fast rate. While this may not be a truly migratory population, the possibilities of trophy-proportioned brown trout can be the same.

Brown trout are known to be one of the more difficult trout and char to fool with a fly and the migratory version of the brown seem to carry that same trait. However, there are times when the predatory urge takes over and these big fish are extremely aggressive while hunting down a swinging fly. However, migratory brown trout are typically driven by the urge to spawn that can temper the interest in chasing a fly. These various moods require a flexible approach from a standard swing speed to a slow presentation that places the fly within easy access to the fish. Generally, post-spawn browns are more aggressive and show an interest in larger streamer-style flies. However, pre-spawn may require a more subtle approach with

smaller flies while making sure to always swing the fly all the way out. Adding some action and a slow strip on the hang down can be productive as well as a hand-retrieve crawl when fishing slower flows. Brown trout are generally fall spawners but may enter a river or tributary well before the spawn and remain for many weeks after.

Migratory Dolly Varden, Arctic char, and even brook trout can be found in many tributaries of the northern Atlantic and Pacific Oceans, providing interesting opportunities for Spey fishing. Dolly Varden migrations typically coincide with the various Pacific salmon runs. While dollies are sometimes caught when targeting salmon, large schools can be encountered. Dolly Varden are typically 6 to 10 pounds, but some northern rivers are known for larger fish. Fresh-run silver Dolly Varden may require a slower swing approach. But as the brilliant spawning colors develop after some time in the river system, Dolly Varden will chase leech-type patterns with some vigor. Dollies are also caught on the top with mouse and similar patterns.

Unique Arctic char migrations are scattered around the northern reaches. When decked out in brilliant

The spectacular beauty of a sea-run Arctic char. Unique fisheries can be found around the globe that are well-suited for Spey techniques. JEFF BRIGHT PHOTO

orange-and-red spawning colors, char are one of the most spectacularly beautiful creatures that swim. Char can readily attack a swung fly fished below the surface when in the river or fishing the current flow as it extends into a lake or bay. The average size of char is highly variable and depends on the environment, and 5 to 9 pounds is considered average. But exceptional individuals of up to or exceeding 20 pounds are possible.

Migratory brook trout can be found in many rivers along the northern Atlantic Coast of North America. Sea-run brook trout do not grow quite as big as other sea-run trout and char but do reach relative trophy proportions for this species. An average sea-run is 2 to 6 pounds, but exceptional migratory brook trout can exceed 10 pounds. Fairly consistent runs exist on some coastal rivers and represent a fun opportunity for light two-hand or single-hand Spey techniques. Sea-run brookies are commonly caught incidentally by salmon anglers.

There are also some larger rivers systems where landlocked brook trout thrive in nutrient-rich waters.

In some instances, these fish can grow to sizes similar to sea-runs. Landlocked brook trout can be caught swinging or swinging and stripping streamer-style flies and even on top using mouse patterns. Some opportunity still exists in the northern Great Lakes for remnant populations of migratory brook trout, referred to as "coasters."

Smallmouth Bass

Smallmouth bass are not traditionally considered a species to be pursued by Spey fishing, but like trout Spey, advancements in equipment and lines provide for equipment setups that match well with smallmouth. Given that smallmouth inhabit a range of rivers in North America both during spawning migrations and as residents, the opportunity to pursue bass by Spey fishing is open to many anglers. Smallmouth are fun to pursue and catch. And while simply catching a smallmouth can be the end objective, Spey fishing for bass also assists in keeping your skills sharp for larger migratory species and can teach the importance of covering specific structure.

A wide variety of flies can be used to fool smallmouth. Simple baitfish or buggy marabou and rabbit strip patterns cover the basic needs for Spey fishing for smallmouth. Weight added to the fly pattern allows it to effectively fish along the bottom and near rocky structure.

An angler works a rocky structure in search of feeding smallmouth bass. Be sure to let the fly hang a few seconds and strip back slowly as the added action can provide the trigger for a smallmouth to eat the fly. NICK PIONESSA PHOTO

Proper rod and line rigging for smallmouth can be as light as a Spey streamer setup for trout in the 300- to 350-grain range Skagit head. But I prefer a rod that handles a 450-grain Skagit for the versatility required by smallmouth fishing. Smallmouth can be caught throughout the water column but working the fly close to structure is typically the most productive. Rigging with a sinking leader or sinking-tip and a weighted fly allows for coverage of various depths and the ability to get down into the structure. Scandi heads are best utilized for surface presentations. Surface fishing for smallmouth can provide for great sport in warmer water conditions.

Holding structure is a key factor when in pursuit of smallmouth. Logs, overhanging brush, boulders, ledges, reefs, drop-offs, and troughs tight to the bank all provide prime bass target areas. When Spey fishing for smallmouth, making precise casts to cover a specific structure may be more important than when pursuing other species. When fishing small to medium-sized waters, casts should land as close to

logs and other structures that define the opposite bank as possible. Casts covering boulders and changes in depth should be made at various angles to completely cover an area. While I still employ a cast and step approach to smallmouth water, there is more of an emphasis on covering structure as opposed to simply covering all the water.

Smallmouth can be caught on a simple swing or by adding action to the fly with a strip, hand crawl, or jigging action by moving the tip up and down. Giving the fly some action by pulling on the line with the line hand and releasing the line back provides enticing movement while maintaining the length of the swing. Often, the speed and action of the fly will be a more important trigger for a take than the pattern selection. Experiment throughout the day to find the right approach. Slow and deliberate tends to be more effective than quick and rapid with respect to fly movement. Often, a smallmouth grab occurs in between strips when the fly is at rest. Always swing the fly out entirely and let it sit a second or two before beginning

There is no water too big for Spey casting and fishing techniques. An angler covers the placid flows of a big river for spring smallmouth. You don't need to cover it all. The key is intently fishing the structure that can be readily reached with your casting abilities. NICK PIONESSA PHOTO

a slow strip back. The slow strip in the hang down can be surprisingly effective.

When fishing deep water or when temperatures are cold, fishing the fly down in the water column with a sinking leader or sinking-tip is typically the best approach. Often, the fly is also weighted to get it down quickly and to increase its action when stripped. A weighted fly with a floating line is an effective rig on smaller waters or where the fly only needs to sink a short distance.

Smallmouth are quite surface-oriented and can move significant distances to attack a surface fly. A buoyant pattern swung and waked on the surface can get a smallmouth's attention. I prefer to add a subtle movement or popping action during the swing that mimics injured or struggling bait. Work the surface fly near any structure, including downed logs, but also be sure to cover deep, slow pools and tailouts where smallmouth can be pulled from the depths to intercept the fly.

There is no need to get too complicated with smallmouth flies. You can't go wrong with combinations of rabbit strip, marabou, schlappen, and rubber legs tied to represent common bait in the river being fished. Bunny buggers, wooly buggers, Clouser Deep Minnows, and various sized game changers round out a good selection of smallmouth flies. Surface patterns typically include a foam or spun deer hair head allowing for an extra disturbance when stripped or popped.

Other Species

Any fish that lives or occupies moving water can be targeted with Spey fishing techniques. The key is matching up the equipment and rigging to meet the size of the fish and the challenges of the proper presentation.

A couple examples of additional opportunities that come to mind are the migratory runs of American or hickory shad into coastal rivers or predators such as striped bass that move into the lower end of rivers to feed. I vividly remember a small river in Maine that pulled stripers in from the bay with nearly every changing tide. When the tide flow was right, the bass would go on a heavy feed. A swung bait fish pattern resulted in arm-jolting strikes and fast action. And don't discount other predators such as resident wall-eye, hybrid bass, or lake trout that may nose up into a river to feed.

Other Applications

While not truly Spey fishing, two-handed rods have wide application to various fly-fishing situations. Thinking outside the box and adapting various elements of Spey can assist in meeting challenges and improving presentations.

Short head lines that load a rod quickly can be quite useful in stillwater fishing situations on lakes, impoundments, or even oceans. Shoreline fishing positions where there is very little backcasting room because of high banks or trees and other vegetation can be quite frustrating when using a traditional fly cast. Roll casting with a single-hand rod provides some relief, but the power of either a two-hand or one-hand Spey cast with a short head line drives the fly further and with less effort. The fly can then be retrieved all the way back before a simple switch cast or forward Spey sends the fly back into the water. An integrated running-line-style line is an advantage when the fly is stripped all the way back to the casting position.

Short head lines not only assist with avoiding back-casting obstructions but also allow you to be at the ready for visual casting situations when roaming a shoreline or beach. False casting can waste valuable time when a feeding or cruising fish is spotted, partic-ularly when fishing near high banks that may restrict the backcast. But more importantly, taking advantage of the ability of the Spey cast to efficiently change directions when sight fishing along a beach can be a significant benefit. A Skagit head combined with waterborne casts work best for fishing along a beach. A stripping basket to hold loose running line is essen-tial to keep the running line out of the sand and surf.

When Spey casting in the surf, it is important to recognize how the movement of the water and wave action impacts the anchor. The water height can be in constant flux so that adjusting the arm position up in higher water levels assists in freeing line for the for-ward stroke. Also, wave action can push or pull on the anchor so that having a minimum of line on the water by adjusting arm position alleviates some of the impact.

The ability to overhead cast a two-handed rod can't be overlooked. While overhead casting is based on the principles of a standard fly cast, the hand movement involving the push of the top hand and, more impor-tantly, the pull of the bottom hand on the forward stroke is nearly identical to the forward stroke of the Spey cast. The motion of the bottom hand pulling in results in significant line speed, like utilizing a haul on a standard one-hand cast. Two-hand overhead cast-ing is capable of shooting line great distances while carrying big, wind resistant flies. Also, two-handed casting that engages the entire body relieves some of the wear and tear on the casting arm muscles and joints caused by all day single-hand casting heavier rods and large flies.

To begin the cast, the rod tip should start low, just off the surface of the water, eliminating any slack in the line. The cast begins with a slow lift off the water that continues into the backcast with a smooth acceleration ending with a hard stop at 1 o'clock or between 1 and 2 o'clock. At this point, the upper hand is positioned back near your face and the lower hand is pushed out. As the line straightens on the backcast, the forward stroke begins with a smooth acceleration by pushing out the top hand and pulling with the bot-tom completing to a definitive hard stop at 11 o'clock or between 10 and 11 o'clock. Immediately after the stop, the rod is lowered, allowing the running line to easily move through the guides.

Similar to single-handed fly casting, the further the rod moves between stopping points on the forward stroke, the more line speed that is generated. Allowing the upper hand to slip back slightly after the rod has stopped on the backcast increases the length of the stroke. Timing is everything as the rod needs to stop first and hand slipped back as the line straightens on the backcast. This process takes some practice and repetition to commit to muscle memory. I find that when overhead casting, slightly more upper hand is engaged than when Spey casting. A more aggressive upper hand allows the rod to move forward for a lon-ger distance creating more speed and casting distance. There is more a feel of controlling the rod with the upper hand while overhead casting as opposed to sim-ply guiding with the upper hand when Spey casting. However, it is critical to keep the bottom hand fully

Overhead casting with a two-handed rod utilizes many of the same casting principles as making a Spey cast. Here I place a deep bend into the rod to launch a large musky fly. NICK PIONESSA PHOTO

engaged on the overhead stroke for a tight loop and to maximize speed and distance.

A common mistake in overhead casting is allowing the rod to edge or creep forward after the stop on the backcast. This acts to shorten the distance of the forward stroke, limiting power and distance. While allowing the top hand to slip back after the stop on the backcast may be more of an advanced move, it is imperative to make sure it doesn't slip forward before beginning the acceleration of the forward stroke. It is equally critical to be sure the forward stroke builds with a smooth movement starting out slowly and moving fastest just before a firm stop. Pushing the stroke too quickly in the beginning diminishes the power of the cast by not allowing the rod to load deeply and can result in a tailing loop and fouled leader.

Since the overhead cast does not provide for an efficient change in direction, it has limited application for swinging a fly. The overhead two-handed cast can be useful in situations that do not require a significant direction change such as dry-fly fishing for trout or salmon. However, the best application for this approach is delivering big flies to large predators in difficult casting situations. Fishing from a boat for musky and pike or working beaches and rock outcroppings for striped bass and other near shore species is the perfect match for the two-handed overhead approach. Given that two-handed rods and casting have become quite popular for conventional gear fishing for large fish, it only makes sense to utilize two-handed rods this way for fly fishing. The use of two-handed rods allows more anglers the ability to chase large predators with a fly.

Rods of 12 and a half feet in length or less are best for overhead casting. Some manufacturers produce rods designed specifically for overhead use. My preference for an efficient two-handed overhead rod for use out of a boat is around 10 feet or even slightly less in length. But when wading surf or fishing on foot, longer rods have an advantage in line pick up and keeping the backcast in the air. Shooting taper style lines work best with overhead casting. When retrieving the fly back to a point where most or all of the head remains outside the rod tip, a 30-foot head is a good match for overhead casting. With the power of this cast, a 30-foot head can be propelled significant distances. In situations where the fly is retrieved all the way back to the casting position, such as alongside the

Two-handed rods provide an advantage when overhead casting large, wind-resistant flies for big musky and pike. Nick Pionessa releases a huge musky caught while using two-hand overhead casting techniques. The efficiency of this approach likely played into the success.

boat when musky, pike, or even bass fishing, a shorter head allows for an easier start to the next cast. At the end of each retrieve when musky fishing, I bring the fly within 2 feet or less of the rod tip. To quickly get the next cast in the air, a 23- to 25-foot head that loads the rod deeply works most efficiently. Heads can either be floating, intermediate, sinking, or some type of blend. Sinking shooting tapers have the widest application that can be used to cover significant depths but also fished fairly shallow with a faster retrieve.

After retrieving the fly all the way back to the boat or casting position if wading, a two-handed rod allows for placing the fly back in the water quickly with only a modest amount of effort. The leverage of a two-handed rod assists in the process. If the fly is retrieved inside the leader at the end of the presentation, simply sweeping the rod while the fly remains in the water allows line to be fed past the tip so that there is enough mass to get the next cast started. With some of the head past the tip of the rod, a roll cast forward allows some more or all of the head to slip past the rod tip. The roll cast can be allowed to touch the water in front of the casting position and/or to remain in the air and move right into the backcast. Allowing the fly to touch or kiss the water allows for an easier set and load of the rod for the backcast but also creates a disturbance on the water that may not be consistent with a stealthy approach.

If all the head is not positioned beyond the tip after the roll cast, the remaining head can be allowed to slip back during the backcast by reducing the pressure on the running line where it is pinched off against the cork. It takes some practice to complete the forward stroke with a single false cast and another false cast can be added if required to properly position the head just outside of the rod tip. Normally, the head and a few feet of running line positioned beyond the rod tip provide for the best rod load. Trial and error may be required to find the sweet spot for running line overhang for each line and rod combination. Integrated heads with a rear taper typically allows for more overhang.

Shooting a long cast relies on managing the running line in a manner that maintains loose coils free from obstructions. Line-grabbing items should be removed or covered in boats and other watercraft to enable consistent casting. Baskets or buckets can be used on windy days to keep line coils from blowing around. Stripping baskets are a valuable tool when wading. The running line should maintain the same position during the cast that it had when stripped in to be smoothly pulled out by the next cast. Wind can cause the coils to flip over, resulting in running line tangles and frustration. Also, make sure that the cast and setup are performed smoothly, allowing the running line to uncoil in a manner that reduces the opportunity for tangles. Quick movements that result in the running line jumping off the surface in which it lays is a common source for running line tangles.

7

TROUT SPEY

Fishing for trout has long been associated with the use of a fly rod and remains the most popular species pursued with fur and feathers tied on a hook. Trout streams and rivers with healthy populations can be found in proximity to many anglers supporting this popularity as opportunities often exist nearby. And sadly, as migratory runs have diminished on some rivers, resident trout have been found by anglers to provide an alternative for swinging a fly.

The development of a wide range of lighter two-hand and single-hand Spey rods along with a variety of heads to match has resulted in a significant growth in the popularity of trout Spey in recent years. In fact, special rods are not required to take advantage of this style of fishing as a 9-foot single-hand rod with a head designed for Spey can work remarkably well on smaller to medium-sized waters.

Swinging a trout streamer through prime holding water along the far bank of an Alaskan river in search of resident rainbows. Trout Spey techniques, both one-hand and two-hand, can be employed on most trout streams and rivers.

151

I Spey cast a weighted streamer to work through a rocky trough along the far bank. Casting to structure along the bank is a productive Spey streamer technique. This approach can require accurate casting to present to the prime holding or ambush lies. NICK PIONESSA PHOTO

The trout Spey movement can generally be classified into four distinct approaches—swinging streamer-style flies to play on the predatory instincts of trout, swinging wet flies or dry flies to represent various aquatic insects during pre-hatch and hatch situations, swinging large flies on the surface, and prospecting suspected holding and feeding lies while dead drifting dries and wets.

Streamers and Baitfish Patterns

Let's first look at swinging streamers and baitfish patterns. This approach can be effective in all water conditions, but I prefer high, off-color water that puts predators more at ease while taking advantage of a situation that tends to favor the hunter. I prefer water that is beginning to recede and clear after a high-water event—water that is still higher than normal but defined enough to identify structure. Water on the rise can also provide a similar opportunity, however, the rising water window may not last for a long period and can be quite short on smaller waters. The best

conditions seem to exist just as water begins to rise and color after a rainfall and may only last for a couple hours until it is too stained and flows are strong. Taking advantage of a rise often results from being in the right place at the right time.

A Skagit or similar weight forward head or integrated line like a streamer switch allow for the use of a sinking-tip or sinking leaders as well as a weighted fly. Sinking-tip or sinking leader length for streamer fishing is typically 7 to 10 feet. There is normally an advantage to sinking the fly quickly when fishing streamers in stained water. Sink rates of 5 to 7 inches per second are a good starting point. And always use sufficient tippet strength to withstand the jolting grab of a big trout. Don't be concerned about a trout being too tippet shy in stained water. I always rig with sufficient tippet strength to hold up to the largest trout believed to exist in the water being fished, typically with a 10- to 12-pound breaking strength. The tippet is normally 2 to 4 feet in length and looped directly to the sinking-tip or sinking leader.

On bigger waters, I prefer a rod that handles a 300-grain to 325-grain Skagit while fishing lighter on smaller streams and rivers. A rod that handles a 300-grain to 325-grain Skagit may be a little heavy for the fight of an average size trout, but streamer Spey is all about looking for top predators—the class of fish that puts a bend in an 11-foot 5-weight. Also, the heavier grain weight head is an aid in handling big, weighted streamers. In most instances, the fly doesn't need to fish right on or near the bottom, but placing it near structure is important for covering specific holding and ambush areas. However, patterns tied to represent a sculpin or other bottom-dwelling creatures are best fished down along the bottom.

On bigger rivers, the focus is on water coverage by making long casts and swinging into the soft inside current. A straight swing with no additional action added to the fly is an effective approach for trout. The speed of the swing is adjusted for factors such as water temperature, clarity of the water, and how active the trout seem to be on a given day. Speed can be controlled by casting angle and mending. Also, using techniques discussed in previous chapters to gain and control depth are critical for fishing deep, dark pools. When fishing a streamer on the swing, I prefer showing the fly on more of a broadside angle by casting across and then pointing at or leading the fly slightly with the rod. The broadside angle gives the predator a better look at the meal-sized offering swimming in its neighborhood. This approach has proven to be more effective than a quartering down cast when fishing a baitfish pattern.

Over the years, I have found that a swing and strip approach often works best in enticing a strike with a streamer. The fly is stripped at intervals as it is swinging across current. The strip adds action to the fly to catch a predator's attention or to give the appearance of bait that is injured or in peril. While we often think of the predator chasing down healthy prey, feeding on the injured or weak is often the most common approach to predation. Short and sharp strips have proven very effective but vary the strip length, speed, and cadence to determine the best approach for a given day. Use a more subtle strip in cold water and a more aggressive one when it's warmer. Experiment each day to find the best approach that matches the trout's mood. Stripping the fly during the swing also makes for an efficient approach as the head is at or near the

Focus on structure that provides a food source and security. The top predators often take up the prime feeding lies. This fish was positioned in a prime water hold where a riffle dumped into deeper soft water.

rod tip as the swing concludes and ready for the next cast. Swinging and retrieving can make a good case for using an integrated Skagit or streamer switch line so there are no loops to contend with if the head is stripped back through the tip.

Stripping and releasing the line back is a good approach for adding action to the fly while maintaining a constant line length to assure complete coverage of a pool or run. Once a short strip has been made, the line is allowed to slide back out under light tension of the fingers against the cork. Always maintain contact so that the grab or take of a fish can be determined.

Rod action can also be used to create motion in the fly. A jigging action by raising the rod tip up and lowering it down creates lifelike movement while maintaining a consistent length in the line during the swing. The jigging action works best in combination with a weighted fly, and while this rod movement provides an enticing up-and-down action in the fly, it also allows for covering uneven bottom structure and pocket water.

When the fly completes its swing, allow it to sit there for a second or two and then add a few strips. Never be quick in taking the fly out of the water. Trout can follow for a distance, or as the fly completes its swing, it may gain the attention of a fish sitting in the soft inside currents. Try stripping the fly slowly, but I have found that two or three quick, sharp retrieves can entice a trout into a snap decision to attack.

Streamer Spey should be employed with purpose by paying specific attention to structure and contour changes. Hit mid-river structure such as logs, boulders, and pockets, making sure to cover prime holds from various angles. Areas where a riffle dumps into deeper, darker flows represent a prime ambush hold and commonly are occupied by an alpha trout that has pushed others out of such a preferred feeding lane. The fly needs to get down into the dark water quickly as the flow rushes out of the riffle. Also, focus on the soft inside flows toward the end of the swing, particularly where there is a contour change as big trout often sit here waiting in ambush.

Another approach for larger rivers is to fish the off side of the pool from the bank that has the deeper, faster water. While this may require difficult wading and problematic casting along or in between overhanging brush and trees, it may be the best way to present to fish holding along the bank on big rivers.

The fly is now allowed to swing into the deep water along the bank—prime holding water for a predator trout. And be patient by slowly stripping the fly back along the bank by adding at least a half dozen retrieves to be sure to cover all fish that can be holding in this prime water. Fishing the off side is a good approach for both high- and low-water conditions. Be sure to use a stealthy approach as trout can react to the noise and vibration of clumsy wading or a heavy foot on the bank. In high water, the subtle soft currents along the bank caused by contours create the perfect holding and ambush spot out of the heavy flows of a swollen river.

On small to medium-sized rivers, casts can usually be made to cover the far bank. Each cast now requires some thought and accuracy, adding a new challenge to the equation. Often, the cast setup takes into consideration obstructions requiring delivery of the fly at various angles and off both shoulders. Attempt to land each cast next to the bank or the structure that defines the bank, such as boulders or a downed log. Mature resident trout are rarely found in the middle of a pool in smaller waters unless the water is significantly off color.

Focusing on obvious structure is very important as most grabs from big fish are encountered near single logs, log jams, divots or pockets, or troughs along a cut bank. When fishing smaller rivers and streams, an active fly is typically more effective than a straight swing. The retrieve can begin almost immediately after hitting the water. The most exciting part of streamer Spey is the arm-jolting strike of a big trout as the fly pulls away from a piece of structure. When the water is clear or clearing, focusing on structure seems to be a must, but in more stained water, trout feel comfortable roaming somewhat and may be found in a wider range of water types.

Many trout streams and creeks are quite small and require more of a hybrid approach to streamer Spey. Smaller waters set up well for one-hand Spey techniques and a very short or micro Skagit head. With the short head, the setup is quite simple and normally results in a single or double Spey, depending on the side of the creek being fished. But just getting the head lined up and making a forward Spey or switch cast often works best in close quarters. Just make the cast and present the fly any way possible. Smaller streams may not accommodate the typical step and cast approach so think of approaching holding water

Angler Chris Lee and an aggressive brown trout fooled by a large tube fly. While large flies can be the key to attracting large fish, be sure to adapt fly size and design to the conditions. NICK PIONESSA PHOTO

in a manner that provides an element of stealth. I also find that smaller waters may require extra attention in quickly attaining the proper depth through mending or high-sticking since the swing path of a small pool is quite short.

Flies of 3 to 4 inches and occasionally slightly longer are common when swinging streamers for trout. While not as big as those used by many one-hand streamer anglers, flies of this size remain manageable in most casting situations. Marabou, schlappen, Arctic fox, and various synthetics tied with methods that create an illusion of bulk and a minimum of materials assist in reducing water and wind resistance when casting. Dumbbell eyes and/or a bulky head aid in attaining an erratic movement of a stripped fly. From a purely casting standpoint, unweighted or lightly weighted flies are easier to cast with a trout Spey rig, but weight on the fly can be of great importance when covering structure or getting the fly into the depths.

Big streamers shouldn't be the only size on the menu. When streamer fishing clear water at or below average flows, going small and subtle can be more productive than larger flies. Small squirrel strip, rabbit strip, or woolly buggers in olive, gray, or brown with a little weight at the head are often irresistible. Even try going extra small with patterns, like the Mayer Mini-Leech. In low, clear-water conditions, swinging and working the fly slowly around obvious structure, drop-offs, and troughs is consistently more productive than using a speedy retrieve. For a stealthier approach in clear water, a long monofilament or fluorocarbon leader with a weighted fly running directly to the head removes the sinking-tip or sinking leader from the equation, potentially providing a more natural look. This approach also provides for more sensitivity to determine the subtle take of a trout when the fly is worked along a slow pool or run.

Swinging Wet and Dry Flies

Swinging small wet or dry flies can be very effective during non-hatch and pre-hatch periods or even during a hatch. For delivering small wets or dries, I prefer floating Scandi-style heads or other similar tapers made for trout Spey. I also prefer a lighter rod for swinging wets than that used for streamers typically handling a Scandi head in the 200 to 270 range. During non-hatch periods, an intermediate or slow sinking leader allows for greater depth for fish positioned down in the water column. An intermediate head or head with an intermediate tip also work well to place the fly lower in the water column.

When fishing a floating line, the leader length is the approximate length of the rod but can be extended longer when additional stealth is needed. Fluorocarbon adds to the stealth factor. The leader is tapered for turnover and presentation. Manufactured knotless tapered leaders right out of a package are effective for this fishing, although I prefer to tie my own for better turnover control. The butt section of the leader should be approximately 60 to 75 percent of the diameter of the end of the fly line or head, typically placing it in the .019-inch to .023-inch range. The general configuration of a hand-tied trout Spey leader uses a 60 percent butt, 20 percent midsection, and 20 percent tippet formula with the diameter of the mid-section being approximately the midpoint between the butt and tippet. The tippet needs to be of sufficient strength to handle the downstream take of a large trout and results in a diameter that is usually .002-inch in diameter greater than when dead drifting for trout with a dry.

For swinging wets, I let the current do the work pushing the line and causing the fly to move. Controlling swing speed when fishing trout wet flies is critical as a fast movement in the water is normally not natural for most aquatic insects. Think in terms of an insect rising from the bottom and being caught in the current as opposed to swimming across the river or stream. Upstream mends in faster flows assist in slowing the swing. An across-stream rod angle also works to reduce the speed of the fly moving across the current. Allow the fly to swing all the way out and sit for a second or two. The fly rising as the current pushes on the line and leader in the hang down often entices a fish to grab.

I rely on more of a down and across casting angle when swinging a wet. This angle, combined with pointing the rod out toward the opposite bank, reduces the broadside angle of the fly to more accurately represent an insect struggling to rise in the current. Rod movement and line control should be aimed at reducing swing speed throughout the presentation. Extra line taken from the reel can be added to the presentation by gently moving the rod tip back and forth. This reduces tension while maintaining the position of the fly in one current lane. This slows the speed and can act to feed a fish in a specific drift.

Swinging wet flies as insect life becomes active just before a hatch can be very effective. Trout may be focused on movement in the pre-hatch period, making a swinging or swimming fly look quite natural.

However, occasionally on slower pools, providing an action to the fly that results in the appearance of a swimming nymph can be very productive. This works best for insect species that swim in the water. Placing downstream mends and leading with the rod creates this swimming motion in slow water.

As the wet fly swings out, the push of the current on the line and leader will naturally raise the fly toward the surface. This movement can entice a strike from a fish that followed or is positioned along the inside seam playing on the instinctive response to a feeding opportunity that is getting away. Subtle action added to a wet fly toward the end of the swing can impart lifelike movement. Using a figure-eight or hand twist retrieve keeps the fly alive as it reaches the hang down.

Fishing the fly down in the water column and then rising it up during the swing produces a realistic representation of an aquatic insect moving to the surface. The Leisenring Lift method developed and made popular by Pennsylvania angler Jim Leisenring matches well with the longer length of a trout Spey rod, providing for great line control. The Leisenring Lift begins by making a cast angling upstream about 15 feet or more above a feeding trout or where it is expected

that a trout is positioned. As the fly sinks, its drift is followed with the rod pointed in its direction with little to no slack in the line but also drifting in the current with no added movement. When the fly is close to the fish or suspected lie, about 4 to 5 feet away, the movement of the rod is checked or stopped and the flow of the current against the line and leader causes the fly to move. At once, the wet fly springs to life with hackles, tails, and wings undulating in the flow. The stoppage of the rod also allows the fly to rise toward the surface. The movement of rising toward the surface is a natural occurrence for many aquatic insect forms, and when properly performed, it is certain to gain attention from an active trout.

Leisenring was clear in his description of the technique that the movement was caused by the stoppage of the rod without any other manipulation. However, I have experimented with a slight raise of the rod tip at the stop point that can accelerate the rise and provide more control over the placement of the fly.

Waking a dry fly can bring trout to the surface with aggressive rises. During caddis or stonefly hatches or egg laying, it is common to see insects skittering or flopping around on the surface. This can often be

The beauty of trout streams and rivers can be found in the surroundings and also what lies beneath. Here a perfect specimen caught while using trout Spey techniques is detained for a couple photos before release.

Spey casting techniques can be quite useful on smaller trout waters where there is restricted space for a backcast. Here a deep shaded pool on a small stream creates perfect holding water. NICK PIONESSA PHOTO

accompanied by erratic splashy trout rises and represents the perfect situation to riffle hitch a bushy caddis or stimulator-style pattern and wake it slowly across the surface. Dry flies for waking should be buoyant and tied on an up-eye hook to accommodate the hitch.

Swinging wets or dries matches up with almost any size trout water, but I find it most enjoyable on slightly larger waters where longer casts can be stretched out. However, there are advantages to Spey casting on smaller waters that restrict backcasting room for a traditional fly cast. Swinging flies on small streams requires innovation to cover a wide range of water. Stealth must be at the forefront by avoiding quick movements and fitting into the surroundings. Fish each swing thoroughly by allowing the fly to work extra on the hang down. Moving the rod tip from side to side keeps the fly moving and swinging when on the hang down and can result in jolting strikes. Rods shorter than 9 feet can successfully be used on smaller waters with one-hand Spey and swinging techniques.

Where legal, the use of two flies can double the chances for a fooling a trout. A simple setup of a two-fly rig begins with tying the point fly to the main tippet with an improved clinch or similar knot. The tippet running to the second fly is attached to the bend of the hook of the point fly with an improved clinch and then to the trailing fly. The distance between the two flies is approximately 12 to 20 inches. When utilizing two flies, the best approach is selecting two very different patterns in terms of size and color to provide options to the fish. Over the course of a day, one pattern usually outperforms the other. A strategic approach to the two-fly setup is to use a small wet fly as the point and a wooly bugger or streamer as the trailing fly. This can provide the appearance of a small baitfish chasing a swimming aquatic insect—the food chain in motion. This in turn may entice a larger trout to enter the chase.

For swinging wets and dries, I rely on my experience of dry-fly fishing and understanding of how various insect hatches impact trout behavior. Some of my wets are generic, but I also carry a range of flies aimed at representing the approximate size and color of common hatches for that river. A working knowledge of insects allows for the ability to select a size and color of fly that is common for the time of year and employs a technique that accommodates the behavior of that insect.

My favorite time for swinging wets is the pre-hatch period where trout feed at various levels of the water column as nymphs and pupae break free from the substrate and become active. Often, trout move up the water column or into shallow riffles as this occurs, making for easy targets with a wet fished just below the surface. Continuing the wet fly swing into the hatch can also be productive. While my preference is to fish a dead-drifted fly during a hatch, a properly timed wet fly can cause a carefully feeding trout to abandon caution and chase down the swinging offering.

At times, the wet fly swing approach has really surprised me as to its effectiveness. There have been a few occasions when normally wary, stream-bred trout seemed to entirely let their guard down. A stealthy approach can go a long way when fishing softer flows, and it's quite important to keep the disturbance from casting to a minimum.

My wet flies are quite simple, usually constructed of a tail or trailing shuck, ribbed dubbed body, and soft-hackle folded back. Sometimes a wing is added. I have not found the need to over-complicate the process.

Swinging Big Flies on the Surface

Large patterns swung on the surface can result in explosive attacks by large trout. Mouse patterns are the most popular and seem to entice big fish on just about any river where trout live. Spey fishing matches perfectly with presenting a mouse on medium- to larger-sized waters. A floating head with enough mass to consistently turn over a bulky pattern is required for accurate and repeated casts. The leader should be long

A beautiful Alaskan rainbow that attacked a mouse pattern as it swam away from a grassy bank. Mouse fishing provides an exciting visual element to Spey fishing. Using a strip set keeps the mouse in the fish's zone if not successfully hooked on the initial attack.

I scan the water for visible rising fish to target with a surface fly. The rise of a trout can be quite subtle, requiring careful observance while identifying likely areas for fish to set up for feeding.

enough to comfortably set the anchor approximately the length of the rod away and with a stiff enough butt to assist in fly turnover. A much heavier tippet is used than when fishing wet flies. In fact, a simple 75 percent butt section and 25 percent tippet are sufficient for fishing a mouse with tippet of enough strength to withstand the vicious take of a large trout.

On medium-sized water, I prefer to cast tight along the opposite bank to represent a rodent that has unfortunately fallen into the water. Be sure to fish the mouse near any structure such as logs and boulders found along the opposite bank, midstream, or near the inside bank. A mouse cannot swim too fast in the water so controlling speed through mending and rod angle provides for a natural presentation.

Wiggling the rod tip from side to side gives the appearance of a mouse swimming on the water's surface, providing an enticing realism to the presentation.

A trout taking a mouse pattern can be explosive—a visual treat for a Spey angler. But other grabs can be more subtle. It seems that some fish attempt to pull the mouse down to drown it as opposed to eating it all at once. This leads to grabs on the surface without a hookup. In this situation, it is always best to keep the mouse swimming like it is trying to get away and set the hook with a strip and rod lift only when the weight of the fish is felt or when certain the fish has solidly taken the fly down.

While I have enjoyed great mousing action during the middle of the day on Alaskan rivers, fishing a mouse pattern at night on waters with big brown trout has become quite popular for single-hand overhead fishing. But there is also the opportunity for Spey fishing mouse patterns at night as well. Safety is the key when fishing at night. Fish with a partner and only work water that is familiar and where depth changes are well known. Everything looks very different at night. A bright head lamp is a must, and an inflatable lifejacket is a good idea on big water. Be aware of wildlife in areas where dangerous game exists.

When Spey fishing at night, extra care must be given to setting the anchor in a safe place. Using a shorter head allows for easier control and safer setup. Practice during the day to develop a rhythm. Even in the dark, a visual of the anchor can usually be made prior to the cast. I attempt to always cast off the downstream shoulder in the dark as a step toward keeping the anchor away from my body. A big trout breaking the nighttime silence with an explosive take is exhilarating and makes the creepiness of being out after dark worth the effort. Spey fishing from a boat at night is another option that can help assist with greater safety.

Dead Drifting Dry Flies

Spey casting with a light two-hand trout rod or a single-hand rod also matches up with dead-drifting dry flies. While this approach isn't preferred when delicate presentations of small dries are required, a forward Spey may be the only choice when backed up to vegetation or other casting obstructions. But the Spey approach can work quite well on large rivers when prospecting and blind casting imitations of bigger mayflies and stoneflies as well as terrestrials such as grasshoppers.

Spey casting is extremely efficient when employing a blind casting surface approach as compared to overhead casting and keeps the fly fishing on the water's surface for a greater period than when a traditional backcasting is involved. A floating Scandi head or other similar taper with a monofilament or fluorocarbon leader of approximately the length of the rod completes the rig. The leader should have a stiff enough butt section to turn over wind-resistant flies, and the leader should taper to a 2X to possibly 4X depending on the size of the fly, size of the expected trout, and water type.

The slightly longer rods typically used for trout Spey provide the ability for line control at longer distances than when using a shorter one-hand rod. Touch

and go casts match up well with the dead-drift dry fly approach. Both the single Spey and snake roll place the fly back in the fish zone quickly after the drift is complete. The cast is made at an upstream angle. The nuance here is that the fly will not swing all the way out before the next cast begins. When the fly begins to no longer dead drift and starts to swing, it is time to pick up and make another cast. The fly may still be at a 45-degree angle when the cast begins. At this point, a roll cast or switch cast can place the fly in the hang down so that the next cast can begin. But in water with a moderate to heavy flow, simply lifting the rod tip up allows the fly to skitter to the inside and the next cast can begin at a slightly cocked upstream angle to the flow of the river that assists in placing the next cast at a slight upstream angle.

When searching with big flies, the precise dead-drift presentation required for selective surface feeding trout is typically not as vital. However, maintaining a reasonable dead drift will raise more fish. To that end, attempting to land the fly line upstream from the fly and placing some slack in the leader greatly assists in attaining a dead drift. Incorporating a reach cast into the forward stroke by pointing the rod upstream as the line is in the air allows the line to land up from the fly. And utilizing a long tippet section of 3 to 4 feet will encourage slack at the end of the leader. With some practice, slack line casts can be added by either underpowering the forward stroke or adding an abrupt stop and slight pull back at the end of the stroke, creating shockwaves in the leader.

Extra-buoyant flies that ride high and keep floating without the benefit of drying off during a backcast work best with this approach. I prefer creating my dries with high visibility materials to be easily seen on the water. The visible grab of a trout taking a dead-drifted dry should be met with a hookset when the fly disappears without feeling the weight of the fish. A high rise of the rod tip while pulling down on the line is usually all that is needed to set the hook. The dead-drift nymphing techniques described in chapter 5 are very effective in the pursuit of trout.

8

FLIES

A wide range of fly styles and types are used for meeting the varied opportunities to use Spey and two-handed techniques. NICK PIONESSA PHOTO

Thoughts and recipes concerning fly designs and patterns already fill volumes. Fly fishers are enthralled with fly patterns. This fascination lies partly in the joy derived from the craft of tying and the beauty of a fine creation on a hook. But it extends to the magic that a particular fly design can be the link to success on the water. We have all felt the renewed enthusiasm in trying a new fly when the others in our box have seemed to fail. Sometimes it's the fly but more often it is the presentation. However, confidence in our fly pattern is what allows us to fish intently and with purpose.

It is impossible to do justice to flies for Spey fishing and other strategies discussed in the book that utilize Spey and overhead casting in a single chapter. However, it would seem remiss to not discuss the most used and effective categories of flies along with some tried and true examples of each style. Some fly styles and patterns are nearly synonymous with Spey fishing being developed side by side with the advancement of this style of fishing. Others have been created for various uses but match well with Spey fishing and swinging a fly.

This chapter can be used as a guide with samples of effective fly styles, many of which have an eye appeal to the angler as well. With an ever-expanding plethora of tying materials available today along with talented tyers that continue to develop and create, there is a nearly endless progression of flies to be combined with modern Spey techniques. Certainly, too many to catalog in any book. The only limit is one's own creativity. Designing or modifying flies to meet a certain situation can be an enjoyable part of the Spey journey.

Spey Flies

Not only does a style of fishing carry the Spey name but so does a style of flies. In his comprehensive and inspiring book entitled *Spey Flies*, Bob Veverka discusses that Spey flies were originated on Scotland's River Spey well over a century and a half ago. This style was developed at a time when each salmon river had a set of flies developed for the specifics of that river. Flies for various rivers were characterized and defined by certain colors, availability of materials, and a distinguishing style.

Top row: Bunny Spey, Sol Duc Spey; Middle row: Bill's Spey, Lady Caroline, Green Highlander; Bottom row: Akroyd, Black Gordon, Gold Riach NICK PIONESSA PHOTO

The original Spey flies had simple dressing, muted colors, and were tied on long shank hooks. Spey fly bodies were typically constructed of blended wool and ribbed with tinsel. The element that caught my eye upon first seeing a Spey fly was the long flowing hackle that could extend beyond the bend in the hook. The hackle gives the fly depth and enticing movement in the water. The hackles commonly used were of Spey-cock and heron. A Spey-cock was specifically bred near the River Spey and are believed to no longer be in existence. Spey-cock feathers were of cinnamon-brown or black in color, and some had gray at the tip. Heron hackles on these early patterns were typically gray or black. The original Spey flies were finished with a teal flank collar and bronze mallard set low on top of the hook.

Another type of fly very similar in general appearance because of its long sweeping hackle is the Dee fly, named for Scotland's River Dee. While this style was similar to the Spey fly, there were notable differences. Dee flies were tied on very large hooks and featured a tail that was not present on the early Spey flies. Bodies consisted of spun fur featuring two or three colors ribbed with wide tinsel. When the body material was picked out and enveloped the tinsel, it created a translucent look. The hackle on the original Dee flies consisted of the longest heron hackle to extend to or even past the bend of the large hook. The wings of a Dee fly were constructed of a quill wing, typically turkey, tied in individually and flat over the body. When looking down at the fly, the wings formed a V and tied in that manner provided good movement as the fly worked through the current.

Spey and Dee flies were developed and mainly used for Atlantic salmon fishing. Roderick Haig-Brown, one of the finest and most influential fishing writers of the twentieth century, mentions using a Spey fly pattern in his 1939 book *The Western Angler*. And decades later, West Coast steelhead tyers, led by Syd Glasso, created beautifully colored and designed patterns that soon proved effective on migratory steelhead as well.

Speys and Dees have largely merged into a style that has assumed the single name of Spey fly. It is a style that represents both elegance and functionality. And classic Spey flies adorned with intricately constructed colorful married wings of quill fibers have evolved as an art form in itself. These are beautiful creations from the hands and vises of the world's best tyers. From a fishing perspective, many anglers continue to utilize Spey flies in their repertoire of flies for salmon and steelhead. Spey style flies have expanded into trout Spey and the pursuit of other species. Today the definition of Spey fly has expanded to include most patterns with long, sweeping hackles that provide both movement and silhouette in the water tied on elegant hooks to enhance the overall appearance. The ultimate Spey fly has a pleasing appearance to the angler's eye while being effective in attracting the take or grab of a fish.

Salmon / Steelhead Wet Flies

It's tricky placing flies used for Spey fishing and two-handed rod casting into definite buckets. The previously discussed Spey flies would also be considered a wet since that style of fly is also designed to be fished in the water column. But in this classification, salmon and steelhead wet flies have a scaled-down look. While the roots of this style of fly clearly lie in the original Spey and Dee ties, smaller subtle patterns have their place.

The typical salmon and steelhead wet fly is generally characterized by a shorter hen or saddle hackle folded back to angle toward the rear of the fly. It can also feature a simple throat of hackle fibers. Most wets also have a wing of hair, feather, or quill the approximate length of the hook and feature a dubbed or floss body typically ribbed with tinsel. Many patterns feature a tail and then a collar over the main hackle.

Wet flies are typically tied on traditional return eye salmon hooks in a range of sizes. Heavy wire hooks add weight to the fly and assist with sinking it into the water column when fishing depth is a factor. Where allowed by regulation, some wet flies are tied on heavy wire double hooks to add weight for greater depth and increase the possibility of a solid hookup. Light wire up-eye hooks work well for fishing higher in the water column and when using a wet fly with a riffle hitch. Wet fly patterns aren't confined to traditional salmon hooks and can be tied on a wide range of hooks.

Wet flies incorporate a wide range of styles and sizes. Colors range from bright and gaudy to subtle and natural. In my own fishing, wet flies fit in best when toning down the size of the presentation for clearer water or pressured fish. Subtle wet flies are also a great choice for going back to a fish that grabbed a larger pattern on a previous cast. Some wets are tied to represent specific food sources.

Top row: Blue Charm, Purple Peril; Middle row: Citation, Winter's Hope, Figure Skater; Bottom row: Green Highlander, Green Machine, Green Butt Skunk NICK PIONESSA PHOTO

I tie and carry a series of wet-style flies that can be fished both below and on the surface. Most of these patterns are tied on a lighter wire up-eye hook to assist in riding on top with a riffle hitch. These patterns are tied with the head of the fly set back from the hook eye to provide extra room for the riffle hitch and to place the point where the tippet comes off the fly more to the rear. This angle pulls the fly to the surface, allowing it to consistently ride high while pushing water and creating a visible "V." Small wet flies often close the deal on an active fish reluctant to commit to larger flies.

Shank Flies / Intruders

Flies first tied on shanks were designed to solve a problem. Large flies tied on long shank hooks provide a fish with extra leverage to twist and turn a hook from its mouth while jumping, shaking its head, or during directional changes when compared to hooking a fish on a shorter shank hook. The solution was to place a free-swinging hook at the rear of the fly, reducing or eliminating the leverage of an extended shank. In the 1940s, European salmon angler Richard Waddington took a step toward addressing this issue by using a long shank with parallel wires, a small loop at the rear, and an up-angled eyelet in the front. At the gap of the end/beginning point of the wire, a treble hook was added, slid to the loop in the rear, and the wire secured with tying thread. The result was the ability to tie large flies while placing a short shank hook at the rear of the materials. Waddington was also one of the first Salmon tyers to construct flies in the round as opposed to an obvious wing on top.

The concept of using a shank to place the hook at the rear of the fly was furthered in the early 1990s by West Coast anglers Ed Ward, Jerry French, and Scott Howell through their development and refining of the intruder style fly. As French explains it, the intruder is more of a platform than an actual pattern. The original ties, inspired by the modern Spey flies being used on the West Coast at the time, featured two distinct trim stations at the rear and front of the fly with a long, attractive section in the middle. The original intruders were big, 5 inches or even longer, and designed to represent the size of food sources that these anadromous fish were eating in the ocean. This was a significant deviation from other West Coast steelhead and salmon flies. And intruders were designed to have a wiggly, lifelike appearance and featured a more durable ostrich herl as compared to marabou that was popular at the time. The large patterns were tied as sparse as possible and were weighted with dumbbell eyes to fish a wide range of water. These large patterns also drove the development of short lines with mass, resulting in the Skagit head.

One of the most prominent features of the intruder that has carried into a broader usage in modern tying is the utilization of a shank with a hook at the rear. Originally tied on cut shanks, today shanks are produced for tying intruder and similar style flies. The original way of rigging the intruder is to insert the tippet through the eye of the shank, fed through the front and rear materials, and then inserted through a nylon loop tied in at the rear of the fly. The tippet is then knotted to the short shank hook and held in place by a short piece of flexible plastic junction tubing. When a fish is hooked, the fly breaks away from the tubing and rides up the leader, reducing the unhooking leverage of a large fly.

Many of today's intruder-style flies use a permanent connection of the hook to the shank using wire,

Top row: Beauly Snow Fly, Scandi Sculpin, Artificial Intelligence; Middle row: Mr. Softie, Blue Moon; Bottom row: Intruder, Mini Trout Intruder, Fauxy Leech NICK PIONESSA PHOTO

monofilament, or gel spun material. A more flexible connection works best to reduce the leverage created by the large, heavy fly. The concept of an intruder fly has greatly expanded into patterns that have deviated from the original design into almost any big fly tied on a shank and supporting French's comments that the intruder is a platform for creation that continues to evolve. The intruder style doesn't just mean big any longer either, as scaled-down versions of buggy flies tied on shanks for trout and bass are sometimes referred to as mini-intruders.

Tube Flies

A tube fly is constructed on a hollow tube and the tippet inserted through the tube, tied to a short shank hook, and then inserted into the tube or connected with junction tubing. Like the concept of a shank, tying on a tube also has its roots in Atlantic salmon fishing. While professional tyer Minnie Morawski of Scotland is credited with tying the first tube flies around 1945, the idea appears to have been first presented by British author and angler Alexander Wanless more than a decade earlier.

The tube fly style has many advantages over tying on a hook for patterns to be used when swinging the fly. The short shank hook tied directly to the tippet is the best strategy for eliminating the leverage of a longer hook and maintaining the connection to the fish. And by controlling the length of the tube or junction tubing, the hook can be placed at the rear of the fly, maximizing the possibility of hooking up when a fish grabs. If a hook becomes damaged beyond the point

Top row: Temple Dog, Cattitude, Marabou Spey Tube; Bottom row: Sunray Shadow, Hybrid Sculpin NICK PIONESSA PHOTO

that it can't be reasonably sharpened, it can quickly be swapped out as compared to a fly tied on a hook that may no longer be usable. Also, a tube typically rides up the leader when a fish is hooked. This greatly adds to the life of a fly when it's out of the fish's mouth during the fight and as the hook is removed.

Tubes are available in plastic and various metals, including brass and copper, providing options for weighting a tube fly. Weight can be easily added to a plastic tube using cones specific for tube flies or simply adding dumbbell eyes. Cones can be added at the tying vice or on the water to convert an unweighted tube to a weighted fly. When tying an unweighted tube fly, I leave a little extra plastic off the front of the tube so that a cone can be slid up the tube and placed on the head of the fly and then use a lighter to flair the plastic around the lip of the tube to hold it in place and create a soft edge to protect the tippet. Plastic tubes are available in various diameters, and any cones or other style of weight or head to be added to a tube need to line up with the proper diameters.

Nearly any style of fly tied on a hook can also be constructed on a tube. I rely on the tube style for many of my Spey fishing patterns. There are many similarities between the advantages of tying on tubes and shanks. I find tying on tubes to be slightly simpler than using shanks. From a fishing standpoint, the greater surface area of the tube and the slight weight of the shank allows the shank style fly to cut the surface tension and gain slightly greater depths when fishing flies with no additional weight added. This is a factor to consider when attempting to place the fly at the desired depth.

The short shank hook can be attached to the tube with two different methods. A straight eye hook can be attached to the tippet with an improved clinch knot and the eye of the hook is pushed into a plastic junction tubing that is then slid onto the rear end of the tube. Some tubes made of a flexible plastic allow the hook eye to be pushed into the tube without the need for junction tubing. The second method utilizes an up-eye short shank hook. A loop connection is formed to the hook by using a no-slip-loop knot. This is accomplished by first forming a loose overhead knot in the tippet and then threading it through the hook eye, then around the hook, and back through the hook eye. The tippet goes back through the loose overhead knot after adjusting the position of the original knot for proper spacing. The no-slip knot is then completed. The knot is then pulled into the tube to position the hook. Advocates of the loop method point to the flexible connection resulting in less snags and a softer feel when a fish grabs the fly.

Dry Flies

Historically, the most popular dry fly patterns paired with Spey fishing were tied with spun deer that created a buoyant base. The well-known Bomber features spun deer hair trimmed with a hackle wound through the body of the fly. This pattern is fished in both a dead-drifted and waking fly approach. For waking the fly, the Bomber is best tied on an up-eye hook. Other deer hair dry flies evolved from the Bomber concept. The Waller Waker, created by well-known West Coast steelhead angler Lani Waller, features a spun deer hair body and two visible wings or posts. The fly is tied to plow along the water's surface cutting a visible "V" to catch a fish's eye and create a clear visual point for the angler to see.

Various spun deer head muddler style flies create enough buoyancy to assist in maintaining a fly on the surface in conjunction with the use of a riffle hitch. Caddis patterns with a deer hair head can be tied in a wide range of sizes for trout, bass, steelhead, and salmon and represent an egg-laying adult skittering across the surface. Tightly spun deer hair for the body of a mayfly, caddis, or stonefly creates effective patterns that can be used with either a dead-drift or waking approach and stay buoyant when Spey cast. Treating a dry fly with flotant may be required to maintain the fly on the surface even when using buoyant spun deer hair.

The popular use of closed cell foam in fly tying has changed the game with respect to tying dry flies for waking on the surface. Well-constructed foam flies are nearly unsinkable, providing the confidence that your fly is always riding properly on the surface. Some dry flies are constructed entirely from foam, and others use a combination of foam and traditional materials. The Little Wang, created by Todd Hirano, is a multi-use skating fly that rides high and is quite visible with its distinct post. The Morrish Mouse, created by Ken Morrish, is a perfect example of an effective surface pattern that uses both foam and natural materials to provide a high-riding, lifelike imitation of a popular food for big trout.

Top: Articulated Emperor Mouse; Middle row: Lemire Grease Liner, Bomber, Parachute Stimulator; Bottom row: Little Wang, Mr. Hanky NICK PIONESSA PHOTO

Most flies tied for waking on the surface are constructed on up-eye hooks. The up-eye holds a riffle hitch in place as the tippet pulling from the side maintains the fly on the surface. Even buoyant flies tend to be pulled under by the tension exerted by waking across the surface. The riffle hitch counterbalances this tendency. Larger, extremely buoyant flies such as many of the popular mouse patterns will remain on the surface without a riffle hitch. This is also the case for popper or other style flies that feature a large buoyant head made of deer hair, foam, or wood.

Tying waking patterns on plastic tubes provides another option for this style of fly. Heating the tip of a needle and poking a hole in the side or bottom of the plastic tube at the front of the fly allows the tippet to be threaded through the tube at an angle. The tippet pulling from the side or bottom creates the same effect as the riffle hitch and, even better, there is no concern of the hitch coming undone. This technique can turn almost any fly tied on a plastic tube into a waking fly.

Trout Wet Flies

Wet flies or soft-hackles designed specifically for trout are often similar in design to those used for salmon and steelhead except scaled down in size. The typical trout wet is also tied more to represent something specific as opposed to a salmon or steelhead wet aimed more at simply eliciting a response. Mimicking specific or generic aquatic insect life can be seen in the typical trout wet fly dress in natural or drab browns, tans, olives, and grays.

Some trout wet flies exhibit a wing of quill, hair, or other material. Spider-style wet flies are tied without a wing. Trout wet bodies are typically fine and sometimes slightly tapered with wire or other material for ribbing to provide the segmentation typically seen in aquatic insects. Most trout wets are hackled with hen, partridge, or other similar soft-hackles that moves in the water to provide life and possibly represent insect legs. Also, some are tied with tails or materials to represent the trailing shuck of an aquatic nymph.

Historically, trout wets have been tied with all natural materials, but with the popularity and plethora of synthetic material that possess flash, shine, or sheen on the market, many productive wet flies incorporate a wide range of man-made items. The flash or shine of some synthetics can represent small bubbles that occur in or around insects when lifting from the bottom and moving toward the surface. A small element of flash can provide a lifelike trigger to a feeding trout.

It can pay to be specific with trout wet fly patterns. Carrying a range of sizes, colors, and styles of wets to meet the popular insects of the streams and rivers that you typically fish can be very important. Based on insect emergence patterns, some activity is more easily represented with a trout Spey approach. I carry a selection to meet the specific insects that match best with the swing or Leisenring Lift approach and some very generic ties that can be used for searching and during low-activity time periods.

Trout Streamers

Streamer patterns illicit thoughts of triggering the predatory instinct of a trout. While aquatic insects and terrestrials are almost always an important part of a trout's diet, most big trout prefer a large meal when possible. Flies tied to represent specific bait for a particular river or simple generic patterns are often the key to connecting with some of the river's largest fish.

Single-hand overhead-casting streamer techniques often involve using huge flies to attract interest from

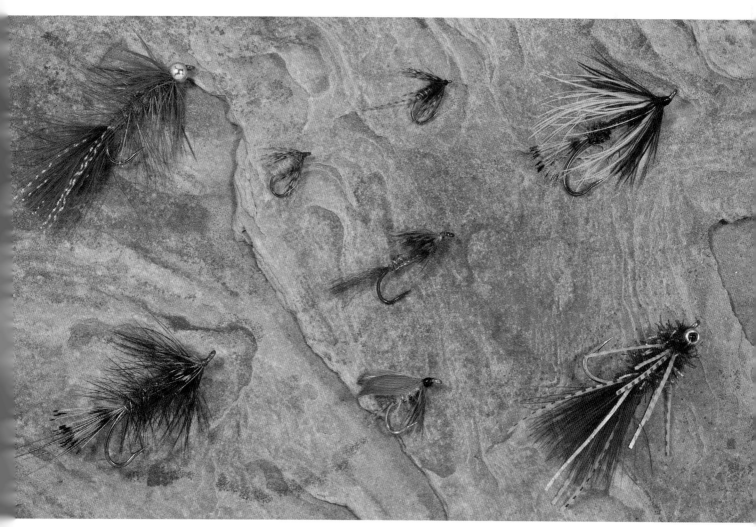

Top row: Bead Head Spey Bugger, American Pheasant Tail, Wingless Royal Coachman; Middle row: Olive Sedge, Iso Emerger Soft Hackle; Bottom row: Woodcutter, Hare's Ear Wet Fly, Ugly Bugger NICK PIONESSA PHOTO

Top row: Cattfish Streamer, Pine Squirrel Leech, Muddler Minnow Spey; Middle: Magog Smelt; Bottom row: SF Streamer, Circus Peanut NICK PIONESSA PHOTO

the largest predators. It's not uncommon for some streamer patterns to be from 5 to 7 inches in length. Modern streamer tyers, such as Kelly Galloup, Tommy Lynch, and Rich Strolis, to name a few, have designed big patterns that show bulk in the water and erratic movement when retrieved. Many of these patterns aim at displaying a bait's vulnerability, in turn attracting a predator to take advantage. However, some of the large streamers tied for one-hand fishing are too big, heavy, or bulky to effectively cast while Spey casting. Skagit-style heads that match with even the heaviest of trout Spey rods cannot comfortably handle Spey casting extremely large flies.

Scaling down the size, weight, and bulkiness of streamer patterns allows for a fly that is much more manageable for Spey casting. Streamers of 3 to 4 inches or slightly longer can still be quite effective for attracting and fooling some of the largest trout in a stream or river. The key element of an effective Spey streamer pattern is to create the illusion of a large fly with a minimum of materials. Construction from materials that flair out and create enticing movement in the water, such as marabou, Arctic fox, and large hackle as well as schlappen, can result in baitfish patterns that swim well and are manageable to cast even when built to 4 inches or more.

Larger streamers can utilize shanks for extra movement and for placing the hook toward the rear of the fly. Double hooks can also be used to increase the likelihood of a hookup when a fish grabs the fly. Weight in the form of dumbbell eyes or other style of weighted head can add to both the design and function of the fly. Weighted flies are preferred when casting next to structure so that the offering quickly gets to the trout's level or when working sculpin patterns along the bottom. But be careful as adding too much weight makes the fly difficult to cast with a trout Spey rig.

Not all effective Spey streamers need to be big. In fact, small, understated patterns have performed quite well in clearer water conditions. Traditional-style streamers or those tied with a low profile are effortless to cast and capable of fooling large trout. My toned-down streamers tend to reflect olives and browns, but I also find that tying smaller patterns to replicate the bait commonly found in a particular river to be an effective approach for tricking a wily wild trout.

Smallmouth Bass Flies

Many of the popular smallmouth flies used on a single-hand double as effective Spey fishing flies. Lightly weighted Clouser minnows work very well when combined with a swing and strip approach. While I like the movement of bucktail Clouser minnows, tying this pattern with synthetics can create a realistic sheen and a more durable fly. Other buggy smallmouth flies that combine the movement of rabbit, rubber legs, and webby hackle are also effective. I tie some of these flies on jig-style hooks to allow for working closely to the bottom without snagging up. Crayfish patterns can also be surprisingly productive with Spey fishing techniques. Working the fly near the bottom and incorporating a sharp strip action so the fly bounces up and down can create an irresistible presentation. Various other streamer patterns used for inland or migratory trout double as smallmouth patterns.

A selection of smallmouth bass flies for Spey fishing isn't complete without a range of surface patterns. I prefer pencil-style poppers made from trimmed deer hair or foam that give the appearance of injured or stunned bait struggling on the surface. Poppers, gurglers, and diver head flies that include feathers, flash, and rubber legs round out a good surface selection. I like to carry some patterns that are a close resemblance to bait common to a particular stream or river and others that act as an attractor. I prefer my surface smallmouth attractor flies to have some wiggle that allows the fly to look alive even during the pause while using a strip and pause approach.

Buggers / Leeches

One of the most common and universal subsurface fly patterns is the wooly bugger. In fact, if my life depended on catching a fish, I would most certainly rely on an olive or brown wooly bugger. The wooly bugger has accounted for success on many occasions and seems to really excel in the swing game. Small wooly buggers have been my secret "go-to" pattern for Great Lakes steelhead for years when larger flies are ineffective or when fishing in extremely clear-water conditions. Due to its effectiveness and ease in tying, this rather mundane pattern's importance, along with its various adaptations, deserves its own classification.

Wooly buggers can be tied in a range of sizes, colors, and styles. My most effective buggers tend to be on the smaller side and tied in natural colors, but large and bright variants have their place. Wooly buggers are typically tied on a 3X- or 4X-long hook, but utilizing the benefits of tube flies, buggers tied on tubes have the advantage of utilizing a short shank hook at the rear of the materials. Due to its rather low-profile adding weight in the form of a bead or cone allows a bugger to sink quickly to cut surface currents or cover specific structure. Using dumbbell eyes on the top of the shank allows the hook point to ride up, reducing the chance of hanging up the on the bottom of the stream or river.

Small variations to a wooly bugger can make this pattern more effective for a given situation. Adding a few additional wraps of longer hackle at the head of the fly gives it a bushier Spey fly look and creates an appearance in the water of the bulky head of a sculpin. A few strands of flash can be added to the tail or at the head to act as an attractant. And cactus chenille can replace standard chenille or dubbing to add flash throughout the body. And don't forget about tying some synthetic legs into the tail or head of the fly. Legs make a wooly bugger extra buggy, and flies with legs have proven especially effective on bass and trout.

The egg-sucking leech is a simple advancement on the standard wooly bugger that adds the appearance of an egg on the front of the fly. The egg-sucking leech is typically a black or purple body with an orange or pink egg made from chenille, dubbing, or a bead and can be tied on a hook or a tube. The egg-sucking leech and its various iterations are quite effective on migratory fish and have been a standard pattern for anglers in Alaska for many years.

Top row: Feather Game Change, Clouser Minnow; Middle: Getting Jiggy; Bottom row: Nick's Pencil Popper, Swinging D

NICK PIONESSA PHOTO

One other very simple fly that can get lumped into the bugger category is the bunny bugger. This fly can be completed with a single strand of rabbit strip. The rabbit strip is tied in at the bend of the hook and then wrapped forward to the head. A dubbing loop can be used to wrap the rabbit fibers forward. This eliminates the hide, creating a neater finish. A colored bead or dubbing can be added to the head to create an egg-sucking bunny bugger. Flash can also be added to the tail before wrapping the rabbit forward.

Game Changers

The Game Changer is a style of fly created by Blane Chocklett, one of today's most innovative tyers. The Game Changer is a platform for tying realistic patterns both big and small that swim and perform like actual bait. Game Changers provide the ability to truly match

the bait in a particular river and swim extremely well with the swing but excel when a swing, strip, and pause approach is utilized.

The basic platform of the Game Changer begins with a series of short, interconnected shanks that create a spine. This allows the fly to move in ways that aren't possible with historic tying techniques. The Game Changer–style fly flows and moves like real bait. It is a platform that can be adapted to nearly any type of fly while creating the basis for future creativity.

Game Changer flies are constructed with a shape typical of bait, meaning wider at the head and tapering down throughout the tail. For best performance, the head is constructed with dense, bulky material and is lighter in the rear. Stiffer material on the inside of the construction props up the material to maintain the profile and impact the action. Game Changers can be constructed from a range of materials, including bucktail, feathers, craft fur, and synthetic brushes. But there is no limit to where this style can go. In his book *Game Changer: Tying Flies that Look & Swim Like the Real Thing*, Blane goes into incredible detail on every step of constructing some of his most productive patterns. The book is an instant tying classic and a must have for effectively constructing this style of fly.

Other Flies

To have a full well-rounded selection of flies to meet all that Spey fishing and use of two-hand overhead casting have to offer, there are a couple other categories of flies that may be needed. First, we'll start small. Nymph patterns often form the basis of rigging when utilizing a dead-drift approach. Slim, low-profile nymphs with beads or other weight sink quickly and work well with any dead-drift or tight-line strategy. This style of nymph can be tied in a range of sizes and configurations. The dead-drift approach can extend to other flies, such as baitfish patterns and crayfish.

Not all nymphs need be small and slender. Larger nymph patterns tied big and bushy with webby hackle, synthetic brushes, and synthetic legs can also be effective for trout and other species. Some of these larger patterns work quite well with a swing the fly approach.

While huge flies used for large predators in fresh or saltwater are nearly impossible to Spey cast, using a two-handed rod and overhead casting may be the best approach for delivering flies up to and exceeding 10 inches in length. Large offerings for pike, musky, striped bass, and a variety of other saltwater species can be efficiently cast with a two-handed rod and a shooting taper.

The most effective large flies tend to move side to side, slide, or dance when stripped. This type of movement gives the appearance of wounded or vulnerable bait and creates the side attack angle preferred by most predators. Large flies can be tied to represent the natural colors to match the bait of the water being fished or in bright colors to enhance visibility in the water or in some combination of both natural and bright. The most effective large flies are tied in a manner that creates bulk and size in the water with an efficient use of materials to allow for ease in casting. Most large

A Game Changer fooled this lake trout on the swing. Realistic patterns combined with a full arsenal of Spey and two-hand overhead casting techniques has few limits as to its effectiveness on a variety of water and fish species.

flies utilize shanks and/or double hooks. Even with the use of two-handed rods, flies that are too heavy with material can be difficult to cast.

Various large fly styles have emerged. In addition to Blane Chocklett's Game Changer, the T-Bone is another effective predator pattern that he developed for musky. The goop head series of flies created by Joe Goodspeed and various patterns developed by Matt Grajewski and Eli Burant, to name a few, have proven quite effective for musky and other freshwater and saltwater predators. Lefty's Deceiver, created by Lefty Kreh in the 1950s, continues to evolve and adapt as new materials are developed and remains one of the most popular large flies for saltwater. Bob Popovic's hollow fly series, developed mainly for salt, may be the ultimate design for size and bulk while minimizing materials. This style can also create an effective bait-fish pattern for freshwater fishing.

SPEY FLIES

▪ AKROYD

(tied by Steve Silverio)
Tag: Silver tinsel
Tail: Topping and tippet strands
Body: Rear-half yellow seal or substitute and front-half black floss
Rib: Oval silver tinsel over yellow seal or substitute with yellow hackle and flat silver tinsel over black floss
Hackle: Black heron or substitute
Wing: A pair of cinnamon turkey tail strips
Cheeks: Jungle cock

The Akroyd is a great example of a classic tie that has endured and can still be found in some fly boxes today. The pattern was originated by Charles Ackroyd in 1878 and is considered one of the best known Dee patterns.

▪ GOLD RIACH

(tied by Steve Silverio)
Tag: Orange silk
Body: Orange wool followed by black wool
Rib: Narrow gold tinsel, gold twist, and silver twist
Hackle: Long reddish-brown Spey cock or substitute black Spey hackle
Throat: Teal
Wing: Bronze mallard strips

A classic Spey fly that exhibits the muted tones and long, flowing hackle of the early patterns.

▪ LADY CAROLINE

(tied by Charlie Dickson)
Tail: Golden pheasant breast feather
Body: Olive-brown dubbing
First rib: Flat, large gold tinsel
Second rib: Oval small silver tinsel
Third rib: Oval small gold tinsel
Hackle: Blue-eared pheasant
Collar hackle: Golden pheasant breast
Wing: Bronze mallard

The Lady Caroline is one of the most recognized Spey patterns, named after Caroline Elizabeth Gordon-Lennox, daughter of the Duke of Richmond and Gordon at Gordon Castle in Scotland. The pattern was most likely developed by the head ghillie at the castle. Developed as an Atlantic salmon fly, it is mentioned by Roderick Haig-Brown as a pattern he used in the Pacific Northwest, first marking the Spey style in the pursuit of steelhead. The Lady Caroline is still readily used for salmon, steelhead, and even sized down as a trout fly.

▨ SOL DUC SPEY

(tied by Charlie Dickson)
Tag: Small, flat silver tinsel
Body: Orange floss
Rib: Oval silver tinsel
Hackle: Blue-eared or white-eared pheasant dyed yellow
Collar hackle: Blue-eared pheasant dyed black or long black schlappen
Wing: Four hot-orange hackle tips

The Sol Duc Spey is the creation of Syd Glasso, first tied in the late 1950s, and named after his home river on the Olympic Peninsula. Influenced by the Spey flies tied for Atlantic salmon, Glasso is credited with developing Spey-style flies designed specifically for steelhead, featuring his careful attention to detail and brighter color schemes. His patterns are still very popular among steelhead and trout anglers.

▨ GREEN HIGHLANDER SPEY

(tied by Charlie Dickson)
Tail: Golden pheasant crest
Tag: Fine, oval tinsel and yellow floss
Butt: Black ostrich herl
Body: Rear yellow floss, front bright-green floss dubbing
Rib: Oval silver tinsel
Body hackle: White-eared pheasant dyed green
Front hackle: Yellow saddle hackle
Wing: Married yellow, orange, green, natural turkey
Eyes: Jungle cock

The Green Highlander is a well-known salmon pattern that originated in the late 1800s. Its bright color scheme has led to its lasting popularity. The original pattern featured a married wing style, and the pattern features a longer Spey hackle look.

▨ BUNNY SPEY

Body: Senyo's Laser Dub
Wing: Rabbit strip
Rib: Medium copper wire
Hackle: Schlappen folded back
Collar: Guinea

The Bunny Spey was one of my first productive swing flies. It combines the very lifelike properties of rabbit strip with a Spey fly look of long, flowing hackles. Initially, this pattern was tied exclusively on hooks but, over time, found it to hook more fish when tied on a tube. It is much more than a steelhead pattern but has worked on salmon, trout, and smallmouth tied in a wide range of colors.

▨ BLACK GORDON

Tag: Fine oval silver tinsel
Tail: Golden pheasant crest
Body: Rear-half red floss, and front-half black angora goat
Rib: Fine oval silver tinsel
Hackle: Long black Spey Hackle
Throat: Teal flank
Wing: Black hackle tips

This is a Spey variation of a steelhead pattern created by Clarence Gordon in the 1930s. It is a good example of a relatively easy-to-tie and functional Spey fly that can be adapted to various sizes and color combinations.

▨ BILL'S SPEY

(tied by Nick Pionessa)
Shank: 30 mm or size 3 hook
Body: Summer Duck SLF
Hackle: Bleach-burned pheasant tail
Collar: Wood duck flank
Eyes: Jungle cock
Wing: Cree rooster cape

Bill's Spey, created by Nick Pionessa and named for his dad who supplied some of the materials for the early versions, can be tied on a hook or shank. The shank style combines the Spey style with the fish-playing advantages of a short shank hook. Bill's Spey is an extremely effective steelhead pattern for clear-water conditions and has proven to be equally successful for smallmouth bass.

SALMON / STEELHEAD WET FLIES

▪ BLUE CHARM
(tied by Charlie Dickson)
Tag: Fine oval tinsel and yellow floss
Tail: Golden pheasant crest
Butt: Black ostrich herl
Rib: Oval silver tinsel
Body: Black floss
Throat: Blue saddle hackle
Wing: Turkey tail with strips of teal on each side set on the upper-half of the wing
Topping: Golden pheasant crest

The Blue Charm is a very popular Atlantic salmon pattern first developed in the 1800s. It is a less complex tie than many of the other patterns of the time and is thought to represent an effort toward simpler salmon patterns. It is often used as a low-water pattern and can be further simplified by substituting a grey squirrel tail hair wing.

▪ GREEN MACHINE
(tied by Nick Pionessa)
Tag: Oval silver tinsel
Butt: Yellow floss then red floss
Body: Spun green deer hair trimmed to size
Hackle: Brown cock neck wound through body

While the Green Machine has the general appearance of a dry fly, its small body is designed to dive under and be fished subsurface with a floating line or with a sinking-tip. This relatively simple fly has produced exceptional results for Atlantic salmon, steelhead, and migratory brown trout.

▪ WINTER'S HOPE
(tied by Charlie Dickson)
Body: Flat silver tinsel
Hackle: Purple over blue saddle hackle
Wing: Two orange hackle tips over two yellow hackle tips

The Winter's Hope is one of the most recognizable steelhead patterns developed by the expert Pacific Northwest angler Bill McMillan. Its sparse tie allows the fly to sink easily yet show a visible profile with

bright colors to boost angler confidence. Classic steelhead patterns tied on a hook have lost some popularity as intruder- and shank-style flies have become popular. However, this style still has its place in the pursuit of steelhead and other species.

▪ GREEN BUTT SKUNK
(tied by Charlie Dickson)
Tail: Died red golden pheasant or red saddle hackle fibers
Tag: Flat silver tinsel
Butt: Green floss or yarn
Body: Black dubbing
Rib: Flat silver tinsel
Hackle: Black saddle or schlappen
Wing: White calf or bucktail or polar bear
Eye (optional): Jungle cock

The Green Butt Skunk is a classic steelhead pattern developed by Dan Callaghan. It is a good example of a simple steelhead wet fly that has produced on numerous rivers and has crossed over as an effective fly for other species.

▪ PURPLE PERIL
(tied by Charlie Dickson)
Tail: Died golden pheasant or purple saddle hackle fibers
Tag: Flat silver tinsel
Body: Purple dubbing
Rib: Flat silver tinsel
Hackle: Purple saddle hackle or schlappen
Wing: Squirrel tail
Eye (optional): Jungle cock

Originally developed by well-known steelhead angler Ken Mcleod in the 1960s, the Purple Peril is a very popular pattern up and down the West Coast of North America. It is a versatile pattern that can be tied in a range of sizes and effectively used in a variety of conditions.

■ FIGURE SKATER
Body: Burnt-orange dubbing
Rib: Small wire
Hackle: Black saddle
Collar: A couple turns of natural teal

The Figure Skater can be used as a wet fly but has excelled as a skater fished with a riffled hitch. Fished as a search fly or a follow-up when a fish shows for a larger pattern, this fly has accounted for numerous solid hookups on steelhead over the years. With the materials tied more toward the rear, there is extra room on the hook to set the hitch. This allows the line to pull from further back on the hook to assist in placing the fly cutting through the surface in a visible V.

■ GREEN HIGHLANDER
Tail: Yellow hackle tips
Tag: Silver tinsel
Butt: Yellow floss and fine black yarn
Body: Rear third yellow floss, and front two-thirds bright-green floss or dubbing
Body hackle: Bright-green saddle hackle
Front hackle: Yellow schlappen
Wing: Golden pheasant tippets, then sparse yellow bucktail, orange bucktail, and natural bucktail or squirrel on top
Eyes: Jungle cock

As noted, the original pattern was tied in the classic married wing salmon fly style but can also be tied in a fishing-friendly version that features a hair wing. I can still remember the Green Highlander protruding from the jaw of my first Atlantic salmon.

■ CITATION
Tail: Brown hen hackle fibers
Body: Summer duck SLF dubbing
Rib: Small gold wire
Hackle: Mottled brown hen hackle
Wing: Pheasant filoplume

This Citation is a simple wet fly and reminder that some productive steelhead patterns can be quite small in stature. A great swing pattern for low, clear-water conditions.

SHANK FLIES / INTRUDER

■ INTRUDER
Shank: 35 mm
Connection: 30-pound Berkley Fireline
Rear: Senyo's Aqua Veil Chenille, schlappen, a few strands of ostrich herl
Middle: Sparkle Braid
Front: Arctic fox in a dubbing loop, ostrich herl, Flashabou, saddle hackle for the wing, and guinea for the collar
Eyes: Medium dumbbell

As described by Jerry French, the intruder is a platform as opposed to a specific pattern. It is the original design of two distinct stations in the back and front. It features a rather sparse tie to sink quickly but active materials for movements and size. The intruder platform is extremely versatile, limited only by our own creativity.

■ ARTIFICIAL INTELLIGENCE
(tied by Greg Senyo)
Shank: 25 mm Senyo Articulated Shank
Wire: Senyo Intruder Wire
Eyes: Double medium bead chain
Hot spot: Crystal chenille
Under wing: Orange Lady Amherst
Overwing #1: Copper Flashabou and copper Holographic Flashabou
Overwing #2: Black-barred orange Voodoo Fibers
Collar: Orange guinea over Senyo's chocolate 1.5-inch Chromatic Brush
Eyes: Orange-dyed jungle cock

The Artificial Intelligence was developed by professional tyer and fly/material designer Greg Senyo. It shows well in the water with a solid silhouette and great movement and flash. The Lady Amherst under wing keeps the Flashabou elevated above the wire and hook to take advantage of its natural buoyancy, enhancing the fly's action in the water. The bulky head pushes water, also adding to its movement. Greg ties this pattern in a variety of color combinations to meet a range of water conditions.

▨ MR. SOFTIE

(tied by Nick Pionessa)

Shank: 1-inch shank or also can be tied on a 1-inch tube or #4 hook

Butt: Small ball of orange dubbing

Rear hackle: Three turns of orange rooster cape

Body: Lateral Scale pearl/black wrapped flat with a small ball of orange dubbing to finish

Hackle: Four or five turns of a fine tip section of a marabou feather, best if sparse and short

Collar: Mottled brown hen saddle folded and wrapped three turns

Flash: A few strands of copper holographic Flashabou and a few strands of black barred orange Voodoo Fibers

Wing: Two black saddle feathers matched, back-to-back and tied in tented. Look for feathers from lower sections of rooster saddles with wider bases and plenty of webbing with a strong taper.

Mr. Softie was developed by Nick Pionessa and can be tied in a variety of color combinations, but the brown and orange has proven to be very effective. The pattern orientates properly in the water with the hook riding up or down when tied on a shank or tube. With the hook point riding up, it is unlikely that Mr. Softie will hang up on the bottom even in the nastiest of structure.

▨ MINI TROUT INTRUDER

Shank: 25 to 30 mm

Hook connection: Berkley Fire Wire

Rear: Pheasant rump over orange angora dubbing in a dubbing loop

Middle: Small black or brown cactus chenille

Front: Large grizzly hen or schlappen over bronze mallard flank

This combination of colors creates a natural buggy pattern with good movement in the water, suggestive of a wide range of trout foods. The Mini Trout Intruder allows Spey anglers a style more closely related to the pursuit of migratory fish to be used in the trout Spey game. The specifics of this fly can easily be changed or substituted to fit specific situations.

▨ BLUE MOON

(tied by Jeff Hubbard)

Shank: 40 mm

Wire: Beadalon or 40-pound Power Pro

Tail: King fisher blue Pseudo Hair tied in to create a shoulder and then black rabbit strip tied in over top

Body: The extra black rabbit strip from the tail wrapped forward toward the front of the shank

First collar: King fisher blue schlappen

Overwing: Blue Flashabou

Second collar: Black schlappen

The Blue Moon was developed by guide Jeff Hubbard. Rabbit strip baitfish and leech patterns are very effective on almost all species and belong in almost any swing box. The color scheme and size of this pattern can be modified to meet the situation. A small tube can be added to the rear of the rabbit strip and the connecting tippet threaded through to eliminate the chance of the hook fouling.

▨ SCANDI SCULPIN

(tied by Justin Pribanic)

Shank: 35 to 40 mm

Hook connection: Maxima Chameleon

Body: Copper braid

Dubbing ball: Red Ice Dub in loop

Gills: Barred ostrich in loop

Wing: Golden olive craft fur, tied Scandi wing style and barred with brown and black sharpie

Flash: Mix of copper, Kelly green, and gold Flashabou

Collar 1: Black or contrasting schlappen

Collar 2: Mallard dyed wood duck

Head: Olive rabbit in loop

A pattern developed by Justin Pribanic that fuses a lifelike representation with both a shank-style platform and Scandi-style wing. The pattern provides a realistic teardrop look in the water with good movement. But most importantly from a casting standpoint, because of the light craft fur wing, the Scandi Sculpin is easy to cast and can readily be adapted to trout Spey situations.

■ BEAULY SNOW FLY

(tied by Steve Silverio)
Shank: Waddington shank
Body: Light-blue pig's wool or seal substitute
Rib: Flat silver tinsel with gold twist
Hackle: Long black heron or substitute
Wing: Large bunch of bronze peacock herl
Collar: Bright-orange mohair

The Beauly Snow Fly is a classic pattern that combines the Spey style with a Waddington shank. Originally tied on a large, long shank hook, this pattern adapted well to the shank style. The pattern is named after the River Beauly.

■ FAUXY LEECH

(tied by Nick Pionessa)
Shank: 40 mm shank
Dubbing ball: To match color of tail
Flash: Flashabou to match tail color, and Micro Barred Voodoo Fibers to match head color
Tail: Craft fur in dubbing loop to be as long as possible
Body: Lateral Scale wrapped like tinsel
Dubbing ball: To match color of wing
Wing: Craft fur in a dubbing loop tied in shorter than the tail and to create more bulk
Head: Wool in the dubbing loop

The Fauxy Leech is Nick Pionessa's advancement on the classic egg-sucking leech. Craft fur provides great movement in the water and can be relied on for its consistency in quality unlike some natural materials. Craft fur is also quite easy to work with in a dubbing loop, and by using various lengths of the material in the loop, length and bulk can readily be adjusted.

TUBE FLIES

■ CATTITUDE

Body: Small cactus chenille to create a ball behind marabou
Underwing: Marabou
Side/top fibers: Ostrich, holographic flashabou
Overwing: Two or four grizzly saddle hackle
Collar: Schlappen folded back

The Cattitude is full of movement in the water and has become one of my most dependable patterns for big and enticing presentations. All the materials flow or flash when in the water, and the cactus chenille props up the materials to create a thicker head tapering to a fine tail. The Cattitude can also be tied on a shank.

■ MARABOU SPEY TUBE

Overwing: Marabou tied in reverse
Underwing: Marabou tied in reverse, color to compliment overwing
Body: Cactus chenille
Flash: A few strands of holographic Flashabou
Collar: Schlappen

A fairly simple yet very effective swing pattern. Tying the marabou in reverse creates a larger profile in the water and more movement. Marabou tends to condense down, ruining its natural movement. While tying on the tube, the pattern begins by first placing the tube in the vice backward to add the marabou and body and then turned around to finish the flash and collar. This pattern has been extremely dependable for steelhead and king salmon.

■ TEMPLE DOG

Body: Senyo's Laser Hair Dubbing
Underwing: One or two colors of long Arctic fox
Hackle: Schlappen
Overwing: Fin racoon
Cone: Medium to fit snug on tube

The development of the Temple Dog style of fly is credited to Scandinavian tyer Hakan Norling. The Temple Dog can be tied in a range of colors and sizes. While known as an important salmon and steelhead pattern, it can be adapted to trout and smallmouth. It's a quite versatile pattern to have in the box. The Temple Dog was originally developed as a tube pattern but can be tied on hooks or shanks.

▩ SUNRAY SHADOW

(tied by Nick Pionessa)
Tube: Plastic 1 to 1.5 inches
Underwing: Squirrel tail
Main wing: Long black goat hair
Overwing: Peacock herl

This simple but very effective Atlantic salmon pattern was first created by Ray Brooks in Norway and was developed to represent a glass eel. The Sunray Shadow is typically fished at a faster speed to entice a strike.

▩ HYBRID SCULPIN

(tied by Nick Pionessa)
Tube: Plastic
Wing: Olive rabbit strip
Dubbing ball: Olive dubbing
Hackle: Marabou
Collar: Olive-dyed mallard flank
Flash: Copper and black Holographic Flashabou
Head: Rabbit in dubbing loop
Pectoral fin: Grizzly hen saddle hackle
Eyes (optional): Dumbbell eyes

This is an extremely versatile fly that has proven effective on trout, steelhead, and smallmouth bass as well as other species. The Hybrid Sculpin has a lifelike movement in the water while maintaining a general sculpin appearance. Dumbbell eyes allow the fly to be worked along the bottom and with the hook set to ride up can fish relatively snag free.

DRY FLIES

▩ BOMBER

(tied by Nick Pionessa)
Tail: Calf tail
Wing: Calf tail
Body: Spun deer hair trimmed to form body
Hackle: Cock saddle wound through body

The Bomber is one of the most popular and dependable dry flies for Atlantic salmon and steelhead. Its buoyant body makes it a good choice for both waking and dead-drift fishing. While Bombers for salmon and steelhead are tied on larger hooks, scaling this pattern down can also make this an effective trout prospecting fly.

▩ LITTLE WANG

(tied by Todd Hirano)
Tail: Moose body hair, a few strands of holographic Flashabou
Butt: Fluorescent green floss
Tinsel: Fine oval silver
Body: Glo Brite floss
Lip: 2 mm closed cell foam cut into tapered piece with widest pointing forward
Flash ball: Cactus chenille or dubbing ball
Wing: Black cow elk hair
Rear post: 2 mm closed cell foam cut into rectangle with V cut out of rear
Front post: 2 mm closed cell foam length to match fly size

This pattern was developed by steelhead angler Todd Hirano. It's a versatile and very effective pattern that can be used in a wide range of water. The fly has a relative low profile in the water that assists in getting a fish to commit to the take. It also rides and floats well with high visibility so that the Little Wang can be fished in a wide range of water types.

■ MR. HANKY

Shank: Length to match size of body
Hook connection: 30-pound Fireline or 30-pound Maxima
Tail: Rabbit strip trimmed of fur
Underbody: Natural rabbit strip crosscut
Upper body: Brown closed cell foam trimmed to shape of mouse
Legs: Brown round rubber legs
Whiskers: Pearl Krystal flash

Mr. Hanky was created by guide and lodge owner Jeff Hickman. It is a very effective mouse pattern for swinging. Trout and salmon often attempt to pull a mouse below the surface without eating the entire fly. The stinger hook positioned to the rear assists in hooking more fish.

■ ARTICULATED EMPEROR MOUSE (tied by Steve Yewchuck)

Shank: 35 mm offset shank
Hook connection: Flexible wire
Tail: Thin, brown leather tip with closed cell foam—as an alternative a tail of coreless paracord with wire running through the center or surgical tubing with braided backing can used for the tail with the stinger added at the end of the tail
Underbody: 2 mm closed cell foam
Body: Montana Fly Company Bunny Brush
Ears and face: 2 mm closed cell foam

The Articulated Emperor Mouse is the creation of professional tyer and fly designer Steve Yewchuck. The head of the pattern is designed to push water and allow the body to stick to the surface when attacked by a big fish. It floats extremely well and is very durable, and the articulated tie is smaller than the original Emperor Mouse but is a good size for Spey casting.

■ PARACHUTE STIMULATOR

Tail: Elk hair
Body: Floss/dubbing or closed cell foam for greater buoyancy
Legs: Round rubber legs
Post: Poly yarn
Hackle: Grizzly tied around post

The stimulator is a well-known attractor pattern for stonefly and caddis. It is a great fly for prospecting with dry fly Spey techniques because of its buoyancy and high visibility. A body constructed of foam or spun deer works best for a consistent high float.

■ LEMIRE GREASE LINER

Tail: Deer hair
Body: Gray/tan dubbing
Throat: Grizzly hackle
Wing: Deer hair extending toward rear of hook

If you are going to wake flies for migratory or resident fish, it is imperative to carry some caddis imitations. The Grease Liner was developed by well-known steelhead pioneer Harry Lemire and is considered one of the most effective waking patterns for steelhead. There are many other variations of caddis waking flies that are also effective. The versatile elk hair caddis can also be a good choice for dead drift or waking.

TROUT WET FLIES

▪ OLIVE SEDGE
(tied by Steve Bird)
Body: Mix of light olive rabbit and olive Antron dubbing with hare's mask for the thorax
Rib: Silver wire
Hackle: Partridge or brahma hen

Periods of caddis emergence represent one of the best opportunities for trout Spey. Fish key in on the movement of pupae lifting from the rocks toward the surface. Simple wet fly spiders like the Olive Sedge are extremely effective as a caddis imitation. It can also be a great pattern for migratory fish in clear-water situations.

▪ AMERICAN PHEASANT
TAIL *(tied by Steve Bird)*
Tail: Three lemon wood duck flank whisks or bronze mallard flank
Body: Ringneck pheasant tail twisted with the tag of tying thread for the rear and peacock herl for the thorax
Rib: Fine silver wire
Hackle: Partridge or brahma hen

In nymph form, the pheasant tail is one of the most effective and popular subsurface flies. As a wet fly tied in various sizes, the Pheasant Tail wet is an effective representation of a wide range of trout foods.

▪ WINGLESS ROYAL
COACHMAN *(tied by Steve Bird)*
Tail: Golden pheasant tippet
Body: Peacock herl at front and rear with red floss in the middle
Wing: White gull or hen
Hackle: Red-brown hen

The Royal Coachman is one of the most recognized patterns in fly fishing. For many years, my brother Jerry and I used a Royal Trude on the swing while fished on and below the surface with tremendous results on large trout. The Royal Coachman wet is an extremely effective pattern for active fish.

▪ WOODCUTTER
(tied by Steve Bird)
Tailing: Four or five pheasant tail swords
Rib: Copper wire
Body: Blended dark-olive hares mask mixed with a pinch of Hareline UV Shrimp Pink in a dubbing loop
Palmer: Brown grizzly, brown saddle, or schlappen
Hackle: Argus or ringneck pheasant church window body spade

Steve Bird, author of *Trout Spey & the Art of the Swing*, calls this his favorite fly. It is an all-around pattern that can represent a wide range of fish food and is effective on summer steelhead as well as trout and is an absolute killer on Steve's home waters of the upper Columbia.

▪ HARE'S EAR WET FLY
Tail: Mallard flank
Body: Hare's ear dubbing
Rib: Fin gold tinsel
Throat: Brown hen hackle
Wing: Slate-gray matched pair from mallard wing

A versatile wet fly constructed in a wing style popular in the patterns tied and developed by Ray Bergman and documented in his greatly influential book *Trout* first published in 1938. Winged patterns work best when imitating diving adult caddis or mayflies emerging in the surface film.

▪ ISO EMERGER SOFT HACKLE
Tail/shuck: Dark brown Antron yarn
Rear body: Mahogany Super Fine dubbing under clear V Rib
Front body: Chocolate-brown dubbing
Hackle: Mottled-brown hen hackle

The trailing shuck on this pattern seems to make a difference in enticing feeding trout. The Isonychia Emerger has worked quite well in the spring, summer, and fall when prospecting in non-hatch periods. This style can easily be adopted to other mayflies.

TROUT STREAMERS

◼ CATTFISH STREAMER
REAR HOOK:
Tail: Marabou
Body: Cactus Chenille
Hackle: Schlappen
SHANK:
Body: Arctic fox, Senyo Laser Dub
FRONT HOOK:
Body: Small beads to cover connection, Cactus Chenile on hook
Hackle: Schlappen over marabou
Eyes: Dumbbell eyes tied on top

For streamer Spey fishing, flies with excess bulk or material create too much resistance for casting with trout-sized gear. I designed this fly so that it looks and fishes bigger in the water as the materials move and pulse in the water. And it is a relatively easy pattern to tie and has proven extremely effective.

◼ MAGOG SMELT
(tied by Nick Pionessa)
Tag: Oval silver tinsel
Tail: Teal
Body: Flat silver tinsel
Rib: Oval silver tinsel
Throat: Red hen saddle
Wing: White bucktail, yellow bucktail, purple bucktail, peacock herl
Cheeks: Teal
Eyes: Jungle cock

The Magog Smelt is a good example of the classic streamer style fly featuring a bucktail wing. While streamer patterns have advanced dramatically to include a wide range of natural and synthetic materials, simple bucktail streamers still have a place for trout and salmon fishing. The Magog Smelt is also a top-producing Atlantic salmon fly.

◼ MUDDLER MINNOW SPEY
(tied by Charlie Dickson)
Tail: Matched turkey wing quills
Body: Flat gold tinsel
Hackle: Blue-eared pheasant
Wing: Matched turkey wing quills
Collar: Natural deer hair
Head: Natural deer hair trimmed

The Muddler Minnow was originated by Don Gapen around 1937 and is one of the best-known trout streamer patterns. The Muddler has spawned numerous other designs but still remains as an important and effective fly that can be easily Spey cast. The version pictured here is tied Spey style and with its buoyant head can be fished on the surface with a riffle hitch.

◼ PINE SQUIRREL LEECH
Tail/body: Pine squirrel Zonker strip
Collar: Pine squirrel Zonker strip palmered—can also be placed in dubbing loop for a finer finish
Head: Medium bead to correspond with color of body, dubbing optional to fill in any gap behind bead

This pattern is about as simple as it gets and can be effectively tied with one material. The Pine Squirrel Leech is a good trout Spey option, especially in clear-water conditions. It is easy to cast and looks great in the water.

◼ SF STREAMER
Wing: Two colors of Steve Farrar SF Blend
Head: Senyo Laser Dub
Eye: Flymen Living Eyes

This is an easy-to-tie trout Spey baitfish pattern. This pattern can be tied in various sizes and color combinations. Tied with living eyes, the SF Streamer is light and easy to cast. The rigidness of the SF Blend keeps the fly from fouling. Dumbbell eyes can be used to add weight.

▣ CIRCUS PEANUT

Tail: Marabou blood quills
Flash: Krystal Flash
Body: Cactus chenille
Body hackle: Schlappen
Legs: Sili legs
Connection between hook: Senyo's Intruder Trailer Hook Wire
Wire bead spacer: Glass Tyers Beads
Eyes: Hareline Painted Eyes

The Circus Peanut was developed by Michigan guide Russ Madden and popularized by Kelly Galloup. This a proven streamer pattern for large trout and can be sized to easily Spey cast with a Skagit or streamer taper head. It can be a deadly pattern with a swing and strip approach.

SMALLMOUTH BASS FLIES

▣ CLOUSER MINNOW

Eyes: Dumbbell eyes tied on top of hook so that hook point rides up
Wing: Two colors of bucktail—darker color to ride on top of fly
Flash: A few strands of Krystal Flash or holographic Flashabou through the middle

The Clouser minnow was developed by Pennsylvania smallmouth guide and expert Bob Clouser. Bucktail creates good movement in the water, and its low profile allows this fly to sink quickly for covering depths and structure, making it much more than an effective smallmouth pattern. It can also be tied with synthetics such as Steve Farrar SF Blend winging material to create a more durable fly with a natural sheen in the water.

▣ GETTIN JIGGY

Eyes: Medium red dumbbell tie in on the underside of a jig hook to ride point up
Tail/body: Olive rabbit strip approximately 2 to 2.5 inches in length—tied in near head and the hook point pushed through the rabbit hide to prevent fouling
Legs: Light olive barred Sili Legs—three full legs on each side tied down in the middle, folded back and trimmed as necessary
Under hackle: Brown schlappen
Hackle: Entire olive saddle including the fuzzy fibers at the end of the hackle
Collar: Olive-dyed guinea

For smallmouth, it is good to have some patterns that can run close to the bottom that have a reduced chance of becoming snagged up. Gettin Jiggy has a sculpin or other bottom-dwelling bait look, and the jig hook provides a dancing action when stripped during the swing.

▣ NICK'S PENCIL POPPER

(tied by Nick Pionessa)
Tail: Bucktail with a collar of deer belly hair
Body: Grey or olive deer over white—white is spun and grey or olive is stacked
Gills: Red deer hair
Eyes: Doll eyes

Nick's Pencil Popper is a good example of an effective surface fly that represents a baitfish struggling at the surface. For years, this has been an extremely effective pattern retrieved on a one-hand rod for smallmouth, but its design is also ideal for a swing or swing and strip approach.

▣ SWINGING D

(tied by Mike Schultz)
Flash: Opal Flashabou Mirage and Lateral Scale
Tail: Saddle hackles tied Deceiver style
Body: Chocklett's Filler Flash and two hen saddle hackles
Cap feather: Mallard flank
Shank 1: 10 mm
Body 2: Chocklett's Filler Flash and two or three hen saddle hackles
Shank 2: 15 mm

Body 3: Chocklett's Filler Flash and two hen saddle hackles

Keel: .025 lead wire wrapped around hook bend

Bump: XL Fizzle Chenille

Body 4: Chocklett's Filler Flash and two hen saddle hackles

Rattle: 5 mm glass rattle

Body 5: Chocklett's Filler Flash wrapped over and through rattle

Collar: Marabou

Flash: Flashabou

Accent and throat: Grizzly hackle tip on each side and Cascade Crest Mirror Wrap

Head: Rainy's Diver Head

The Swinging D was developed by Michigan guide and shop owner Mike Schultz. It can be Spey casted or delivered with overhead two-hand casting. The Swinging D is designed as a smallmouth bass fly that can be quite effective with a swing, strip, and twitch approach but has a wide application to other species as well.

BUGGERS / LEECHES

■ BEAD HEAD SPEY BUGGER

Tail: Olive marabou with a few strands of Krystal Flash

Body: Olive Ice Dub

Hackle: Olive saddle hackle with extra wraps at the head folded back

Bead: Medium gold

The Wooly Bugger is possibly the most versatile fly pattern of any style. It has been used to catch a wide variety of fish species in numerous color and size combinations. Olive or brown color schemes seem particularly effective and are an important pattern in low, clear water. The Spey bugger is tied with a reverse saddle hackle with extra turns of the longest fibers at the head.

■ UGLY BUGGER

Eyes: Dumbbell ties on top of shank

Tail: Marabou and Sili legs

Body: Cactus chenille

Legs: Sili legs

A very simple fly that has proven productive on both trout and smallmouth bass. It can be tied in a range of colors and sizes and is effective on the swing or working it slowly along the bottom. It can also be used with a dead-drift approach.

GAME CHANGERS

■ FEATHER GAME CHANGER

(tied by Blane Chocklett)

Shank: Flymen Fish Spines

Tail: Barred rooster saddle hackle

Body: Barred rooster saddle over Finesse Body Chenille

Pectoral fin: Barred hen hackle tip

Eyes: Jungle cock

The Game Changer platform is extremely versatile. Shank size and a wide range of materials can be adjusted to create effective flies that swim like the real thing from a couple inches to over 10 inches in length. The feather Game Changer pictured here is between 3 and 4 inches long. It can be easily Spey cast and is irresistible to resident trout, smallmouth bass, and migratory species.

CONCLUDING THOUGHTS

The forefathers of Spey could not have envisioned how well Spey and two-handed casting has flourished into the twenty-first century and its development into meeting the challenging requirements of so many fly-fishing situations. Spey will continue to evolve with new ideas, technology, and future generations of anglers that recognize the angling value and enjoyment gained through this style of fishing. My hope is that *Modern Spey Fishing* will be recognized as a significant element of this development.

Going forward, the health of our fisheries will play an important role in the future of Spey. Looking at fisheries worldwide, there are many that are well-managed, healthy, and supporting outstanding sport angling. But man's impact on the planet is becoming very apparent. The effects of climate change piled on

Always remember to enjoy the journey and the friendships that bring us together on the water. Chris Garcea and Jules McCann enjoying the lighter side of the pursuit. NICK PIONESSA PHOTO

top of habitat degradation, overfishing, and poor past management practices are taking a toll on the quality experience that once existed on certain rivers. Especially hard hit in recent years are the anadromous runs of Pacific steelhead and Atlantic salmon. Many Pacific salmon runs have also been reduced significantly.

We are moving into a time when being a complete Spey fisher is not simply about learning the craft of casting, presentation, and fly tying. Those are no longer enough. There needs to be an elevated concern and care for special fisheries that we as Spey anglers hold dear. There are many rivers and fisheries that need more than the occasional visit. These places need advocates to prevent irreversible loss. There will always be fish and fisheries to apply the use of Spey, but some are simply too special and unique to lose. To be a complete Spey fisher, get informed and get involved. Support can come in the form of a voice, a helping hand as a volunteer, or with financial backing. For many fisheries, the time is now, and we can't wait any longer.

INDEX